UNCOVERING LONDON'S HIDDEN HISTORY

Julian Shuckburgh

First published in 2003 by
HarperCollinsPublishers
77-85 Fulham Palace Road
London W6 8JB

The Collins website address is:
www.collins.co.uk

Collins is a registered trademark of HarperCollins Publishers

Photography © 2003 Getmapping plc
Text © 2003 Julian Shuckburgh

Getmapping can produce an individual print of any area shown in this book, or of any area within the United Kingdom. The image can be centred wherever you choose, printed at any size from A6 to 7.5 metres square, and at any scale up to 1:1,000. For further information, please contact Getmapping on 0845 0551550, or log on to www.getmapping.com

A CIP catalogue record for this book is available from the British Library.

ISBN: 0 00 716638 9

07 06 05 04 03
987654321

Designed and edited by Essential Works Ltd, 2003
Jacket design, Two Associates
Colour origination by Colourscan, Singapore
Printed and bound by Johnson Editorial Ltd, Italy

With thanks to Peter Bull, Barbara Saulini, Nina Sharman, Katie Cowan, Martin Brown and Dan Gritten

CONTENTS

INTRODUCTION

When you fly in to London's Heathrow airport, depending on the direction of the wind that day, you not infrequently pass quite low over central London, and if you are sitting by the window, and it's a cloudless day and the sun is shining, you can have a stunning view of the city. But things look different from above, and it is sometimes hard to recognise places that you know intimately at ground level. Look, there's the Tower of London! Is that really Battersea Power Station, can that be Holland Park? Is that my neighbourhood, my street, my house? And of course there's not enough time to work it out, as the plane soars rapidly westwards across the huge city.

Getmapping's extraordinary photography of London from above, begun in 1998 and completed as part of their famous Millennium Map of Britain, allows us time to see. And what a revealing vision it is. No street atlas can convey the complexities of this vast metropolis, and no traveller on the ground can comprehend all the connections and shapes of its structure. Of course we all know that London has some huge green parks, which stand out most visibly in the overall view: Hyde Park, split by the curving Serpentine, the circular Regent's Park to the north of it and

Battersea below. Then to the east there's the tear-drop shape of Victoria Park above, and Greenwich and Blackheath to the south. But what are all those black lines, sweeping across the city in every direction? Are they roads? No, of course not, they're the railways. What a dominating feature they are, how ruthless the 19th-century railway companies were allowed to be in carving through miles of residential London with their straight and curving lines, destroying thousands of houses on the way. These are the first thoughts that the photographs bring to mind: how did these patterns emerge, what caused the shaping of this great city around its swirling river, its endless streets and roads, its occasional grand avenues and stately squares? What history lies beneath?

There are many ways of recounting London's growth through the twenty centuries since the Roman army first built a bridge across the Thames, and many great books have used them. Here we explore a wide range of political and social themes, illustrating them with photographs of the areas and buildings they relate to. Some are local accounts of the history of particular streets and squares, such as Fetter Lane, Knightsbridge and Docklands. Many are designed to demonstrate the endlessly recurring patterns in London's history – the riots and protests that have occurred repeatedly over the last eight

hundred years, the role of immigrant communities who have played such a significant part in London's story over the centuries, the expansion of burial places for the dead, from the earliest churchyards in the centre to famous cemeteries such as Kensal Green and Highgate, and the even larger and more numerous late 19th-century ones further out, like Putney Vale and Plaistow. Then there are factual topics which may surprise even the best-informed Londoners, such as the rubbish sites, the huge numbers of street markets, museums, churches, mosques, synagogues, restaurants offering foreign cuisines, the locations of London's buried rivers, and the houses where famous people lived in past times.

For the last two hundred years, public and private transport has been a subject of crucial concern to London's inhabitants and working population, and London's current mayor, Ken Livingstone, was elected largely on the basis of his promise to find ways of improving the chaotic tube and bus systems, and reducing the horrific rush-hour traffic congestion. We show the history of this long drama, and portray in the photographs where Livingstone's schemes will operate – the extension of railway lines, the introduction of new trams, and the controversial congestion zone for road traffic.

London is constantly changing, as has always been the case, and Getmapping has to update its photographs every few months to allow the Millennium Map to be accurate. We can see many changes in motion here: the restructuring of Trafalgar Square to remove traffic from the northern side, the building of new skyscrapers alongside the Canary Wharf tower, and the dominating presence of the Millennium Dome. We examine some of the past plans, unrealised, to alter the shape of London; and speculate about some of the major changes that may lie in the near future, such as the development of sites in Shepherd's Bush and Thames Gateway, and the plans to win the right to stage the 2012 Olympic Games.

I am grateful to several institutions, such as the London Museum, the London Transport Museum, and the British Library, for help with my text; and to the authors of numerous books of which the most valuable are Peter Ackroyd's *London: The Biography* (2000), Robert Gray's *A History of London* (1978), *The London Encyclopaedia,* edited by Ben Weinreb and Christopher Hibbert (1983), and Felix Barker's *The History of London in Maps* (1990).

Julian Shuckburgh, July 2003

THE ORIGINS OF LONDON

Although human beings roamed along the Thames for thousands of years before London came into existence, the town itself is not recorded in history until the Roman army founded it as a military base shortly after their second invasion of Britain in AD 43. Until then the wide river ran through a gravelly valley surrounded by lime and oak tree forests. From around 3900 BC, tribes and communities inhabited isolated settlements all the way from Dartford in the east to Harmondsworth in the west, carving out clearings in the woodland. It has been hard to uncover evidence of their lives, because for the last 2,000 years a vast city has emerged in this space. Nonetheless, much survives. For instance, hand-axe tools made of flint dating from as far back as the Palaeolithic Era (450,000 to 8300 BC) have been found in Thurrock, Dartford, Becontree and Wanstead, and in Piccadilly, Wandsworth, Acton and Southall. In the latter part of the Bronze Age, c.1600 BC, much larger areas were settled by farming communities, dotted all along the Thames. As the population expanded, other activities, such as trading in bronze and iron, began to develop. However, evidence suggests that the area of London itself does not appear to have been a main tribal or trading centre. These were set well back from the river in places such as Ilford and Woolwich.

The Romans initiated the creation of London by constructing a bridge across the Thames. Their purpose was military: to enable the army based in the south-east to control the British population whose main resistance to the invasion was located in Colchester, in eastern Essex. They chose a spot just to the east of today's London Bridge, where the reeds and mud flats of Southwark were supported by a sand and gravel bank – where Duke Street Hill still rises above the neighbourhood.

On the northern bank the land was much more stable, and it was here – in the area between Gracechurch Street, Cornhill and Lombard Street – that the construction of Londinium began. All of its timber, clay and mud brick buildings, with their thatched or tiled roofs, were destroyed by Queen Boudicca when she led the rebellion of the Iceni in AD 60. In the following 150 years, however, the Romans built a vast forum and basilica, of Kentish ragstone and brick, a massive fort by Cripplegate, the governor's palace where Cannon Street Station now stands, and a defensive wall around the city.

After the collapse of the Roman Empire (c.410), most of eastern Britain fell under Saxon control. *Lundenwic*, as London was then called, retained its role as an important port, and the Saxons developed a trading town to the west of the Roman city walls, along the Strand. Churches like St Martin-in-the-Fields may well have been founded in this period. Moreover, in the 11th century, under the reign of Edward the Confessor, the Westminster area began its development.

The real growth of the London we know today began after the Norman Conquest in 1066. A stark, uncompromising symbol of Norman strength, The White Tower, at the centre of the Tower of London, was completed in 1088.

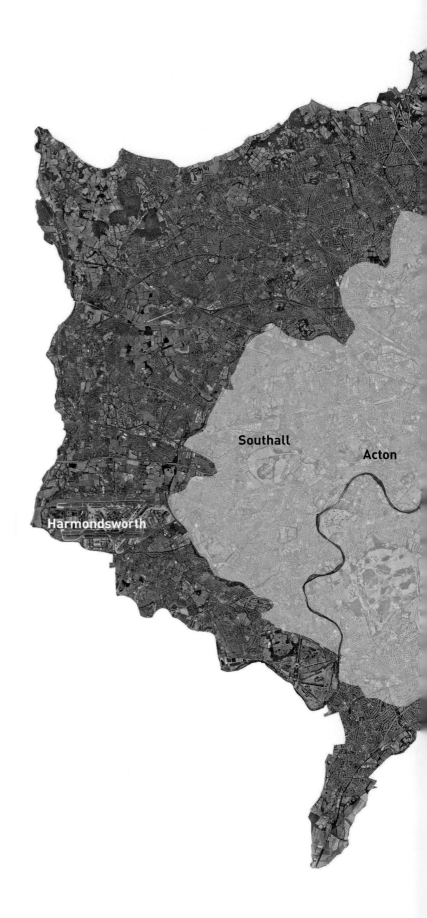

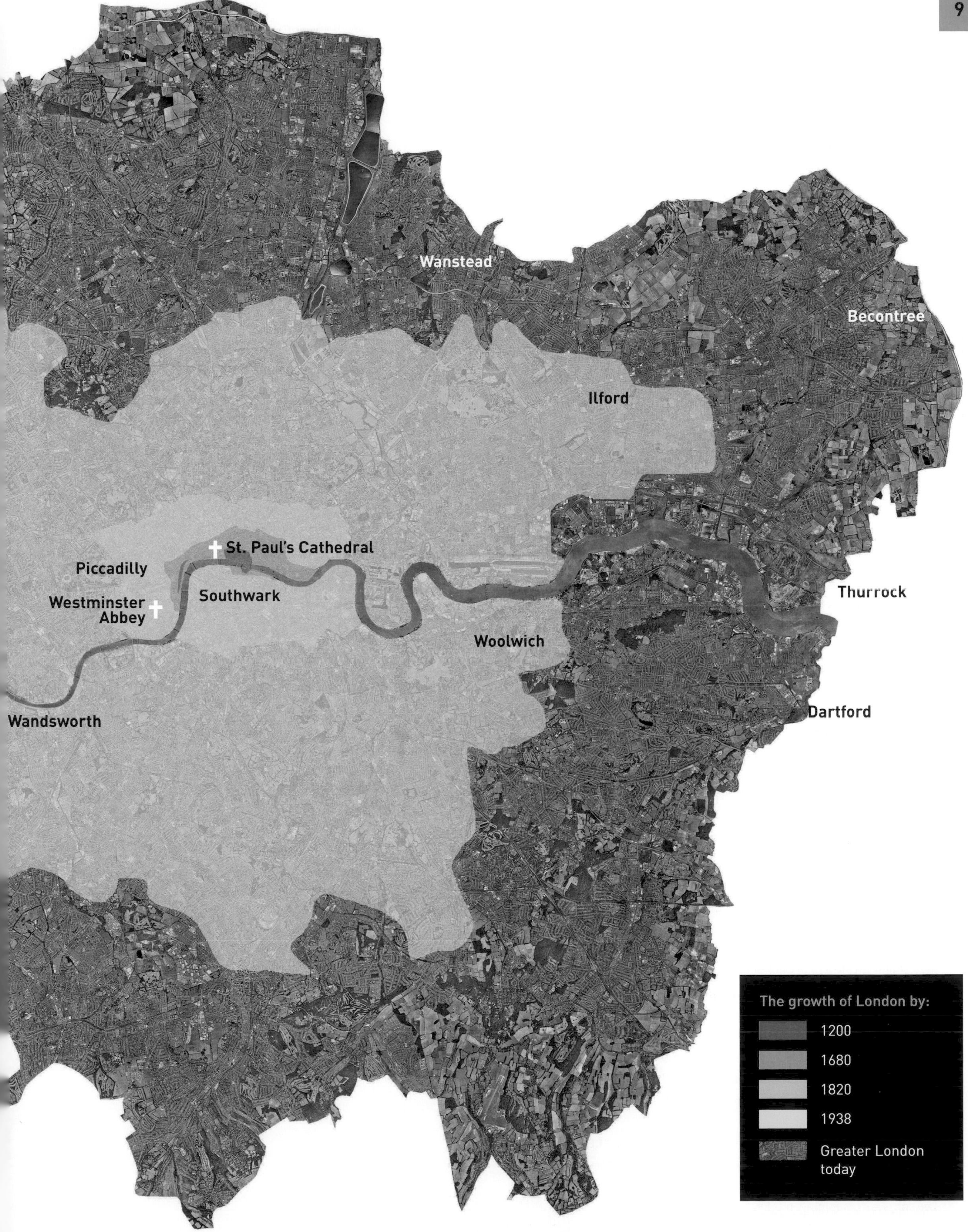

Wanstead

Becontree

Ilford

St. Paul's Cathedral

Piccadilly

Westminster Abbey

Southwark

Thurrock

Woolwich

Dartford

Wandsworth

The growth of London by:

1200

1680

1820

1938

Greater London today

LONDON'S GEOLOGY

The story of present-day London's terrain and physical structure begins some three-quarters of a million years ago, when the Thames started to flow on its present course through the area. Throughout the long Ice Age millennia, both its course and the level of its flow of water varied as the climate changed. During the coldest eras, rainwater froze on the land, lowering the level of the sea, but when these northern ice sheets began to melt, the river flowed faster, and gradually eroded its way through a deeper channel, corresponding to the lower sea level. In milder times, the sea level rose, and the river ran more sluggishly, flooding wide areas and infiltrating them with gravel and other deposits. When the cold returned, the river narrowed and its flow speeded up, leaving its deposits spread over the flood plain. These massive changes occurred many times over several hundred thousand years, creating several different levels of gravel throughout the London basin. The slopes of present-day London, such as Whitehall to Trafalgar Square, or Exhibition Road up to Kensington Gardens, are the consequence of these variations in gravel levels. The gravel deposits attracted early man to the area, providing the stone from which to make useful tools and weapons.

Below London's gravel lie rock and clay formations dating much further back through time, of which the predominant one is London Clay. It dates from the Tertiary Period, 45 million years ago. Levels of Claygate Beds and Bagshot Sands remain on the tops of most of London's high points, such as Hampstead Heath, Harrow on the Hill and Shooters Hill. Until they were eroded during the glacial periods, these features were much more widespread and can still be found south-west of the city. Chalk from the Cretaceous Period (90 million years ago), of which the Chiltern Hills to the west of London and the North Downs to the south are made, reaches no further than Watford, Epsom and Dartford.

London Clay dominates the outer reaches of the London area, and the gravel of the river terraces forms its inner structure. For two thousand years these two substances, combined with chalk, have provided the elements from which London's bricks have been manufactured, the basic material with which London's buildings are made. As Peter Ackroyd puts it: 'It is almost as if the city raised itself from its primeval origin, creating a human settlement from the senseless material of past time.'

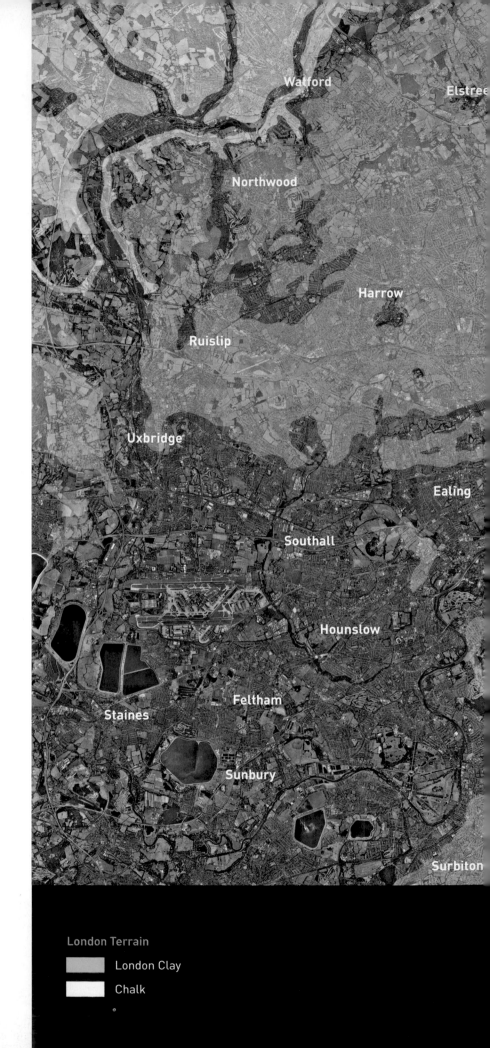

London Terrain

London Clay

Chalk

Barnet
Enfield

Loughton

Edmonton
Chingford
Chigwell

Wanstead

Ilford

Highgate
Hackney
Dagenham

Hampstead
Barking

West Ham

Paddington

Hammersmith
Woolwich

Greenwich

Richmond
Clapham
Bexley

Dartford

Wimbledon
Chislehurst

Kingston
Streatham

Mitcham
Bromley

Beckenham
Orpington

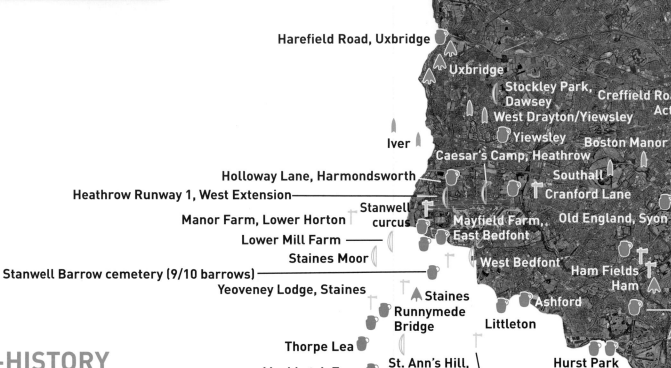

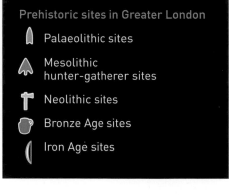

Prehistoric sites in Greater London

- Palaeolithic sites
- Mesolithic hunter-gatherer sites
- Neolithic sites
- Bronze Age sites
- Iron Age sites

Harefield Road, Uxbridge

Uxbridge

Stockley Park, Dawsey

Creffield Road, Acton

West Drayton/Yiewsley

Iver

Yiewsley

Boston Manor

Caesar's Camp, Heathrow

Southall

Holloway Lane, Harmondsworth

Heathrow Runway 1, West Extension

Cranford Lane

Stanwell curcus

Manor Farm, Lower Horton

Mayfield Farm, East Bedfont

Old England, Syon

Lower Mill Farm

Staines Moor

West Bedfont

Stanwell Barrow cemetery (9/10 barrows)

Ham Fields

Ham

Yeoveney Lodge, Staines

Staines

Runnymede Bridge

Ashford

Littleton

Thorpe Lea

Muckhatch Farm

St. Ann's Hill, Chertsey

Staines Road Farm, Shepperton

Hurst Park

PRE-HISTORY

Until about 8,500 years ago, when rising temperatures led to the melting of the last ice sheets, Britain was part of the European continent. Animals and human beings moved northwards whenever improvements in the climate allowed. Even before the evolution of *Homo sapiens,* groups of people roamed the area, hunting and scavenging; and their flint tools, some associated with the remains of mammoth and woolly rhinoceros, have been found in such places as King's Cross, Leadenhall Street, Southall and Crayford. Biologically modern people from Europe probably didn't migrate here until the end of the last glacial, around 10,000 BC.

As the air warmed and the ice melted, the Thames and other rivers flooded the London basin and people were forced back up the slopes of the surrounding valleys. Communities formed in the forests fringing the western end of the Thames, in areas such as Staines and Stanwell, where they carved out large clearings and built stone monuments and wooden trackways.

A huge range of prehistoric finds have been uncovered in the London area, reflecting the great changes that occurred over these millennia: sharks in Brentford, wolves in Cheapside, crocodiles in Islington, mammoth in King's Cross, elephants in Trafalgar Square, lions in Charing Cross, buffaloes by St Martin-in-the-Fields, bears in Woolwich, flint axes and tools in Southwark, a hunting camp on Hampstead Heath, and neolithic pottery in Clapham.

The population evidently increased after about 1600 BC, when farming communities began to compete for the more favourable land, and field systems were laid out. In Bermondsey, traces of prehistoric criss-cross ploughing have been found on the valley floor, showing that farming skills had already become quite sophisticated. Timber trackways were built on the riverside marshes, giving access to the water meadows. But from the surviving evidence, it seems unlikely that the central London area was a population centre, or engaged in tribal and trading activities. It is more likely that such centres were either on higher land above the river, such as Ilford, or downstream at Woolwich. The name 'London' is of pre-Roman origin and has been connected with a word meaning 'wild' or bold' in the Celtic language of the time, but it seems the town didn't exist until the Romans created it some 50 years after the birth of Christ.

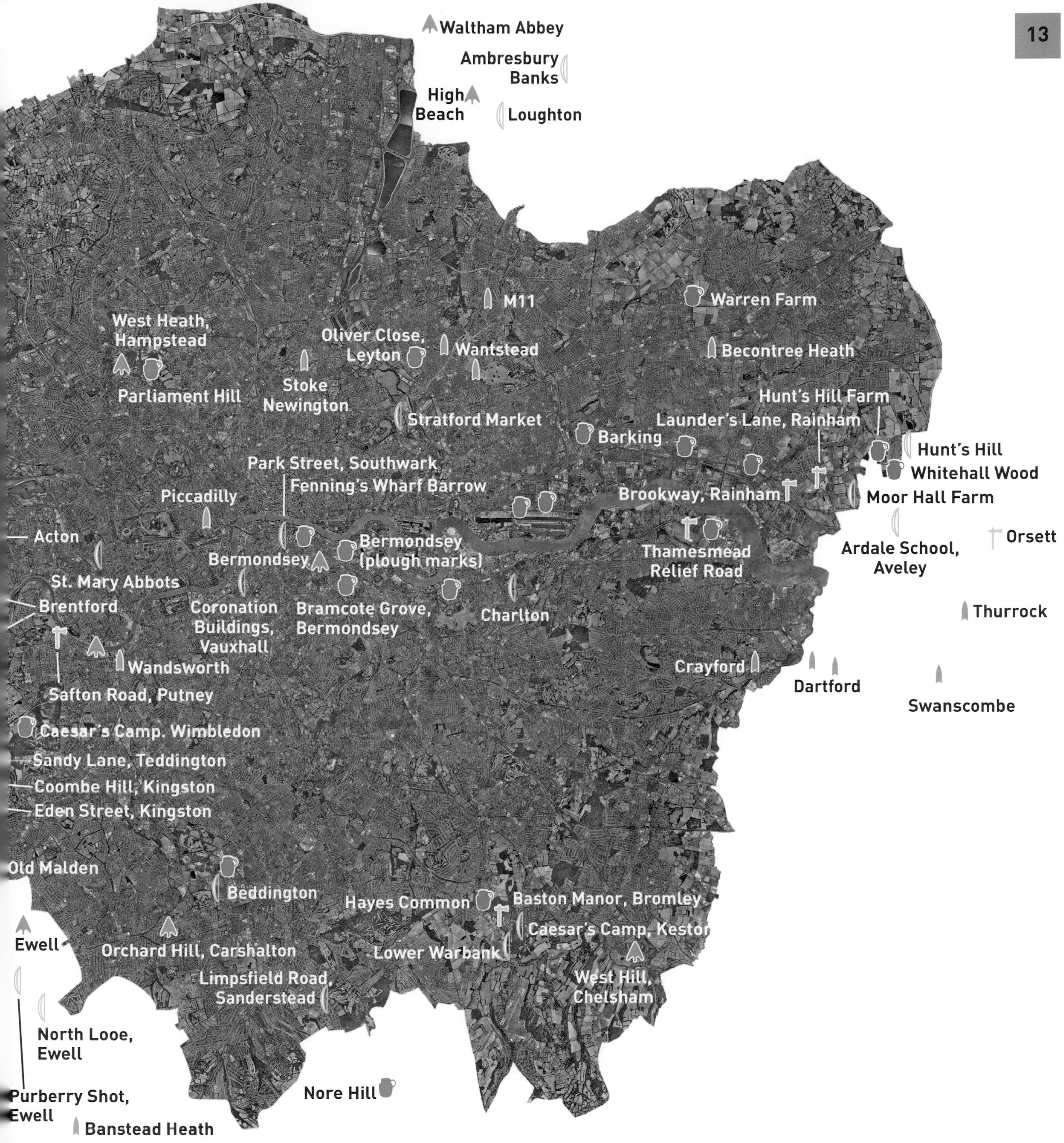

Waltham Abbey

Ambresbury Banks

High Beach   Loughton

M11   Warren Farm

West Heath, Hampstead

Oliver Close, Leyton   Wantstead   Becontree Heath

Parliament Hill   Stoke Newington   Hunt's Hill Farm

Stratford Market   Launder's Lane, Rainham

Barking   Hunt's Hill

Park Street, Southwark   Whitehall Wood

Fenning's Wharf Barrow   Brookway, Rainham   Moor Hall Farm

Piccadilly   Orsett

Acton   Ardale School, Aveley

St. Mary Abbots   Bermondsey   Thamesmead Relief Road

Brentford   Bermondsey (plough marks)   Thurrock

Coronation Buildings, Vauxhall   Bramcote Grove, Bermondsey   Charlton

Wandsworth   Crayford   Dartford

Safton Road, Putney   Swanscombe

Caesar's Camp. Wimbledon

Sandy Lane, Teddington

Coombe Hill, Kingston

Eden Street, Kingston

Old Malden

Beddington

Hayes Common   Baston Manor, Bromley

Ewell   Caesar's Camp, Keston

Orchard Hill, Carshalton   Lower Warbank

Limpsfield Road, Sanderstead   West Hill, Chelsham

North Looe, Ewell

Purberry Shot, Ewell   Nore Hill

Banstead Heath

Palaeolithic c.450,000–8300 BC
Mesolithic c.8300–4500 BC
Neolithic c.4500–2300 BC
Bronze Age c.2300–650 BC
Iron Age c.650 BC–AD 43

Cripplegate

Fort

Newgate

Amphitheatre

Cheapside

Ludgate

St. Paul's Cathedral

Bath-house

Site of Palace

Site of Temple of Mithras

River Walbrook

ROMAN LONDON

Several factors influenced the Roman invaders in their choice of a site for the future Londinium. The valley was fertile, and the navigable river headed east towards the North Sea and the mouth of the River Rhine, one of Europe's most important waterways. It made for ideal trading headquarters, linked inwards to a prosperous farming and timber area, and outwards to the Roman Empire. The site was stable and rivers and springs supplied plentiful freshwater. It was protected in the west by the River Fleet and in the south by steep slopes leading down to the Thames.

The first version of Roman London was burned to the ground by Queen Boudicca in AD 60. The Romans persevered, however. They maintained Londinium as the Governor's headquarters, and over the next 50 years a grander and more ambitious town was built. In addition to the

basilica and forum, and the fort in Cricklewood, street systems were laid out, shops and commercial buildings constructed, and residential areas created as the population expanded. The port also became hugely active in trade. A devastating fire severely damaged the town in about AD 125, after which the growth of trade and population declined, but not enough to deter the Roman authorities from their biggest building project yet – the construction of a massive city wall, completed by about the year 210. Over two miles long, and enclosing an area of 330 acres, it rose at least 20 feet high, and was 8 feet thick at the base, with a deep ditch outside and earth piled high within. A few small sections can still be seen.

By the end of the third century, political unrest was growing in the Empire and Londinium's great days were over. In 410, the British appealed to the Emperor Honorius (393–423) for military help against the northern invaders, but he refused. Londoners were now on their own.

The development of Roman London

by AD 125

by AD 375

Cornhill

Basilica

Forum

Leadenhall

Aldgate

Riverside wall
built during
4th century AD

London Bridge

Tower
of London

R i v e r   T h a m e s

Norman London
1: Fleet Prison
2: Tower of Montfitchet
3: Baynard's Castle
4: St. Paul's
5: Jew's Cemetery
6: The Tower
7: Winchester Palace
8: Lambeth Palace
9: Westminster Palace

St. Mary's Priory
Priory of John of Jerusalem
St. Mart
St. Bartholomew's Priory
St. Bartholomew's
St. Giles's
The Temple
St. James's
St. Peter's Abbey

Saxon London

Main Area of Saxon
Lundenwic (7th–9th century)

Norman London

City Wall

Monastery

Hospital

Other important building

Marshland

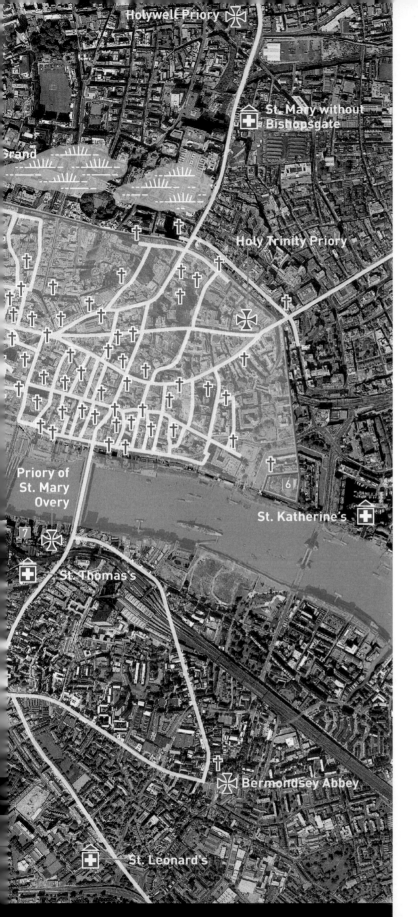

SAXON AND NORMAN LONDON

After the Roman legions departed, Pict and Anglo-Saxon invasions accelerated throughout northern and eastern England, and by the end of the fifth century the whole of eastern Britain was under Anglo-Saxon control. But curiously there is little evidence that the invaders had any desire to take over the city of London. Their purpose was to grab land for farming. They had little interest in trade with the outside world, and they regarded cities as useless extravagances. Only in the sixth century did Anglo-Saxons begin to occupy the city, mainly on the western side of Walbrook (meaning 'stream of the British').

After the Anglo-Saxons' conversion to Christianity, a bishop for the East Saxon people was appointed. Ethelbert of Kent (560–616) built a church dedicated to St. Paul in London as the bishop's cathedral. But Ethelbert's capital was Canterbury, and St. Augustine based the church's archiepiscopal see there. Canterbury's primacy in the church of England has survived to this day. Lundenwic, as London was now called, was a port and a market place, but not a religious centre. When Ethelbert died, paganism returned for a time, and the London and Rochester bishops were forced to flee to France.

The Vikings began to invade northern England at the end of the eighth century, and attacked London in 842, inflicting what the Anglo-Saxon Chronicle records as 'a great slaughter'. Twenty years later, their armies gathered in East Anglia and defeated the Anglo-Saxons. In 871 the Vikings wintered in London. They were eventually overcome by King Alfred the Great (871–899), who after 886 began to reinforce London's fortifications, making it one of his many *burhs* (Anglo-Saxon for fortified town). New streets were laid out between Cheapside and the Thames, and around Cannon Street to the east of Walbrook.

One hundred years later, in 994, another Viking invasion led to ravaging of the south-east and a siege of London, but the city held out, and became the country's main anti-Viking centre. By 1016, despite London's resistance, the Danish king Canute (d.1035) had become King of England. Major developments in the city now began, the bridge was rebuilt, new streets stretched north from Cheapside, new quays were erected on the river, and many small parish churches were constructed. There are a number of Danish survivals outside the city walls, such as St. Clement Danes in the Strand, St. Bride's in Fleet Street, and settlements in Greenwich and Woolwich.

In 1060, under the reign of Edward the Confessor (1042–66), the building of Westminster Abbey began and was completed 15 years later. Then came the Norman Conquest of 1066, and within 15 years work had begun on the White Tower, and other great enterprises. By 1200, London suburbs stretched west to Westminster and south to Southwark, a new stone-built London Bridge was under construction, and work had begun on the magnificent romanesque St. Paul's Cathedral, which survived until the Great Fire in September 1666.

The church in London c.1300

1:	All Hallows Barking
2:	All Hallows Bread Street
3:	All Hallows Grasschurch
4:	All Hallows the Great
5:	All Hallows Honey Lane
6:	All Hallows the Little
7:	All Hallows Staining
8:	All Hallows on the Wall
9:	Holy Trinity the Little
10:	St. Alban Wood Street
11:	St. Andrew Castle Baynard
12:	St. Andrew Cornhill
13:	St. Andrew Hubbard
14:	St. Anne (or Agnes) Aldersgate
15:	St. Antonin
16:	St. Audoen
17:	St. Augustine Papey
18:	St. Augustine at St. Paul's Gate
19:	St. Bartholomew the Little
20:	St. Benet Fink
21:	St. Benet Grasschurch
22:	St. Benet Sherehog
23:	St. Benet Woodwharf
24:	St. Botolph Billingsgate
25:	St. Christopher
26:	St. Clement Eastcheap

27:	St. Dionis Backchurch
28:	St. Dunstan in the East
29:	St. Edmund Lombard Street
30:	St. Ethelburga
31:	St. Faith under St. Paul's
32:	St. George Botolph Lane
33:	St. Gregory by St. Paul's
34:	St. Helen
35:	St. James Garlickhithe
36:	St. John the Evangelist
37:	St. John Walbrook
38:	St. John Zachary
39:	St. Katharine Colemanchurch
40:	St. Katharine Trinity nr. Aldgate
41:	St. Lawrence Jewry
42:	St. Lawrence Poutney
43:	St. Leonard Eastcheap
44:	St. Leonard Foster Lane
45:	St. Magnus Bridge
46:	St. Margaret Bridge Street
47:	St. Margaret Lothbury
48:	St. Margaret Moses
49:	St. Margaret Pattens
50:	St. Martin Ludgate
51:	St. Martin Orgar
52:	St. Martin Outwich
53:	St. Martin Pomary

54:	St. Martin in the Vintry
55:	St. Mary Abchurch
56:	St. Mary Aldermanbury
57:	St. Mary Aldermarychurch
58:	St. Mary at Axe
59:	St. Mary Bothaw
60:	St. Mary le Bow
61:	St. Mary Colechurch
62:	St. Mary Fenchurch
63:	St. Mary at Hill
64:	St. Mary Magdalen Milk Street
65:	St. Mary Magdalen Old Fish Street
66:	St. Mary Mounthaw
67:	St. Mary Somerset
68:	St. Mary Staining Lane
69:	St. Mary Woolchurch
70:	St. Mary Woolnoth
71:	St. Matthew Friday Street
72:	St. Michael Bassishaw
73:	St. Michael at Corn
74:	St. Michael Cornhill
75:	St. Michael Crooked Lane
76:	St. Michael Paternoster in the Riole
77:	St. Michael Queenhithe
78:	St. Michael Wood Street
79:	St. Mildred Bread Street
80:	St. Mildred Poultry

New Hospital of St. Mary without Bishopsgate ('St. Mary Spital'), 1197

Hospital of St. Mary of Bethlehem, c.1247

101

Bishopsgate Street

8

30
17

Houndsditch

89 Convent of St. Helen (Augustinian nuns), before 1216
58
34

52

Abbey of St. Mary and St. Francis (Franciscan nuns or 'minoresses') c.1293-4

20

Priory of Holy Trinity Aldgate, 1107-8

12

100

90 Cornhill

Aldgate Street

40

74

3

Fenchurch Street

39

Hospital of Friars of the Cross ('Crutched Friars'), 1269

21 27 62 7

Minchen Lane

49

85

Mart Lane

Syvethe Lane

13 13 32 63

28

1

24

Petty Wales

106

Tower of London

Hospital of St. Katherine by the Tower, 1148

81: St. Nicholas Acon
82: St. Nicholas Coldabbey
83: St. Nicholas Olave
84: St. Nicholas in the Shambles
85: St. Olave by the Tower
86: St. Olave Old Jewry
87: St. Olave Silver Street
88: St. Pancras
89: St. Peter Broad Street
90: St. Peter Cornhill
91: St. Peter the Little Paul's Wharf
92: St. Peter Westcheap
93: St. Stephen Coleman Street
94: St. Stephen Walbrook
95: St. Swithin
96: St. Thomas the Apostle
97: St. Vedast
98: St. Andrew Holborn
99: St. Botolph without Aldersgate

100: St. Botolph without Aldgate
101: St. Botolph without Bishopsgate
102: St. Bride
103: St. Dunstan in the West
104: St. Giles without Cripplegate
105: St. Sepulchre
106: St. Peter in the Bailey
107: St Clement Danes

MEDIEVAL LONDON

After the Norman invasion London's population more than doubled, perhaps to 80,000 people, tightly packed within the Roman walls. The streets laid out in earlier centuries remained in place, with narrow lanes joining them between the many hundreds of new houses, parish churches and religious establishments. A number of monastic precincts were founded; remnants of a handful still survive, such as St. Bartholomew in Smithfield and St. Helen's Bishopsgate. Hospitals, most connected to priories, went up beside the Tower, next to St. Bartholomew, and on various sites outside the Wall.

All along the Thames waterfront, where the Roman riverside wall was decaying, land was gradually reclaimed to create wharves and quay fronts, narrowing the river in places by more than 100 yards. The bridge, which remained the only link between London and the southern counties, had been rebuilt in stone starting in 1176, and was a remarkable engineering achievement led by Peter of Colechurch, head of the Fraternity of St. Thomas. It took 33 years to complete, and before long it was entirely lined with houses and workshops along its outer edges. Several times over the next centuries parts of it collapsed under the weight of these buildings, and because of the intense compression of the river below, narrowed by the bridge's 19 arches. But through many restorations it survived to 1832, almost until the reign of Queen Victoria. On the south side, Southwark began to grow, the land largely owned by the archbishop of Canterbury, the abbot of Bermondsey and the bishop of Winchester, but it was a sleazy area, renowned as the haven of criminals and prostitutes.

Upstream from the city, Westminster began to develop as a separate town, stretching from the river Tyburn to Charing Cross, and dominated by the abbey and the royal palace next to it. Henry III (1216–72) enlarged the palace and rebuilt the abbey, and Richard II (1377–99) reconstructed Westminster Hall to provide space for royal courts and government offices. William Caxton's first printing press was set up in the abbey precinct in 1476. Although Westminster and the city were joined by the Strand, people usually travelled from one place to the other on the river.

Thus the tradition became established that the city was Britain's capital and the centre of its trade, while government was conducted at the monarch's base in Westminster.

Scotland Yard

Whitehall Palace

The Strand

Somerset House

Arundel House

The Temple

Bridewell

Fleet Street

Holborn Bar

Holborn Street

NEWGATE

LUDGATE

ALDERSGATE

Grey Friars

The Shambles

St Bartholomew

Aldersgate Street

Black Friars

The Fleet

St Paul's Cathedral

Baynard's Castle

Paul's Wharf

Fish Wharf

R i v e r   T h a m e s

TUDOR LONDON

When William Shakespeare first came from Stratford to London in the late 1580s, in his mid-20s, the medieval city had been radically changed by Henry VIII's dissolution of the monasteries (1536–40), and by a devastating plague in 1563 which had killed over 20,000 people, nearly a quarter of the population. New housing and workshops were built over many of the monastic areas, often by immigrants who set up centres producing tiles, pottery and glass. Despite the plagues, the population was growing rapidly.

Legislation passed in 1574 prohibited theatres within the city walls. London's first purpose-built theatre was the Curtain in Shoreditch, built in 1577, followed by the Rose, the Hope, the Globe and the Swan on the south bank, west of Southwark. Shakespeare probably lived within the city, perhaps in Cornhill, within easy walking distance of the theatres.

The nobility and rich merchants were tending by this time to move westwards, taking over the former residences of bishops and priors along the Strand towards Westminster. The Earl of Somerset demolished the

Tudor London

Monastic precincts

✠ Monasteries

⚖ Legal inns

○ Other institutions

🏠 Remarkable house

🏠 Fair or large house

🏠 Houses

🏠 Tenement/divided house

🏠 Cottages

RIPPLEGATE

Guildhall

Austin Friars

BISHOPSGATE

The Stocks

Holy Trinity

Corn Hill

ALDGATE

Lombard Street

East Cheap

Tower Street

Billingsgate

London Bridge

Tower of London

residences of the bishops of Lichfield and Llandaff, and built a magnificent renaissance palace, Somerset House, overlooking the river, completed by 1550. Other large houses were built along Holborn Bar, and close to the legal quarter around Fleet Street. New but cheaper housing was going up to the north and east too, around hamlets such as Ratcliffe, Shoreditch, Whitechapel and Limehouse, and giving birth to the East End. This is where the growing population of craftsmen and semi-skilled workers were largely housed, joined by shipwrights and sailors. The city itself contained a broad mixture of rich and poor, merchants and craftsmen, living close to one another. The West End was much more exclusive.

London was now divided into three areas. Within the city walls was the medieval mixture of affluent citizens, craftsmen and paupers. In the East End was the growing army of workers serving the city's diverse trade and manufacture. But if you were rich and titled, you headed west. Enterprise and commerce, fuelled by immigrations from outside London, created the foundations of the metropolis that we know today.

STUART LONDON

At the beginning of the reign of James I (1603–25), the cramped and crowded city remained contained within its medieval walls, with an affluent suburb developing westwards towards Westminster, and the poor living in the East End. By the end of the century, after the Civil War in the 1640s, the Great Plague in 1665 and the Great Fire in 1666, London would be changed almost beyond recognition.

The East India Company established an anchorage at Blackwall in 1614, which led to further developments in the area. Stepney became the centre of the shipping industry, and cheap housing went up to accommodate shipwrights, carpenters, anchorsmiths and ropemakers, as well as merchant sailors and their officers. By 1680 the population of the East End had risen from around 40,000 to 250,000.

By the middle of the century massive developments had also taken place in the West End. In 1608, Robert Cecil, Earl of Salisbury, acquired land near St. Martin-in-the-Fields from the king, where he built 'many fair houses in a gentle row' and created St. Martin's Lane. In 1631 the Earl of Bedford began to develop Covent Garden, appointing Inigo Jones as his architect, and producing one of the finest large-scale plans ever created in London. Leicester Square was built up in the 1670s, and named after the grand house built 40 years earlier by the Earl of Leicester, where the Empire cinema now stands.

During the Civil War (1642–46) London was the headquarters of the Parliamentarians, and although the city was ringed with a vast new system of forts and ditches to defend against possible invasion by the Royalist army, no such event took place. The nearest anyone got to conquering London was Prince Rupert's victory at Brentford, five miles from Westminster, but he retreated when confronted by the 24,000-strong Parliamentarian army under the Earl of Essex at Turnham Green in Chiswick.

Twenty-three years later, one in four Londoners were wiped out by the Great Plague, a monstrous catastrophe that began in the slums of St. Giles in February 1665 and lasted some 11 months, killing perhaps as many as 100,000 people. Then, at three o'clock in the morning on 2 September 1666, a fire broke out in a bakery in Pudding Lane, and over the next three days, fed by a strong easterly wind, spread west along the river bank, and then all around the city. When finally the wind dropped on 6 September, 460 acres had been virtually burned to the ground, and some 13,300 houses destroyed, as well as St. Paul's Cathedral, 87 churches, 52 company halls, and much else.

After this devastation, the reconstruction of London took place with remarkable speed and efficiency. By the end of the century new town planning laws were in place, hundreds of streets had been widened and laid out, thousands of new houses (made of brick because timber was now banned) had been built and a number of major new public buildings completed. Sir Christopher Wren's new St. Paul's Cathedral was finished by 1710.

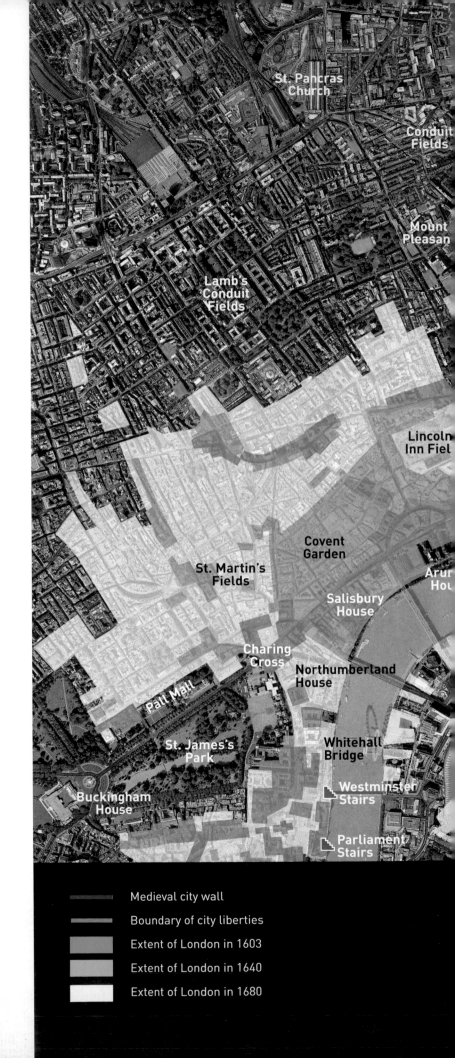

St. Pancras Church

Conduit Fields

Mount Pleasan

Lamb's Conduit Fields

Lincoln Inn Fiel

Covent Garden

St. Martin's Fields

Arur Hou

Salisbury House

Charing Cross

Northumberland House

Pall Mall

Whitehall Bridge

St. James's Park

Westminster Stairs

Buckingham House

Parliament Stairs

Medieval city wall

Boundary of city liberties

Extent of London in 1603

Extent of London in 1640

Extent of London in 1680

ISLINGTON

Finsbury
Fields

SHOREDITCH

BETHNAL GREEN

CLERKENWELL

New
Artillery
Ground

Charterhouse

Moor
Fields

Ely
Place

Spitalfields

WHITECHAPEL

St. Paul's Cathedral

Goodman's
Fields

The Temple

ssex
ouse

Queenhithe

Old Barge
House

Paris
Garden

Billingsgate

The Tower

Bankside

London
Bridge

St. Katharine's
Hospital

Execution
Dock

Hermitage
Stairs

Pickleherring
Stairs

Savory
Dock

WAPPING

St. George's
Church

ROTHERHITHE

London Wall

Smithfield

Guildhall

Lothbu

Fleet Street

St. Paul's Cathedral

Cheapside

London Wall

Queenhithe and former
mouth of the River Fleet

THE GREAT FIRE

The king's baker, Thomas Farriner, lived with his family in a baking house in Pudding Lane, just to the north-east of London Bridge. A fire broke out there, in the middle of the night of Sunday, 2 September 1666. One of his workmen aroused the household, and the baker, his wife and child escaped over the neighbouring rooftops. But there was a strong wind that night, and it had been a hot and dry August, so all the neighbouring timber houses were unusually vulnerable. The flames spread rapidly westward along the river, reaching Three Cranes Walk (where Southwark Bridge now stands) by the following afternoon. It was soon out of control, advancing west towards the Fleet river and north beyond Cornhill and the Royal Exchange. That night it reached St Paul's, which unfortunately happened to be surrounded by wooden scaffolding.

Over the next two days, fire-fighters under the orders of the Duke of York attempted to halt the fire by pulling down houses on either side of the Fleet river, a strategy which failed there but succeeded in Tower Street, stopping the flames before they reached the Tower of London. Most Londoners simply fled, camping in the neighbouring fields, in Highgate, Finsbury and Islington. The fire raged for three more days, but by Friday the wind had dropped, and the fire-fighters managed to dowse the flames.

The destruction had consumed five-sixths of the city. But reconstruction now began, and proceeded with energy and a new optimism. Medieval, corrupt and plague-ridden London had gone. A new, rational era lay ahead.

The spread of the Great Fire, 1666

by Monday 3rd September

by Wednesday 5th September

✝ Churches destroyed and not rebuilt

✝ Churches rebuilt

Royal Exchange

Cornhill

Leadenhall

All Hallows
by the Tower

London Wall

London Bridge

Thomas Farriner's
bakehouse,
Pudding Lane

Tower
of London

R i v e r   T h a m e s

St. Pancras,
Euston Road
(1818–22)

Foundling
Hospital
(1742–52)

St. James,
Clerkenwell
(1788–92)

St. Luke's
Hospital
(1782–4)

University College,
Gower Street (1827)

St. Luke,
Old Street
(1727–32)

Middlesex
Sessions House,
Clerkenwell
(1779–82)

St. Marylebone
Church (1813–17)

St. George,
Queen Square (1703–23)

St. Botolph, Aldersgate
Street (1789–91)

All Souls,
Langham Place
(1822–4)

British
Museum
(1823–47)

St. George, Bloomsbury Way
(1716–23)

St. Mary,
Wyndham Place
(1823)

St. Peter,
Vere Street
(1721–4)

12

26 **38** **1**

13

28

5

37

2 **16**

St. Mark,
North Audley Street
(1825–8)

St. George,
Hanover
Square
(1720–4)

35

7

Skinners' Hall
(façade 1790)

27

41 **9** **25**

23

Burlington
Arcade
(1815–19)

30

21

31

Grosvenor Chapel (1730)

24

36 **34** **32**

St. John,
Waterloo Road
(1823–4)

33

14

40

22

20

10

18

St. George the
Martyr, Borough High
Street (1734–6)

4

17 **15**

St. George's Hospital,
now Lainsborough
Hotel (1827)

Buckingham
Palace
(1824–30)

General Lying-in
Hospital, York Road (1828)

Holy Trinity,
Trinity Church Square
(1823–4)

St. Peter,
Liverpool Grove
(1823–4)

St. Peter, Eaton Square
(1824–7)

St. John,
Smith Square
(1713–28)

St. Luke,
Sydney Street
(1820–4)

Royal Hospital
(ancillary buildings 1814–19)

Place of worship

Public building

Hospital

Educational establishment

Museum or gallery

Theatre

Club

Shopping development

Area of Georgian development

Geffrye Museum, Kingsland Road (1715)

St. Leonard, High Street (1736–40)

Wesley's Chapel, City Road (1777–8)

Christ Church, Spitalfields (1714–27)

11

St. Botolph, Aldgate (1741–4)

St. Anne, Limehouse (1714–25)

Trinity House, Tower Hill (1793–5)

St. George-in-the-East (1714–22)

29

Royal Mint (completed 1807–9)

Guy's Hospital (1722–80)

St. John, Wapping (1756)

34: United Services Club, now Institute of Directors (1827)
35: Covent Garden Market (1828–30)
36: Athenaeum Club (1829–30)
37: St. Dunstan's in the West (1829–33)
38: Goldsmiths' Hall (1829–35)
39: Fishmongers' Hall (1831–3)
40: Charing Cross Hospital, now Charing Cross Police Station
41: National Gallery (1834–8)

GEORGIAN LONDON

In the course of the 18th century occurred the most dramatic changes in London's history, largely funded by a massive growth in the economy and the wealth of individuals, who made their fortunes from trade and the acquisition of colonies in America, India, the Pacific and Africa. Apart from the vast expansion of building, new systems of sewerage were introduced, as well as street lighting, paving, crime and fire control, public open spaces, and many other improvements. In the city itself, the Stock Exchange opened, the activities of the Bank of England were expanded, many private banks were founded, and numerous insurance companies were established, making London the leading financial capital in Europe.

A vast range of manufacturing industries were housed in different regions all over the city, the more noxious ones, such as leather tanning and glue-making, being compelled by new legislation to locate themselves well away from the centre, in places like Blackwall and Rotherhythe. Breweries were established in Chiswick, Hammersmith and Greenwich. Clerkenwell became home to a huge range of crafts, including clockmakers, upholsterers, locksmiths, jewellers, surgical instrument makers and coach builders. A directory of traders in Westminster in 1749 lists tailors and dressmakers, shoemakers, carpenters, butchers, bakers, candlestick makers and distillers, all providing for the needs of the middle and upper classes.

But there was much poverty in the city too. The wages of working-class people were barely enough to support them, and the rapid influx of workers from the rest of Britain created desperately overcrowded housing in the poor areas. Infant mortality was agonisingly high, death rates exceeded birth rates, and yet the population continued to increase. Crime rates were also rising rapidly. By the end of the century, London was twice the size it had been in 1700, and the population was close to a million. The rich moved west along Oxford Street and Piccadilly, while the poor were confined to districts around the old city – St. Giles, Southwark, Bermondsey, Whitechapel, Spitalfields and Clerkenwell. Fine housing was developed in Mayfair up to Oxford Street, and all the way along the north of the old city, from Marylebone to Shoreditch. Everywhere, grand churches and public buildings in the Georgian style were going up, such as the Adelphi (completed 1773), the Bank of England (1734), the Mansion House (1753), St. George's, Hanover Square (1724), the Admiralty (1726) and many others.

VICTORIAN LONDON

In the course of Queen Victoria's reign (1837–1901), London's population grew from around one and a half million to over seven million, and expanded outwards into the surrounding counties of Essex, Hertfordshire, Middlesex, Surrey and Kent. The chaos of shipping in the Pool of London was gradually alleviated by the opening of docks further down river, starting with the West India Docks on the north side of the Isle of Dogs in 1802, and in due course many more on both sides of the river as far as Tilbury (1886). Funded by booms in the economy, building developments advanced in areas such as Chelsea, Bayswater, King's Cross, Camberwell and Clapham, and, as the century progressed, outwards towards Streatham, Hammersmith, Marylebone, Hornsey, Tottenham, Walthamstow and Stratford.

The most significant development of the century was in transport for the general public. In 1800 it comprised coaches, hackney carriages and ferry boats, affordable only to the middle classes. Everyone else walked. The revolution began in 1829, when the first omnibuses (meaning 'for all') began to operate down the Marylebone Road between Paddington and the City. By the middle of the century, well over a thousand buses were traversing the city. London's first railway, from London Bridge to Deptford, opened in 1836, extending later to Greenwich. Initially the railway companies were focussed on mainline trains across Britain, and reluctant to invest in suburban lines, which were thought less lucrative. Moreover, the vast demolitions which the railways required (over five per cent of London's built-up areas were appropriated) worsened the already desperately crowded living conditions of many Londoners. The world's first underground railway system opened in 1863, between Paddington and Farringdon, and the first tubes (more deeply tunnelled) in the 1880s. In the last quarter of the century, trams were developed in many suburban areas.

The City itself was transformed, as London became the financial centre of the British Empire. Banks and insurance companies built grand headquarters around the Bank of England, and Queen Victoria opened the classical Royal Exchange in 1844. In Westminster, Whitehall too was developed out of all recognition to provide government offices on the scale the empire required. All over London, new public buildings went up: schools, hospitals, churches, libraries, town halls, prisons, department stores and mansion blocks of flats. By the end of the century, the overall pattern of today's London had been laid out.

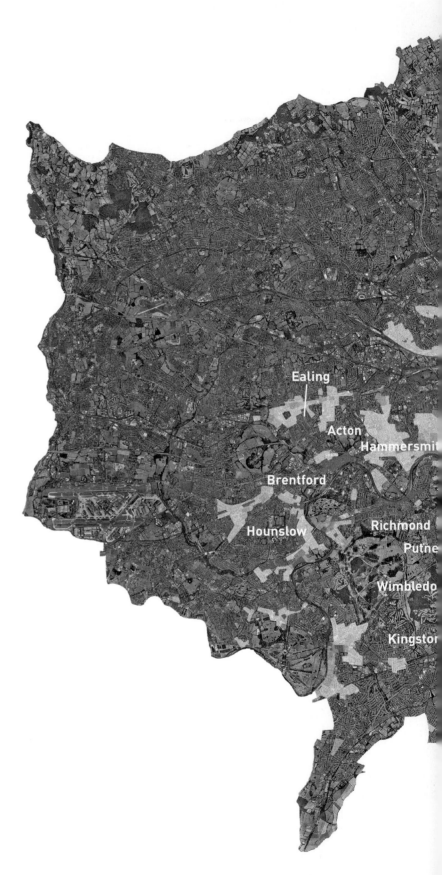

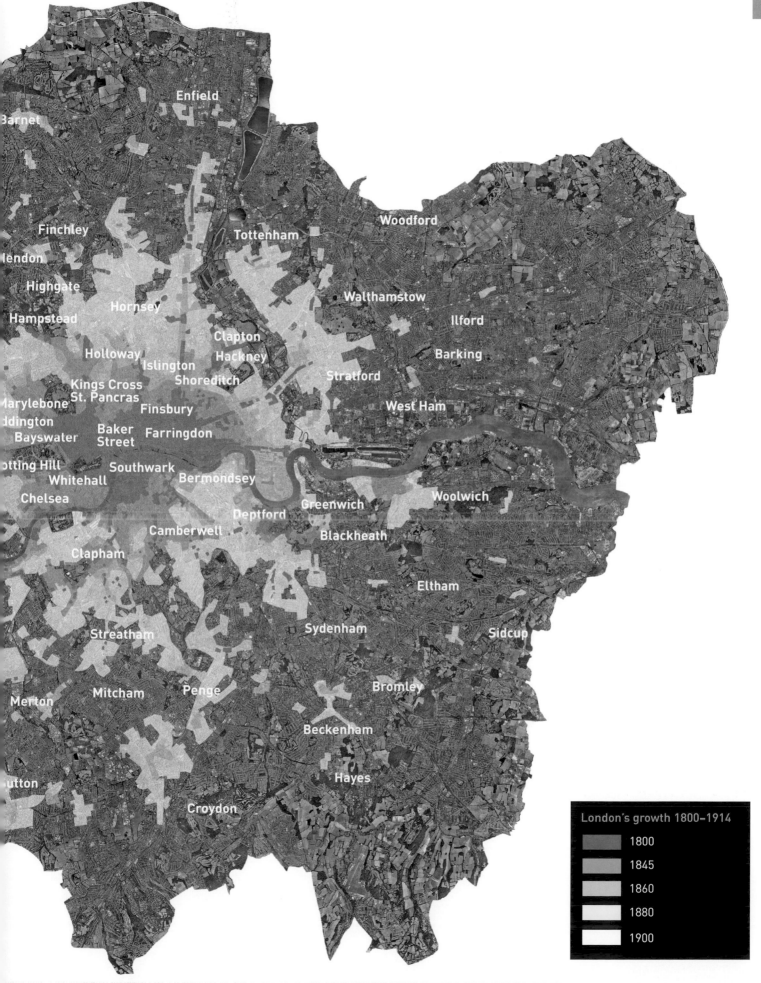

Barnet

Enfield

Finchley

Hendon

Highgate

Hornsey

Hampstead

Tottenham

Woodford

Walthamstow

Ilford

Clapton

Hackney

Holloway

Islington

Shoreditch

Stratford

Barking

Kings Cross

St. Pancras

Marylebone

Finsbury

West Ham

Paddington

Baker
Street

Farringdon

Bayswater

Notting Hill

Southwark

Whitehall

Bermondsey

Chelsea

Greenwich

Woolwich

Deptford

Camberwell

Blackheath

Clapham

Eltham

Streatham

Sydenham

Sidcup

Merton

Mitcham

Penge

Bromley

Beckenham

Sutton

Hayes

Croydon

London's growth 1800–1914

1800

1845

1860

1880

1900

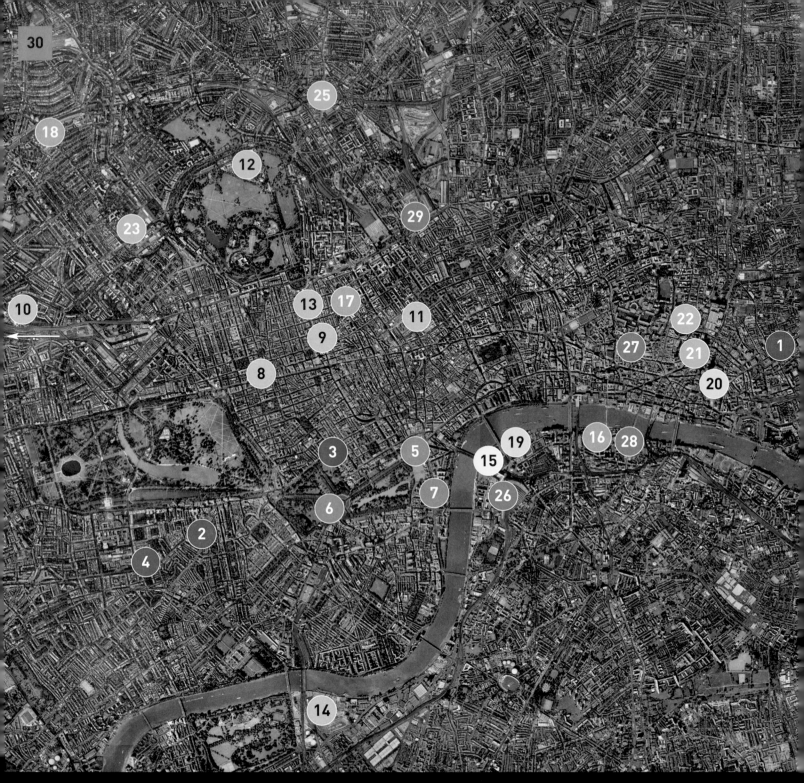

20th-century London buildings and architects

1. Whitechapel Art Gallery,
   Charles Harrison Townsend, 1901
2. Harrods,
   Stevens & Munt,
3. Ritz Hotel, 1905
   Mewès & Davis, 1906
4. Victoria & Albert Museum,
   Alfred Waterhouse, 1909
5. Admiralty Arch,
   Sir Aston Webb, 1910
6. Buckingham Palace,
   Sir Aston Webb, 1912
7. Cenotaph,
   Sir Edwin Lutyens, 1919
8. Selfridges,

   R. F. Atkinson, 1928
9. Broadcasting House,
   G. Val Myers, 1932
10. Hoover Building,
    Wallis Gilbert & Partners, 1932
11. Senate House,
    Charles Holden, 1933
12. Penguin Pool, London Zoo
    Berthold Lubetkin, 1934
13. Royal Institute of British Architects,
    Grey Warnum, 1936
14. Battersea Power Station,
    Sir Giles Gilbert Scott, 1937
15. Royal Festival Hall,
    Sir Leslie Martin, 1951
16. Tate Modern,
    Sir Giles Gilbert Scott, 1963

    (converted by Herzog & de
    Meuron, 2000)
17. Post Office Tower,
    Eric Bedford, 1965
18. Alexandra Road Housing Estate,
    Neave Brown, 1969
19. Royal National Theatre,
    Sir Denys Lasden, 1975
20. Lloyds Building,
    Richard Rogers, 1979–84
21. National Westminster Tower,
    Richard Seifert & Partners, 1980
22. Broadgate,
    Arup Associates, 1982–4
23. The Mound Stand, Lord's Cricket
    Ground,
    Michael Hopkins & Partners, 1985–7

Buildings by decades
- 1900–9
- 1910–19
- 1920–9
- 1930–9
- 1950–9
- 1960–9
- 1970–9
- 1980–9
- 1990–

24. Canary Wharf Tower,
Cézar Pelli, 1986
25. Grand Union Walk Housing,
Nicholas Grimshaw & Partners, 1988
26. Continental Train Platform (Eurostar),
Nicholas Grimshaw & Partners, 1993
27. 88 Wood Street, EC2,
Richard Rogers, 1993–2001
28. Shakespeare's Globe Theatre,
Theo Crosby, 1997
29. British Library,
Colin St John Wilson, 1997
30. Millennium Dome,
Richard Rogers, 1999

THE 20TH CENTURY

Two world wars had a powerful effect on London in the course of the 20th century. The Blitz in 1941 wiped out large areas of the City, the East End and the West End, but nowhere near as much as had been destroyed in the Great Fire in 1666. By the middle of the century, the population had started to decline, and the introduction of a welfare state had introduced widespread improvements in housing, health and the social conditions of the poor. After 1918, the London County Council began the most ambitious programme of housing development in London's history. Private companies followed its lead by buying cheap land on the outer edges, and introducing hundreds of thousands of 'semi-detached' homes all around London. Improved public transport allowed these suburban dwellers to travel in to work. Later in the century, the efficiency of these transport systems declined, largely because of poor management and inadequate investment, leading to chaotic traffic jams in the rush hours.

Meanwhile, despite wild variations in the state of the national economy, the city maintained its position as one of the world's leading financial centres. In the first half of the century, the old Victorian manufacturing industries gradually moved out of the East End and relocated in suburbs such as Holloway, Camden Town and Hackney, particularly after the bombing damage in the Second World War; and most of them eventually left London altogether. The port of London, on which the city's economy had depended for centuries, declined rapidly in the late 1960s and was in due course replaced with one of the largest and most ambitious developments in the city's history – the London Docklands. In 1946, London's status as an international city was enhanced when a new airport was opened in Heathrow. The M25 motorway orbiting around Greater London was completed in 1986.

Twentieth-century developments have also made a significant impact on the appearance of the city. The Festival of Britain in 1951 initiated the development of the South Bank as a cultural centre, stretching east to include the Globe Theatre (modelled on the Elizabeth playhouse) and Tate Modern, a giant gallery created from a former power station, across the river from St Paul's Cathedral. The City contains massive skyscrapers built from the 1970s onwards (although the largest by far is at Canary Wharf in Docklands). Oxford Street and Knightsbridge have both become homes to giant department stores.

Regent's Park

St. James's Park

Kensington Gardens

Hyde Park

Green Park

Richmond Park

Bushy Park

Greenwich Park

ROYAL LONDON

London's royal history begins shortly before the Norman Conquest, when in 1060 Edward the Confessor built a palace in Westminster so that he could oversee the construction of Westminster Abbey on the site of the old monastery of St Peter. He died only a few days after it was completed and consecrated. There is no evidence that his successor, King Harold, spent any time there before he died at the Battle of Hastings (1066).

Although London immediately pledged its loyalty to the new Norman regime, William the Conqueror had no doubt that a display of power was required to enforce this pledge. Shortly after his coronation, work began on the White Tower, which lies at the centre of the Tower of London (see pages 34–5), and still conveys a sense of impregnable and irreversible conquest.

A royal residence existed in Greenwich from at least the 13th century, although its origins are unknown. Henry VIII was born there, and married his first wife, Catherine of Aragon, there, but he later spent more time in Bridewell or his new Nonsuch Palace in Sutton (demolished in 1682), and later at Hampton Court, which he acquired from the disgraced Cardinal Wolsey. Elizabeth I, James I and Charles I all resided at Greenwich. The surviving Queen's House, designed by Inigo Jones, was completed in 1662 for James's wife, Queen Anne of Denmark. In William III's reign, what remained of the palace was transformed into the magnificent Royal Naval College, which is now part of the University of Greenwich. William resided at Kensington Palace, which he bought from the Earl of Nottingham in 1689, and enlarged under the designs of Sir Christopher Wren. It remained one of the royal residences until the death of George II in 1760.

In Westminster, Henry VIII had transformed York Place into Whitehall Palace, and in 1531, on the site of the medieval leper hospital of St James, he began the construction of St James's Palace, which became the monarch's official residence when Whitehall Palace burned down in 1698.

Buckingham Palace was built in 1703 by the Duke of Buckingham, and purchased by George III 60 years later. His successor George IV hired John Nash, the creator of Regent Street, to 'improve' the house, a long-term task which he began on the grandest scale and at vast expense, evoking the rage of the Duke of Wellington who had become prime minister in 1828. Queen Victoria was the first monarch to live in the palace at the start of her reign in 1837, and under her aegis in 1847 the forecourt was enclosed behind an east front built between the projecting wings. This front was remodelled in 1913, when the Victoria Monument was raised in the Mall.

The wide variety of royal parks are one of London's finest assets, including Greenwich, Hampton Court and Richmond in the outer areas, and Green Park, St James's Park, Kensington Gardens, Hyde Park and Regent's Park within.

Royal London properties
 1: Hampton Court
 2: Kensington Palace
 3: Buckingham Palace
 4: Tower of London
 5: Queen's House (Greenwich)
 6: Clarence House
 7: Marlborough House
 8: St James's Palace
 9: Lancaster House
10: Bridewell
11: Nonsuch Palace
12: Whitehall Palace

Phases of construction

1189–1272

1272–1399

1509–1547

post 1547

Devereux
Tower

St. Peter
and Vincula

White
Tower

Tower
Green

Bell
Tower

Bloody
Tower

Wakefield
Tower

Traitor's
Gate

Cradle
Tower

Brick
Tower

Constable
Tower

Salt
Tower

Develin
Tower

THE TOWER OF LONDON

Built by Norman masons and Anglo-Saxon labourers, the White Tower was constructed in the 1070s by William I, by the river in the south-east corner of the London Wall. Its primary purpose was to dominate the city, visually and physically, although it could also protect London from Danish attacks, and provide Britain's rulers with a safe haven in the event of civil disorder.

In the reign of the absent king Richard I (1189–99), his chancellor, the Bishop of Ely, embarked on a massive extension of the Tower, doubling the size of the walled area by digging new and deeper ditches to the north and east, and erecting a new tower, the Bell Tower, on the south-west corner. King John (1199–1216) resided there frequently. During the long reign of his successor, Henry III (1216–72), a wide range of further extensions and improvements were made. First, two new towers were built on the waterfront and a new wall enclosed the west side of the so-called Inner Ward. In 1238, after Henry had been forced to retreat to the Tower in the face of hostility from his barons, he began his most ambitious programme – the construction of a new wall around the entire site, once again doubling its area, and enclosing the church of St. Peter ad Vincula. The wall was surrounded by a flooded moat, and reinforced by nine new towers. The work was completed by his son, Edward I (1272–1307), who added new royal lodgings in the upper section of St. Thomas's Tower, and also introduced the first non-residential function to the Tower when he constructed a large new building to house the royal mint. It was also used as a prison, a treasury and a showplace for the king's animals.

During the 15th-century Wars of the Roses, the Tower was a centre for regal celebrations, such as Richard III's coronation in 1483, and Henry VII's victory at Bosworth in 1485. Its walls were also witness to horrific deaths, such as the murder of the 'princes in the tower' (c.1483), and the death in 1478 of the Duke of Clarence, allegedly drowned in a barrel of wine.

Henry VIII was the last king to make improvements to the royal lodgings, which were only used once before the Tower graduated to the role of a prison and place of execution. Over the next century, a large number of political and religious prisoners were held there, including Sir Thomas More, Ann Boleyn, Thomas Cromwell, Catherine Howard, Lady Jane Grey, Princess Elizabeth (the future Elizabeth I), and – the last person to the executed on Tower Green – Robert Devereux, Earl of Essex (1601).

A number of minor additions were made over the next 200 years, most of which have subsequently been removed. The Tower today looks very much as it did in medieval times, largely due to careful restorations that began in the mid-19th century. During the Second World War, bombs damaged several parts of the site, Rudolf Hess, Hitler's deputy Reichsführer, was confined in the Queen's House for four days in May 1941, and the spy Joseph Jakobs was executed there on 14 August 1941.

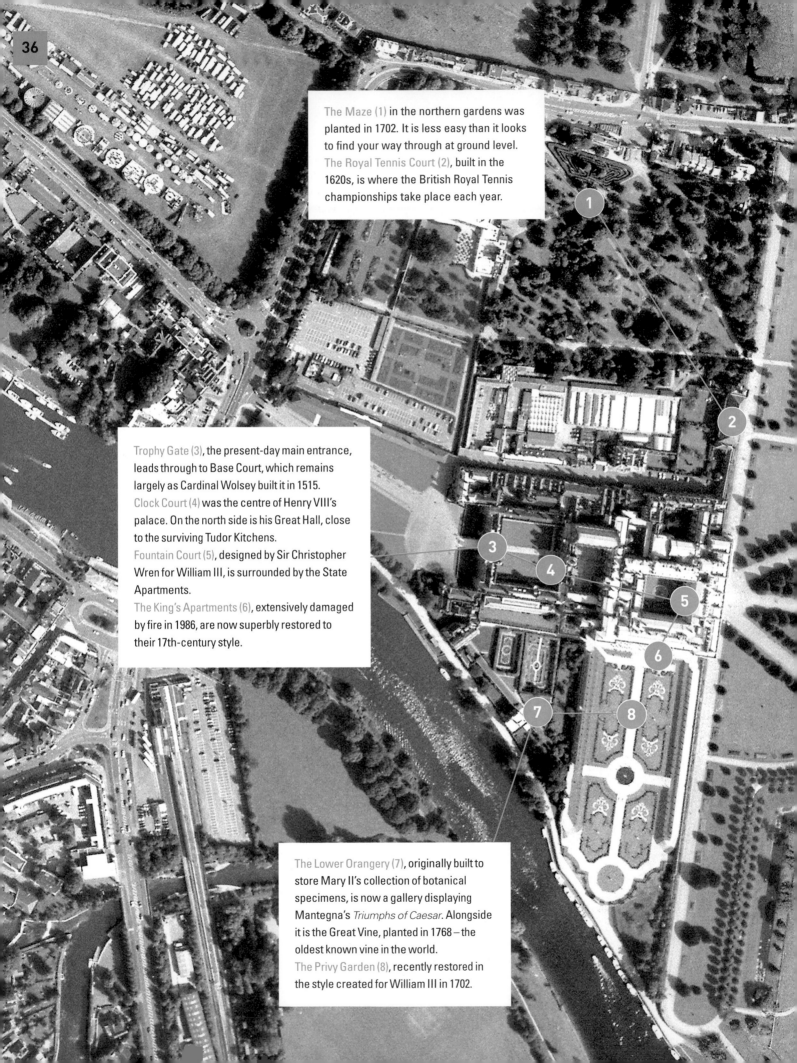

The Maze (1) in the northern gardens was planted in 1702. It is less easy than it looks to find your way through at ground level.
The Royal Tennis Court (2), built in the 1620s, is where the British Royal Tennis championships take place each year.

Trophy Gate (3), the present-day main entrance, leads through to Base Court, which remains largely as Cardinal Wolsey built it in 1515.
Clock Court (4) was the centre of Henry VIII's palace. On the north side is his Great Hall, close to the surviving Tudor Kitchens.
Fountain Court (5), designed by Sir Christopher Wren for William III, is surrounded by the State Apartments.
The King's Apartments (6), extensively damaged by fire in 1986, are now superbly restored to their 17th-century style.

The Lower Orangery (7), originally built to store Mary II's collection of botanical specimens, is now a gallery displaying Mantegna's *Triumphs of Caesar*. Alongside it is the Great Vine, planted in 1768 – the oldest known vine in the world.
The Privy Garden (8), recently restored in the style created for William III in 1702.

Long Water (9), in the home park, was dug for Charles II in the 1660s. The park contains a herd of 270 deer, a 19th-century golf course, and an oak tree which is thought to be over 1,000 years old.

HAMPTON COURT PALACE

The first recorded royal connection with Hampton occurred in 1503, when Henry VII visited the country residence there of the Abbots of the Knights Hospitallers of St John of Jerusalem. In 1514 the estate was acquired by Thomas Wolsey, the Archbishop of York and chief minister to the new king, Henry VIII, and he began to build the most lavish and grandiose residence of any nobleman in Britain. A year later, as the building progressed, he was created a cardinal, and appointed Lord Chancellor. He donated the estate to the king in 1525, and after his fall from grace in 1529 Henry VIII began his own schemes, rebuilding and extending what Wolsey had begun, and completing it by 1540. Half a century later, it was still among the most impressive palaces in Europe. The Duke of Württemberg, who visited Hampton Court in 1592 during Elizabeth I's reign, called it 'the most splendid and most magnificent royal edifice to be found in England, or for that matter in other countries'.

To house his mistress, Lady Castlemaine, Charles II added some rooms in the south-east corner of the palace; but the first major changes, by Sir Christopher Wren under instruction from William III, involved rebuilding the king's and queen's main apartments on the site of the old Tudor lodgings. There were long delays before these apartments were completed in the reign of George I, and in 1732 his son George II added new lodgings, designed by William Kent and known as the Cumberland Suite.

No further monarchs resided there, but the buildings were maintained, and occasionally improved and restored, over the next half century, and in 1838 Queen Victoria opened the palace to the public. Further and more far-reaching restorations were implemented in the last quarter of the 19th century, including many of the original Tudor features.

In 1986, a devastating fire (reportedly caused when a candle fell over in the attic bedroom of an elderly lady grace-and-favour tenant) swept through the King's Apartments and caused extensive damage. The restoration allowed many important discoveries to be made about the history of Hampton Court, and the King's Apartments now look just as they did in the reign of William III. The palace today contains many fine works of art from the Queen's collections, including magnificent tapestries from the Tudor period, works by Bronzino, Corregio, Van Dyke and Rubens acquired by Charles I, and fine 18th-century furniture, clocks and barometers.

THE STORY OF FETTER LANE

In the Middle Ages, Fetter Lane ran parallel to the river Fleet, northwards from Fleet Street, surrounded by fields but just within the city boundary. The source of the name is uncertain: it could be derived from the Norman 'defaytor', meaning defaulter or beggar, or other old French words like foutre (blackguard) or feutriers (felt-makers). Or it could simply refer to the fetters (chains or shackles) manufactured there for the Knights Templar who resided nearby.

John Stow, who wrote *A Survey of London* in the 16th century, claimed that a Roman road had existed on the site before the Dark Ages, a view supported when a Roman urn filled with coins was uncovered below the street. In 959, the local king granted a lease of the land to the west to the abbots of Westminster. Its official existence is first recorded as 'a new lane called Faiteres Lane' in 1329, and other references to its properties from later in the century have survived. In the early 1400s, a famous inn called Le Swan on Le Hope opened on the northern corner by Holborn, which survived (as The Black Swan) until the mid-18th century, after which it became a distillery.

In the earliest surviving map of London (*c.*1550), engraved by Frans Hogenberg, Fetter Lane appears with about a dozen houses on each side, some with wide gaps between them, and fields and trees behind. Two-thirds of the way down, an arch from Clifford's Inn crosses over the road.

The Great Fire of 1666 finally stopped at Fetter Lane. During the Gordon Riots in 1780 (see pages 138–9), the distillery at the top of the road was set ablaze by anti-Catholic rioters. Charles Dickens wrote a vivid account of the dreadful deaths that ensued as workers ran out of the building with their clothes on fire, and rolled in the alcohol mistaking it for water.

Clifford's Inn, where Shakespeare's Justice Shallow, from *The Merry Wives of Windsor*, 'heard the chimes of midnight' in his misspent youth, was the longest surviving Inn of Chancery. It was founded in 1344 when the property was let to law students by the widow of the 6th Baron, Robert de Clifford. They purchased the freehold in 1618. An ugly 1930s block of offices and flats now stands where its hall once stood. Leonard and Virginia Woolf lived here between 1912–13.

The street has also been home to an interesting variety of other people: the composer John Dowland, whose beautiful songs and lute music were popular in their day, lived the last few years of his life there, and was buried at St Anne's, Blackfriars in 1626; Thomas Hobbes, the author of *Leviathan*; the poet John Dryden; Charles Lamb, who went to school in an alley off the lane; Samuel Coleridge who lectured there; not to mention Samuel Butler, Tom Paine, William Cobbett, and Keir Hardie. The Blitz in 1941 flattened the whole street, and since it was rebuilt the private dwellers have gone, replaced by business premises, stationers, printers and coffee shops.

Buildings and institutions in Fetter Lane

1: Clifford's Inn, demolished in 1934, rebuilt as offices and flats
2: Former Public Record Office (built 1851–66), now London University
3: Corner of Fetter Lane and Plough Place (formerly Plow Yard)
4: 5–11 Fetter Lane (Elan house) Formerly the Horseshoe and Magpie Alehouse (18th century), now the Hogshead pub
5: 12 Fetter Lane A butcher's shop c.1420
6: 52 Fetter Lane Former office of *Queen* magazine, 1870's, later merged with *Harpers & Queen*
7: 77 Fetter Lane
8: 82–5 Fetter Lane Surviving 19th century terraced houses, with shops below
9: 83 Fetter Lane Tucker's Sandwich Bar, former premises of beer retailer, coffee houses etc.
10: 98 Fetter Lane Printer's Devil pub (19th century)
11: 108 Fetter Lane Mucky Duck pub, formerly the White Swan, where William McGonagall, 'the worst poet in the English language', stayed c.1877
12: St. Dunstan's House, 133–7 Fetter Lane Office of Commercial Department of High Court of Justice. 1886, demolished and rebuilt 1976 (much hated)
13: 183 Fetter Lane
14: 184 Fetter Lane
15: Great New Street, formerly Nevill's Court (opposite Rolls Buildings)
16: Magpie Alley, off north side of Norwich Street
17: West Corner of Fetter Lane and Holborn Former Black Swan Inn
18: Corner of Fetter Lane and New Fetter Lane Statue of John Wilkes (1727–97), Lord Mayor and 'champion of English Freedom'
19: Just south of Rolls Buildings Former Bonds Stables, large yard for coaches and horses, next to the Bolt & Tun Inn, 1660s
20: Just west of corner of Fleet Street and Fetter Lane St. Dunstan's in the West Church and churchyard, early medieval, rebuilt 1833. Now both Anglican and Romanian Orthodox
21: Norwich Street, off Fetter Lane Associated Press, formerly Solicitor's Law Stationery Society (Oyez)
22: Clifford's Inn Gatehouse, off Fleet Street

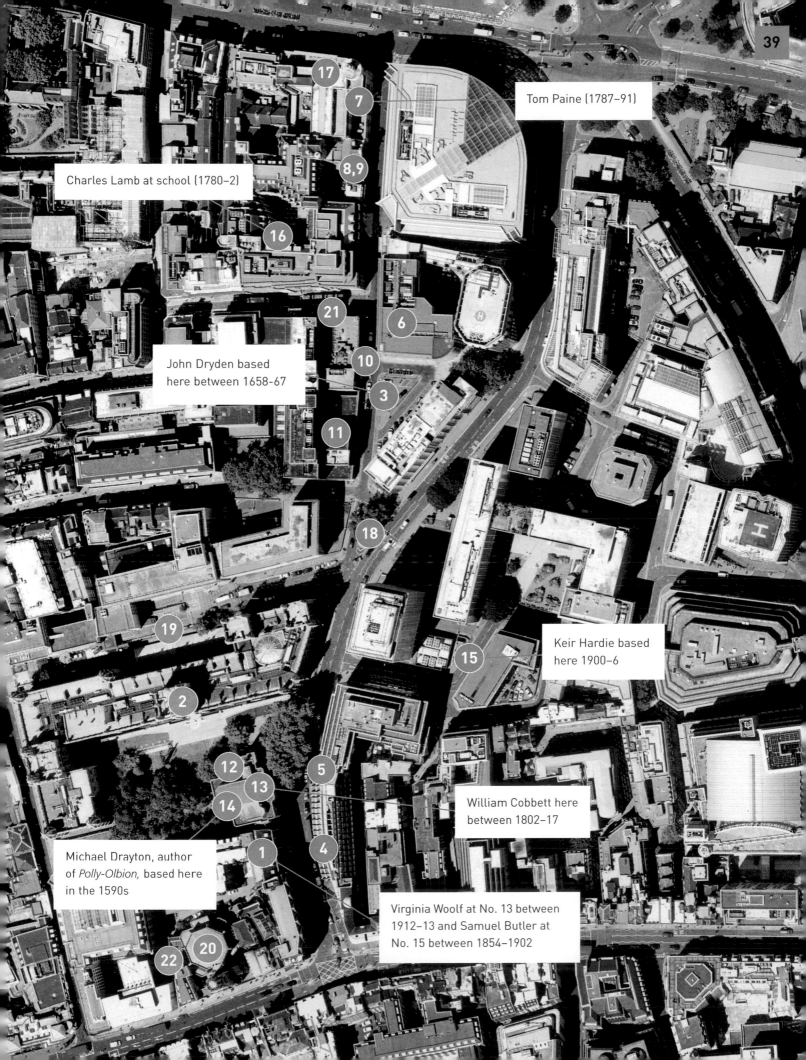

Tom Paine (1787–91)

Charles Lamb at school (1780–2)

John Dryden based
here between 1658-67

Keir Hardie based
here 1900–6

William Cobbett here
between 1802–17

Michael Drayton, author
of *Polly-Olbion,* based here
in the 1590s

Virginia Woolf at No. 13 between
1912–13 and Samuel Butler at
No. 15 between 1854–1902

Territorial Army bases

Army barracks

Other military locations

Territorial Army bases
1: RFCA Greater London, Duke of York's
Headquarters, Chelsea
Central
2: 144 Parachute Squadron RAMC
3: 68 (Inns of Court and City Yeomanry)
Signal Squadron
4: Intelligence & Security Group,
Intelligence Corps
5: University of London Training Corps
South West
6: B Squadron 256 (City of London) Field

7: D (London Irish Rifles) Company,
The London Regiment
8: W Squadron The Royal Yeomanry
9: 31 Signal Regiment
10: The London Regiment
11: 210 General Support Squadron,
Royal Logistic Corps
12: 253 Provost Company,
Royal Military Police
13: C (City of London Fusiliers) Company,
The London Regiment
14: F (Royal Green Jackets) Company,

15: A (London Scottish) Company,
The London Regiment
North West
16: 20 Intelligence and Security Company
West
17: F (Royal Green Jacket) Company,
The London Regiment
18: 10 (London) Company, 4 Battalion,
The Parachute Regiment
19: 83 (London) Signal Squadron
South East
20: D (London Irish Rifles) Company,

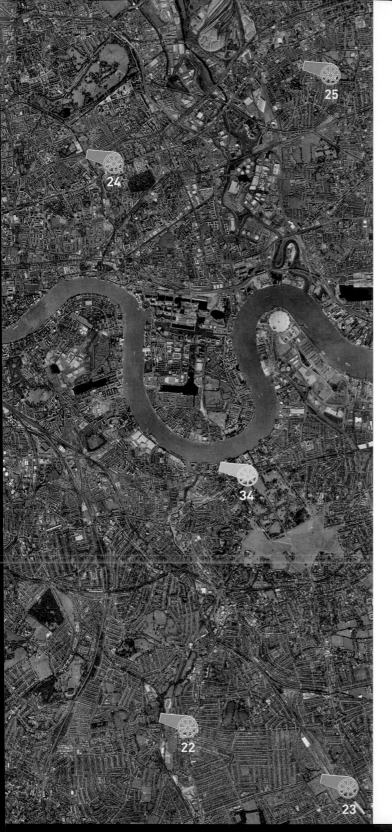

MILITARY LONDON

Modern Londoners don't see much of the British Army, except on ceremonial occasions such as Trooping the Colour on Horse Guards Parade, or the Changing of the Guard, performed daily in the summer around the Mall by the Queen's Guards regiments, the Grenadier, Coldstream, Welsh, Scots and Irish Guards, dressed in their theatrical 18th-century uniforms. But in fact there are army bases located all over Greater London, housing different regiments and battalions. The most noticeable are Wellington Barracks along Birdcage Walk, where the Queen's household regiments are based, and Chelsea Barracks, close to the Royal Hospital, where army veterans have been lodged for two and a half centuries. And there are 22 other barracks housing different regiments of the voluntary Territorial Army. The Ministry of Defence is housed in a vast modern white building on Whitehall, where the Tudor Whitehall Palace once stood. Opposite is the Horse Guards, where the Duke of Wellington commanded his army in the war against Napoleon.

The oldest regiment in the British Army, the Honourable Artillery Company (HAC), established by Henry VIII in 1537, is based in Old Street just outside the old Roman Wall. The HAC was the first Regiment to be given the privilege of marching through the City of London with 'drums beating, colours flying and bayonets fixed', and during the 17th century its responsibilities included maintaining law and order within the City.

In its entire history there have been remarkably few military confrontations in London. The only successful military attacks on the city were carried out by Queen Boudicca in AD 60, and Olaf of Norway in 1013 (see pages 8 and 50). Mobs assaulted the establishment more than once in the 14th century, the Peasants' Revolt (1381) being the best remembered. John of Gaunt's palace, the Savoy (where the hotel now stands), was burned to the ground, and hundreds of merchants, bishops, ministers and foreign traders were slaughtered. In 1642, during the Civil War, Charles I's nephew Prince Rupert defeated the parliamentary army at Brentford (see page 22) but never got further than Chiswick. Twenty-five years later, on 12 June 1667 (remembered as 'the Black Day'), the Dutch navy attacked Sheerness and sailed up the Medway to Chatham, threatening London, but they retreated after sinking several Royal Navy ships and towing the flagship back to Holland.

During the First World War, the German air force dropped hundreds of tons of bombs on London, first from airships (Zeppelins) and later from aircraft, inflicting severe damage in many parts of the capital. But it was nothing compared to the destruction of the Blitz in 1940 (see page 30), when nearly 30,000 bombs were dropped between September and November, killing or badly injuring 20,000 Londoners.

21: 256 (City of London) Field Hospital (Volunteers)
22: 101 (London) Engineer Regiment (Explosive Ordnance Disposal)
23: 106 (Yeomanry) Regiment Royal Artillery
East
24: D Squadron, 256(City of London) Field Hospital (Volunteers)
25: G (Royal Green Jackets) Company, The London Regiment

Army barracks
26: Wellington Barracks, Birdcage Walk
27: Chelsea Barracks, Turks Row
28: Hyde Park Barracks, Hyde Park
29: Horse Guards, Whitehall

Other military locations
30: Ministry of Defence, Whitehall
31: National Army Museum, Royal Hospital Road
32: Guards Museum, Wellington Barracks, Birdcage Walk

33: Imperial War Museum, Lambeth Road
34: National Maritime Museum, Park Row
35: Royal Regiment of Fusiliers, Tower of London

Bomb damage in the City 1939–45

Affected areas

City boundaries

Roman wall

✝ St. Paul's Cathedral

THE SECOND WORLD WAR

Hitler's decision to bomb London in August 1940 was primarily an effort to eliminate the Royal Air Force fighter planes before launching an invasion across the Channel, so the first attacks were on airfields outside the city, like Croydon. But on 7 September his strategy changed and the Luftwaffe switched its attacks to the city itself. Since the fighter planes were saved they were able to fight back, with such success that on 17 September Hitler decided to postpone the invasion.

But London paid a heavy price. On the first evening 600 bombers soared in waves over the eastern side of the city, and wide areas in West Ham, Millwall, Limehouse, Rotherhithe and Woolwich went up in flames. The next night they came back, bombing the West End and Westminster, and the

nightly raids continued for a total of 57 days until 3 November, and slightly less frequently until 16 May 1941. The attacks resumed in 1944, this time with V1 flying bombs and V2 rockets. The destruction was massive, and London's defences virtually non-existent. To begin with many citizens were filled with acute anxiety and panic, but as time went by most Londoners adopted an air of resilience and defiance. Strangers risked their lives for one another, and as everyone suffered class distinctions were set aside.

Large areas in virtually every part of London were severely damaged, but the worst was in the City and the East End. Although St Paul's Cathedral survived almost unharmed, acres around it were entirely flattened and reverted to wasteland. Buckingham Palace, the Guildhall, the Middle

The Tower

Temple, Lambeth Palace, and the House of Commons were all hit. Gas, water and electricity supplies were destroyed.

When I first came to live in Chelsea in the summer of 1946, in a flat in Old Church Street, the surrounding areas were still full of bomb sites, stinking with dust and heaped with broken bricks and the remains of the former residents' possessions, but they were also filled with wild flowers, ragwort, lilies of the valley and lilacs, as the land travelled back to its ancient natural origins.

The last bombing raids took place in March 1945, in Stepney and along the Tottenham Court Road. And then the war was over. Nearly 30,000 Londoners had been killed, over 100,000 houses destroyed, and the old city flattened. A huge task of reconstruction lay ahead.

CHRISTIAN LONDON

When Henry VIII introduced the Reformation from 1536, and the dissolution of the monasteries began in London, there was massive destruction of the ancient Catholic priories, convents and monasteries, with their land made over to favoured aristocrats and institutions. The demolition of churches, abbeys and monastic hospitals created chaos, as their sites were either rebuilt or left rotting.

Within 30 years the reconstruction was well in hand, and by the time of the Great Fire a hundred years later, 89 churches existed within the City walls, only to be burned down. More than 50 of these were rebuilt, all of them designed by Sir Christopher Wren (most notably, St. Paul's Cathedral). In 1711, Parliament commissioned the construction of many more, and a further boom was initiated by the Church Building Act in 1818. By the end of the 19th century there were nearly 600 Anglican churches throughout Greater London, as well as 134 Baptist chapels, 163 Wesleyan chapels, and 52 Presbyterian churches. Westminster Cathedral (completed in 1903) and 145 Catholic churches served the Catholic community. The Greek and Russian Orthodox communities also worshipped in London, the former at the Greek Orthodox Cathedral of St. Sophia (finished in 1882).

Bombing in the Second World War (as well as terrorist attacks in the 1990s) destroyed a large number of Wren's masterpieces, though some have been restored. Today, the City contains a mere 38. As church attendance dropped during the 20th century, many Victorian churches have been converted to flats.

From the eighth century until 1973, the country residence of the Bishops of London was Fulham Palace, a glorious amalgam of architectural styles, from Tudor to Victorian. Since 1197 the Archbishops of Canterbury have resided at Lambeth Palace. A 12th-century crypt chapel survives, and the 17th-century Great Hall houses the palace library, the first public library in England (partly destroyed under Oliver Cromwell, and again in the Second World War). Until the 18th century, the palace was near the river bank, and archbishops came and went on the archiepiscopal barge, mooring where the river police pier now stands.

Over 100 men have held the post of Archbishop of Canterbury since St. Augustine in 597, including Thomas à Becket (1162–70), and Robert Runcie (1980–91). The 104th, Archbishop Rowan Williams, was enthroned on 27 February 2003. His roles include the post of diocesan bishop of Canterbury, primate of the Church of England, and leader of the Anglican Communion, with some 70 million members worldwide. His Catholic counterpart, the Cardinal Archbishop of Westminster, resides in Archbishop House behind Westminster Cathedral.

But very large numbers of churches still exist throughout London, particularly in the districts which became residential in the 19th century. In Camden, for example, there are nearly 100, and nearly 40 in Campden town alone (see opposite).

Christian churches in Camden Town
1: St. George's Cathedral (Antiochian Orthodox), Redhill Street
2: St. Pancras Old, St. Pancras Gardens/Pancras Road (c.1050, oldest building in the borough)
3: Church of Our Lady of Hal (RC, Portuguese; also Belgian connections), 165 Arlington Road
4: St. Aloysius (RC), 20 Phoenix Road, (frequently closed because of 'arson and vandalism')
5: St. Mary the Virgin (Somers Town), Eversholt Street/Aldenham Street
6: Camden Town Methodist, 89 Plender Street
7: Camden Kingdom Hall (Jehovah's Witnesses), 7 Pratt Mews
8: Danish Church of St. Katharine, St. Katharine's Precinct, Regent's Park
9: All Saints (Greek Orthodox), Camden Street/Pratt Street
16: Scientology, 68 Tottenham Court Road
17: American Church in London, 79a Tottenham Court Road, W1 (also London Chinese Lutheran)
18: Greater World Spiritual Centre, 3–5 Conway Street
19: Regent Square United Reformed, Regent Square
20: King's Cross Methodist, Crestfield Street
21: Holy Cross, Cromer Street
22: El-Shaddai Bible Church (Pentecostal), Camden Centre, Bidborough Street
23: St. Mary's with St. George's German Lutheran, 10 Sandwich Street
24: St. Pancras, Euston Road/Upper Woburn Place, WC1 (1822, restored 1953)
25: Trinity Camden Town United Reform, Buck Street
26: New Covenant, Castlehaven Community Centre, 33 Hawley Road
27: St. Michael's Camden Town, Camden Road
28: Holy Trinity, Hartland Road
29: Rochester Square Spiritualist Centre, Rochester Square
30: St. Andrew's Cathedral (Greek Orthodox), Kentish Town Road/Bartholomew Road
31: St. Paul's, Camden Square
32: Kentish Town Congregational, Kelly Street
33: Church of Christ, Hope Chapel, Prince of Wales Road
34: Luther Tyndale Memorial, 9–11 Leighton Crescent
35: Salvation Army Chalk Farm Corps, 16 Haverstock Hill
36: St. Saviour's, Eton Road
38: Friends House (Quakers), 173 Euston Road
39: St. Anne's (RC), Laxton Place, Longford Street

London synagogues

1: The Great Synagogue, Duke's Place, Aldgate, was first established in the 18th century, to serve the large Ashkenazi Jewish community.

2: Hambro Synagogue, off Fenchurch Street, was founded after a dissent among the nearby Great Synagogue congregation in 1707.

3: The New Synagogue in Great St. Helen's, Bishopsgate, built in 1838, was moved to and reconstructed in Tottenham in 1915.

4: The Bayswater Synagogue was founded in 1863 in Chichester Place, just off the Harrow Road.

5: Central Synagogue, Great Portland Street, was established in 1855 as a branch of the Great Synagogue, and became an independent congregation in 1870.

6: The Ashkenazi Borough Synagogue in Walworth, founded in 1825 and incorporated in the United Synagogue in 1870, was subsequently converted into a museum.

7: North London Synagogue was founded in John Street, Barnsbury in 1868, but closed later in the century when many of the Ashkenazi community moved north to Highbury.

8: The East London Synagogue in Rectory Square, Stepney Green, was converted into apartments in 1996, but remains a Grade II listed building.

9: The New London Synagogue at 33 Abbey Road was formerly the St. John's

JEWISH LONDON

Jews first settled in London after the Norman Conquest, escaping from a pogrom in Rouen in 1096. The first evidence that they had settled in a Jewish quarter dates from 1128. Under the law of the time, Christian merchants were not allowed to lend money, which was regarded as 'usury'; but the Jewish immigrants, who had been excluded from the trade guilds, were permitted to do so, with the result that they were hated and blamed for the only activity allowed to them. In 1189, and again in 1215, mass slaughters took place around Old Jewry and Gresham Street, and in 1272 hundreds of Jews were hanged, having been accused of forging coins. In July 1290, under a royal edict, they were expelled from England altogether.

Over the succeeding centuries Jews gradually returned, and in December 1655 Oliver Cromwell convinced his governing Council that it would be just to allow the legal readmission of Sephardim Jews from Spain and Portugal, whose first synagogue was built on Bevis Marks, just inside the city wall. It survives, virtually unaltered, today. Later in the 17th century, Ashkenazi Jews from central and eastern Europe began to immigrate, and their Great Synagogue was established around 1690 a few hundred yards away in Aldgate. But they were an unpopular community, and bore endless prejudice and 'Jew-baiting' over the succeeding centuries. In 1753 the Jewish Naturalisation Act, attempting to remove the disabilities they confronted, was passed by Parliament, but repealed later in the year due to public hostility. Their civil rights were only gradually restored until the Jewish Disabilities Act was passed in 1853, allowing Lionel de Rothschild to take his seat as a Member of Parliament. In July 1870 another Act created the United Synagogue for Ashkenazi Jews.

By this time, the Jewish population had grown and spread out of the City to Covent Garden, and to eastern areas such as Bethnal Green, north towards Stoke Newington, and to Kilburn to the west. By the 20th century there were Jewish communities in Hampstead, Golders Green, Finchley, Hendon, Hammersmith and Ealing. The Ashkenazim union today comprises 13 major synagogues and over 50 minor ones, located all over London. The Sephardim Jews still have their synagogue in Bevis Marks and another in Bryanston Street. In addition, there is the West London Synagogue of British Jews in Seymour Place off the Edgware Road, and the Saatchi Synagogue in Maida Vale, founded in 1998 to attract unaffiliated Londoners to traditional Judaism. The Jewish community in London is the second largest in Europe, totalling around 200,000 people.

Wood United Synagogue, founded in 1888.

10: The New West End Synagogue in St. Petersburg Place first opened in 1879, and is now part of the United Synagogue. The building is Grade II listed.

11: Dalston Synagogue in Poet's Road, Canonbury opened in 1885.

12: The Western Synagogue was founded in the 18th century, and moved to several different buildings, including the Haymarket in Westminster and St

Alban's Place, Kensington.

13: Maiden Lane Synagogue was one of the smaller early 19th-century synagogues providing for Ashkenazi communities moving westwards.

14: The Bevis Marks Synagogue, built in 1701 by the Sephardic Jewish community, is the oldest surviving synagogue in Britain.

15: The synagogue in Upper Bryanston Street was opened in the 19th century as a branch of the ancient Bevis Marks

Synagogue in the City.

16: The North Western London Reform Synagogue opened in Upper Berkeley Street in 1820 for the congregation of Jewish 'dissenters'. In 1991 it merged with the nearby Marble Arch synagogue in Great Cumberland Street.

Buddhist Temples
1: Buddhapadipa Temple
2: Dorjechang Buddhist Centre
3: Kagyu Samye Dzong London
4: London Buddhist Centre
5: London Buddhist Vihara
6: North London Buddhist Centre
7: Santisukha Vihara
8: Tisarana Hihara
9: Zoroastrian House

Hindu Mandirs
10: Aden Depala Mitra Mandal
11: Caribbean Hindu Society
12: Ganpathy Temple
13: Highate Hill Murugan Temple
14: Hindu Centre London
15: Hindu Centre/Radha Krishna Temple
16: Hindu Cultural Society
17: Hindu Mandir
18: Hindu Society
19: Iskon London
20: Krishna Yoga Mandir
21: Kutch Satsang Swaminaryan Temple
22: London Sevashram Sangha
23: London Shri Murugan Temple
24: Mahalakshmi Temple
25: Radha-Krishna Temple
26: Shri Nathji Sanatan Hindu Mandir
27: Southeast Hindu Association
28: Swaninaryan Hindu Mission
29: Swaminaryan Hindu Mission-
    East London
30: Swaminaryan Temple
31: Swaminaryan Temple

Muslim Mosques
32: Al-Nehar Mosque and Education
    Centre
33: Anjuman-e-Islamia Jamia Mosque
34: Azizia Mosque
35: Balham Mosque
36: Battersea Mosque and Islamic
    Centre
37: Bow Central Mosque and Islamic
    Centre
38: Brixton Mosque and Islamic Centre
39: Bromley-by-Bow Mosque
40: Central Mosque of Brent
41: Central Mosque Trust and Islamic
    Cultural Centre
42: Charlton Mosque
43: Chingford Mosque
44: Dalston Mosque
45: Ealing Mosque
46: East London Markazi Mosque
47: East London Mosque
48: Finsbury Park Mosque
49: Forest Gate Mosque
50: Green Street Mosque
51: Harringay Mosque
52: Hounslow Mosque and Islamic Centre
53: Ibrahim Mosque
54: Ilford Mosque
55: Imam Hussain Mosque
56: Ishaatul Islam Mosque
57: Islamic Centre Mosque
58: Jamia Mosque East Ham
59: King's Cross Mosque and Islamic
    Centre

60: Leytonstone Mosque
61: Madina Mosque Trust
62: Mosque and Islamic Centre
63: Mosque and Islamic Centre of Brent
64: Mosque and Muslim Welfare
    Association
65: Muslim Community Centre/Mosque
66: Muslim Cultural Society Mosque
67: New Peckham Mosque
68: Noor-ur-Islam Mosque
69: Peckham Mosque
70: Shaha Jalal Mosque
71: Suleymaiye Mosque
72: Sultan Selim Mosque Complex
73: The Mosque (Chaucer Road)
74: The Mosque (Chesham Place)
75: The Mosque (Denmark Road)
76: The Mosque (Hackney Road)

77: The Mosque (Hertford Street)
78: The Mosque (Linthorpe Road)
79: The Mosque (North Gower Street)
80: The Mosque (Sandringham Road)
81: The Mosque (Willoughby Road)
82: Tottenham Mosque
83: The Turkish Mosque (Newington
    Green)
84: Turkish Mosque (Shacklewell Lane)
85: Upton Lane Mosque/Quwwat Ul Islam
    Society
86: Walthamstow Mosque
87: Wembley Mosque and Welfare
    Association
88: Wimbledon Mosque

Sikh Gurdwaras
89: Central Gurdwara (Khalsa Jatha)

Buddhist Temples

Hindu Mandirs

Muslim Mosques

Sikh Gurdwaras

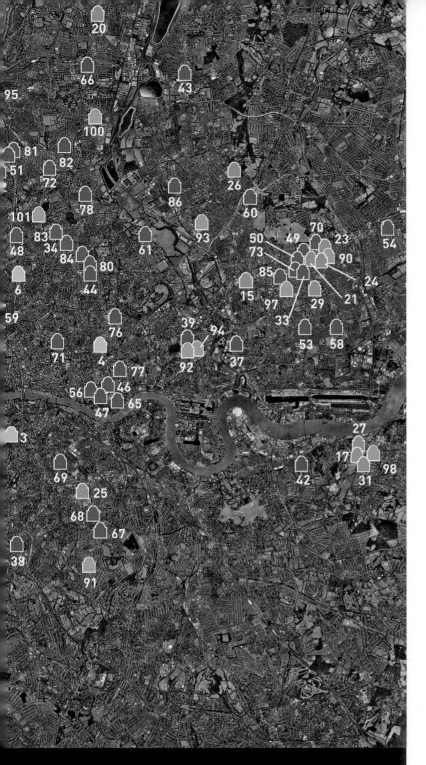

OTHER LONDON RELIGIONS

Modern London is by any standards one of the most multicultural cities in the world, and home to a very wide range of religions other than Judaism and Christianity. The most dominant are Buddhist, Hindu, Islamic, and Sikh.

Indians first arrived in London in the 18th century, many as servants of colonial families. In 1849, Maharajah Duleep Singh was exiled to Britain after the Anglo-Sikh wars, and by 1913 a Sikh temple had opened in Shepherd's Bush. The majority of Sikh immigrants, mainly from Punjab in north-west India, came in the 1920s, and in the 1950s and 1960s, and many have played prominent roles in Britain's recent history. A new temple, the largest outside India, opened in Havelock Road, Southall, in 2003.

The first Buddhist mission to Britain was established in 1908, and the London Buddhist Vihara, the first Buddhist monastery to be established outside Asia, opened in 1926. The lay Buddhist movement Soka Gakkai International was founded in London in the 1960s, though it has now moved to Taplow in Berkshire. The London Buddhist Centre is located in Bethnal Green.

Hinduism, particularly the Swaminarayan movement, has the greatest number of followers, and the main Hindu communities are in Wembley and Harrow. Their roots go back to the 1950s, when Hindu devotees from different parts of London began to meet regularly, and their first mandir (temple) opened in Islington in 1970. In that decade the community grew rapidly with the influx of refugees from Uganda and Kenya, and today there are 26 mandirs across London. The largest Hindu temple outside India was erected in Neasden in 1995, a magnificent building made of Carrara marble and Bulgarian limestone.

Muslim communities began to form in the 19th century, mainly in Shoreditch and Whitechapel. The first formal London mosque opened in Commercial Road in 1941, replaced in 1985 by the current East London mosque in Whitechapel Road. Other more recently opened mosques are in Finsbury Park and Wandsworth; and the most striking is the London Central Mosque on the edge of Regent's Park, presented by the government as a gift to the Muslim community in 1944, and designed by the British architect Frederick Gibberd. The building was eventually completed in 1977. Its members originate from 29 different Muslim nations. Muslims are by far the largest minority religious community in London, with a population estimated at around one million, with ancestral roots in the Indian subcontinent, the Middle East, Africa, eastern Europe and the Caribbean.

90: Dashmesh Darbar Gurdwara
91: Gurdwara Baba Budha Sahib Ji
92: Gurdwara Sikh Sangat (Ia Campbell Road)
93: Gurdwara Sikh Sangat (Francis Road)
94: Gurdwara Singh Sangat (Harley Grove)
95: Maha Sabha
96: Nanak Darber
97: Ramgarhia Sikh Gurdwara
98: Ramgarhia Sikh Temple
99: Ramgarhia Welfare Darbar
100: Shiromani Akali Dal
101: Sikh Sangha Gurdwara Society
102: Siri Guru Singh Sabha (Avarn Road)

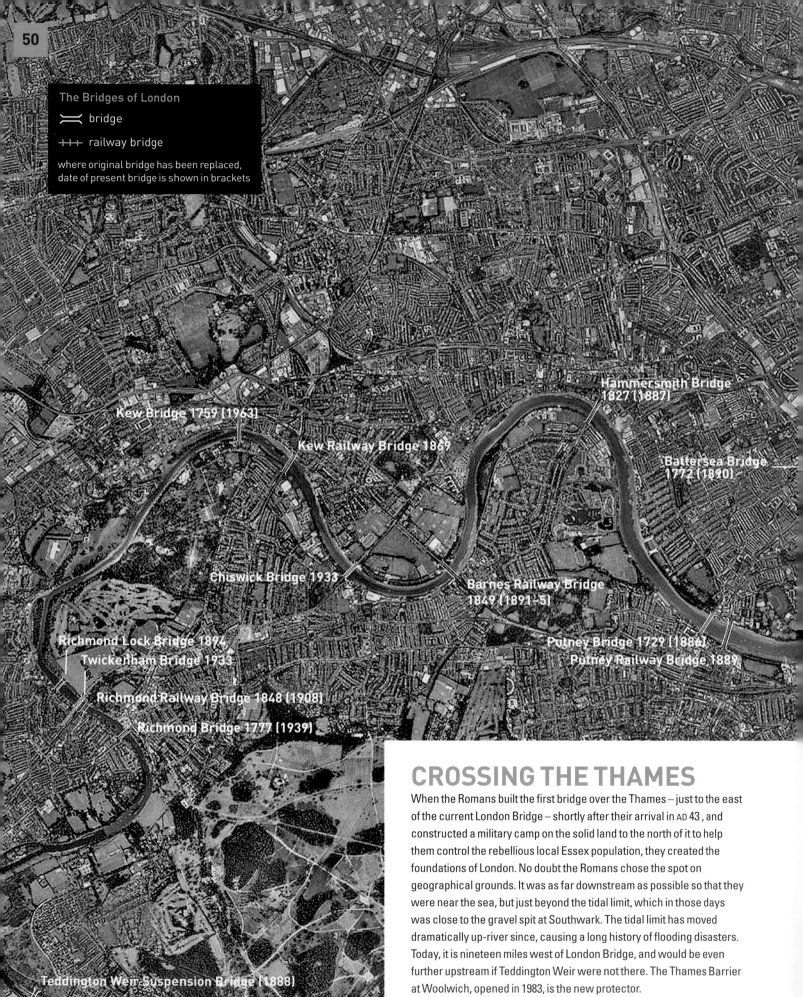

The Bridges of London

⊨ bridge

+++ railway bridge

where original bridge has been replaced,
date of present bridge is shown in brackets

Kew Bridge 1759 (1963)

Kew Railway Bridge 1869

Hammersmith Bridge
1827 (1887)

Battersea Bridge
1772 (1890)

Chiswick Bridge 1933

Barnes Railway Bridge
1849 (1891–5)

Richmond Lock Bridge 1894

Twickenham Bridge 1933

Putney Bridge 1729 (1886)

Putney Railway Bridge 1889

Richmond Railway Bridge 1848 (1908)

Richmond Bridge 1777 (1939)

Teddington Weir Suspension Bridge (1888)

CROSSING THE THAMES

When the Romans built the first bridge over the Thames – just to the east
of the current London Bridge – shortly after their arrival in AD 43, and
constructed a military camp on the solid land to the north of it to help
them control the rebellious local Essex population, they created the
foundations of London. No doubt the Romans chose the spot on
geographical grounds. It was as far downstream as possible so that they
were near the sea, but just beyond the tidal limit, which in those days
was close to the gravel spit at Southwark. The tidal limit has moved
dramatically up-river since, causing a long history of flooding disasters.
Today, it is nineteen miles west of London Bridge, and would be even
further upstream if Teddington Weir were not there. The Thames Barrier
at Woolwich, opened in 1983, is the new protector.

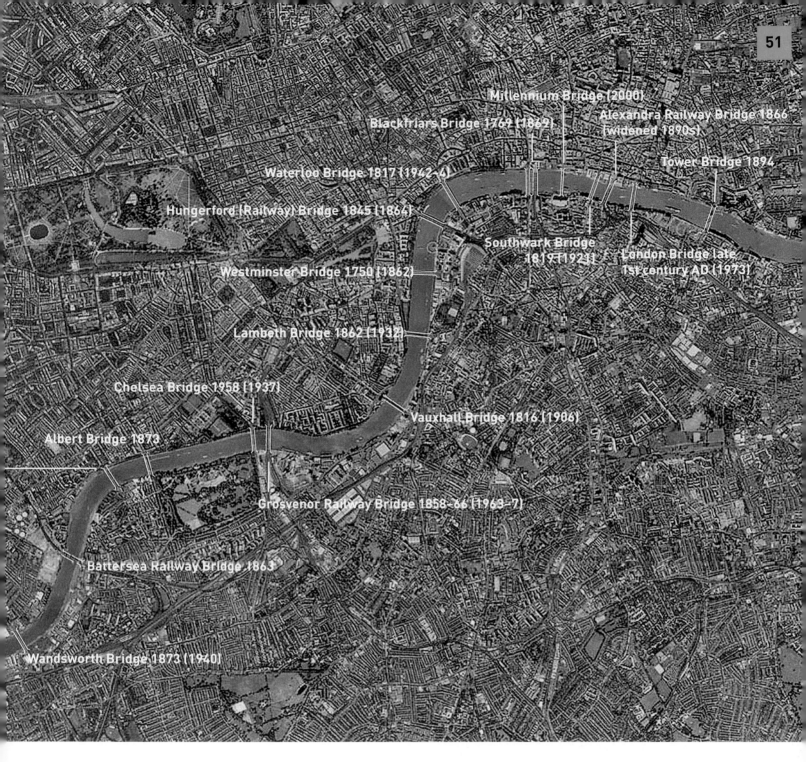

Millennium Bridge (2000)

Blackfriars Bridge 1769 (1869)

Alexandra Railway Bridge 1866 (widened 1890s)

Waterloo Bridge 1817 (1942–4)

Tower Bridge 1894

Hungerford (Railway) Bridge 1845 (1864)

Southwark Bridge 1819 (1921)

London Bridge late 1st century AD (1973)

Westminster Bridge 1750 (1862)

Lambeth Bridge 1862 (1932)

Chelsea Bridge 1958 (1937)

Vauxhall Bridge 1816 (1906)

Albert Bridge 1873

Grosvenor Railway Bridge 1858–66 (1963–7)

Battersea Railway Bridge 1863

Wandsworth Bridge 1873 (1940)

Very little is known about the structure of the first bridge. No remains have been discovered, and its position can only be deduced from the subsequent growth of the city and the alignment of the roads. It was replaced in Saxon times, and we know that in 1014 Olaf of Norway, supporting King Ethelred the Unready's campaign to recover London from the Danes, sailed his fleet up the Thames as far as the well-fortified bridge, tied ropes and cables to its wooden piles, and rowed off downstream, bringing the bridge crashing down. This event gave rise to the original version of the nursery rhyme *London Bridge is falling down*. A stone bridge with 20 arches was constructed in its place by 1209 (see page 19), and survived until 1832.

No new Thames crossings were erected until the 18th century: Putney Bridge (1729), Westminster Bridge (completed in 1750),

Blackfriars (1769) and Richmond (1777). Kew Bridge (1759) and Battersea Bridge (1772), both made of wood, were replaced with stone bridges in 1903 and 1890, respectively. The first iron bridge went up in Vauxhall in 1816, soon followed by Waterloo Bridge in 1817 and Southwark Bridge in 1819. The first railway bridge was Grosvenor (1858–66), next to Chelsea Bridge (1858), which brought the Brighton trains to Victoria Station. Lambeth Bridge went up in 1862. Tower Bridge, a modern symbol of the city, was erected in 1885–94.

Today, at least 30 bridges cross the Thames in London, the most recent being the pedestrian Millennium Bridge. All have undergone major reconstructions and repairs over the last 150 years, none more unusual than the replacement of London Bridge in 1972, when the old one was transported to and re-erected in Lake Havasu City, Arizona.

Regent's Canal

Grand Union Canal

Westbourne

Tyburn

Counters Creek

Falcon Brook

THE OTHER RIVERS

Apart from the Thames, a number of other rivers and streams exist in the London area, of which the best known are the Tyburn and the Fleet. Most of them are buried under the city, and have been converted into the subterranean sewer and drainage system. Every now and then, when prolonged or heavy rain occurs, they flood areas in Gospel Oak, Wandsworth and Battersea.

Among those still visible, the River Roding flows into the Thames at Barking, joined by Mayes Brook, and the River Lee comes down to Canning Town. The Ravensbourne, with its source in Bromley, is joined by the Pool and the Quaggy, and reaches the Thames between Deptford and Greenwich. To the west, Hogsmill River runs from Epsom to Kingston upon Thames, the Crane runs from Edgware to Isleworth, and the River Brent, partly linked to the Grand Union Canal, flows in opposite Kew Gardens. Wandsworth has two rivers, Beverley Brook and the Wandle.

The Fleet has its source in Hampstead. From ancient times it marked the boundary between the City and Westminster, and was evidently navigable by boat at least as far north as Kentish Town. It flowed through St. Pancras, around Clerkenwell Hill, and roughly down where Farringdon Road now runs. By the 17th century, it had become a foul and

Other rivers

━━ canal

━━ underground river

••• presumed course
of underground
river

Regent's Canal

Islington Tunnel

Fleet

Walbrook

Neckinger

Peck

Effra

polluted dump for muck and rubbish of every kind, and although several attempts were made to clean and restore it, eventually by 1765 it was wholly covered over.

The only river inside the City is the Walbrook, flowing from springs in Shoreditch and Hoxton, under the Wall and beneath the Bank of England, and running out just to the west of Cannon Street Station. It was covered over completely in the 15th century, though its name survives in Walbrook Lane. The Westbourne, springing from Highgate and running through Kilburn and Bayswater, was dammed in the 18th century to form the Serpentine in Hyde Park, and its waters can still be seen rushing

through an overhead conduit at Sloane Square station. The Tyburn too is carried through pipes at Baker Street and Victoria tube stations. Stamford Brook used to flow into a moat surrounding the mansion that stood in Ravenscourt Park, bombed and destroyed in the Second World War. It then flowed south to Hammersmith, where a low-level sewer now joins the Thames. These rivers may be invisible, but they are not dead.

54

Kensal Green
Queen's Park
Kilburn Park
St. John's Wood
Camden Town
Mornington Crescent
King's Cross St. Pancras
Maida Vale
Euston
Regent's Park
Euston Square
Warren Street
Westbourne Park
Warwick Avenue
Marylebone
Baker Street
Great Portland Street
Goodge Street
Royal Oak
Edgware Road
Tottenham Court Road
White City
Ladbroke Grove
Paddington
Bayswater
Marble Arch
Leicester Squa
Latimer Road
Lancaster Gate
Oxford Circus
Piccadilly Circus
Bond Street
Wood Lane
Holland Park
Queensway
Green Park
Charing Cross
Shepherd's Bush
Notting Hill Gate
Down Street
Dover Street
Goldhawk Road
Hyde Park Corner
Westminster
Kensington Olympia
High Street Kensington
Knightsbridge
Natural History Museum
Brompton Road
St. James's Park
Hammersmith
Earl's Court
Sloane Square
Victoria
Gloucester Road
South Kensington
Pimlico
Baron's Court
West Kensington
West Brompton
Vauxhall
Fulham Broadway

UNDERGROUND LONDON

Underneath London there is network of holes and tunnels and spaces almost as complex as the city above, but no overall plan of them exists. So every time a tube extension is planned, or any deep-laid building, or water mains or internet cables, the engineers have to research endless old documents to try to avoid fracturing them. The underground rivers (see page 52), most of which are integrated with the sewerage systems installed in the 19th century, are fairly well documented. This system resulted in an ever-growing pollution of the Thames, and in the 1870s intercepting sewers were built to carry the waste to outfalls downstream of the city. These still need constant repair.

The underground railways began in the 1860s, and the electrified tubes in 1905 (see page 62). They were expanded hugely in the 1930s to cater for London's growing suburban population. The Victoria Line was opened in 1968, and the Jubilee Line finally completed in 1999. There are today over 100 miles of underground tube lines across London. Not all of them are for public transport: theRoyal Mail has recently put up for sale its own 6-mile line for transporting post, completed in 1927, running from Paddington to Mount Pleasant, and on to Whitechapel. Over the last 150 years a number of lines and stations have been closed, but still lie there dark and deserted. During the second world war the tube was a useful haven for citizens during bombing raids, priceless works of art were

London Underground

━━━━ Bakerloo
•••• railway on surface

━━━━ Central
•••• railway on surface

━━━━ District
•••• railway on surface

━━━━ East London

━━━━ Hammersmith & City
•••• railway on surface

━━━━ Jubilee

━━━━ Metropolitan

━━━━ Northern

━━━━ Piccadilly
•••• railway on surface

━━━━ Victoria
railway on surface

▢ Deep level WW2 shelter

⬯ Ghost stations

stored in disused lines beneath Aldwych, and the Goodge Street tunnel housed the headquarters of the American military command.

Since the 1930s a number of subterranean fortresses have been constructed in different areas, to accommodate government staff in the event of war, including the Cabinet War Rooms (now open to the public), and the emergency control centre in the northern section of Kingsway tram tunnel.

Under the river, a number of tunnels were dug in the 19th and 20th centuries, of which the most remarkable was Marc Brunel's Thames Tunnel (1825–43), for which pedestrians paid a penny to walk from Wapping to Rotherhithe. It was subsequently converted to a railway

tunnel, and restored in 1997. Other foot tunnels exist in Greenwich (1902) and Woolwich (1912) and another, from Greenwich marshes to Blackwall, was superseded by the construction of Blackwall Tunnel in 1897, to which a second bore was added in 1967. A tunnel from Rotherhithe to Wapping was begun in 1805, but never completed, and the present-day Rotherhithe Tunnel was opened in 1908.

Dollis hill ①
⑬ Childs Hill ②
HIGHGATE
Highbury Barn ⑲
Cricklewood ⑯
Hampstead Heath
Willesden Green ⑧
Barnsbury
⑳
Highbury Station
Brondesbury
⑧
Zoological Gardens ㉝ ③ Camden Town ⑤
Kilburn
Kings Cross
Kensal Rise ⑥
St Pancras
Angel
HARLSDEN
Euston Station
Bank
Kensal Green ⑱
Oxford Circus
⑱
Wormwood Scrubs ⑦
Paddington Stn
㉝
Charing Cross
Shepherd's Bush ⑪
KENSINGTON
Victoria Station ⑯
⑩ ㉒ Elephant and Castle
⑳ Hammersmith
BEL-GRAVIA
Turnham Green ⑫
Watham Green
Ebury Bridge ②
CHELSEA
⑨ Barnes
FULHAM
BRIXTON
Putney Common ⑮
WANDSWORTH
CLAPHAM COMMON
⑤ ⑭ Putney
Clapham Junction ⑲
Brixton ③

1911 bus routes of the London General Omnibus Company

1: Tower Bridge Road – Dollis Hill
2: Child's Hill – Ebury Bridge
3: Brixton (George Canning) – Camden Town
5: Putney – Barnsbury
6: Kensal Rise – Shoreditch
7: Liverpool Street – Wormwood Scrubs
8: Willesden Green – Seven Kings
9: Liverpool Street – Barnes
10: Elephant and Castle – Stratford
11: Shepherd's Bush – Liverpool Street
12: London Bridge Station – Turnham Green
13: London Bridge Station – Hendon
14: Putney – Wanstead
15: Putney Common – Plaistow

Map labels:
Hackney Station 22
Dalston Junction
22
22
Old Ford 25
14
10
8
Shoreditch 6
25
Bow
25 Liverpool St. Stn.
22
6
7 9 11
9 11
9
7 25
6 22
8 14 15 17
10
8 10 14
Limehouse
15 17
Poplar
15 17
15 17
10 12
13 12
22
12 13 London Bridge Station
1 Tower Bridge Road
Camberwell Green
DULWICH
Herne Hill

BUSES

In 1829 a coachbuilder called George Shillibeer (1797–1866), who had seen similar vehicles operating in Paris, introduced the first omnibus service in London. Using a long, thin coach carrying up to twenty passengers, and drawn by three horses, the first route ran from Paddington via Regent's Park to the City. The experiment proved popular, and in the 1830s a number of rival bus operators sprang up, competing for passengers by lowering Shillibeer's original one shilling fare, and developing different designs for the vehicle. By 1850 there were more than 1,300 buses operating in London, and in 1855 an Anglo-French enterprise called the Compagnie Generale des Omnibus de Londres was set up, and bought out most of the independent operators. By the end of the century, the company was carrying 50 million passengers a year.

When the internal combustion engine was invented, horse-drawn buses were replaced by motor-driven ones. The London General Omnibus Company (LGOC) held a virtual monopoly of this new vehicle, and the first double-decker bus, a 34-seater, made its inaugural journey in August 1909. By the beginning of the First World War there were some 2,500 motor buses operating across London, with enough space to carry 46 passengers each. The top decks of double-deckers were originally open to the air, exposing passengers and the driver to the elements, but roofs were authorised in 1925.

In the 1920s, bus transport became even more popular, and new independent operators began to challenge the LGOC's dominance. The competition caused chaos, and in 1924 the London Traffic Act imposed limitations on the number allowed to operate in congested areas. In 1933, all of London's bus companies were merged under London Transport, creating the largest bus fleet in the world. The RT-type bus was introduced in 1939, and mass-produced in the 1950s. The Routemaster, of which over 500 still operate today, was introduced in 1956.

Until 1935, it was possible to hail a London bus anywhere along its route. By 1939, 380 miles of bus routes had been converted to the fixed stop scheme, and a further 970 miles awaited their 'request' or 'compulsory' signs. Today, bus stops are a familiar part of the London landscape, with some 17,000 (some with electronic information systems) within Greater London. In 1993 buses were re-privatised, with different companies operating different routes; but in recent times there has been a sharp drop in the popularity of bus transport. The introduction of congestion charges in central London may eventually reverse this tendency, and finance new improvements to the service.

16: Victoria Station – Cricklewood
17: Ealing – East Ham
18: Kensal Green – Camberwell Green
19: Clapham Junction – Highbury Barn
20: Hammersmith – West Norwood
22: Hackney Station – Putney
24: Victoria Station – Hampstead Heath
25: Victoria Station – Old Ford
33: Oxford Circus – Zoological Gardens

TRAINS

Although London's first railway, built south of the river from London Bridge to Greenwich and opened in 1836, was designed to enable workers to commute to work from the suburb, most of the new railway companies were more interested in developing inter-city lines, mainly because they were expected to be more profitable. By the 1850s, the various railway companies had constructed rail networks all over the country, with London as their centre. But only two of the first London railway termini, Fenchurch Street and London Bridge, were built anywhere near work centres.

The construction of the railways, which required the demolition of vast areas of housing, had a devastating effect on the living conditions of thousands, particularly in areas such as King's Cross and south of the river. At various periods governments intervened to alleviate this damage, mainly by encouraging the development of the suburbs, and by requiring railway companies to introduce low fares for workmen, particularly on London's east side.

By 1866, four railway bridges had been built over the Thames to bring trains to the centre of the City and the West End. The railway companies were in intense competition with each other, and as a result considerably more stations were constructed than were actually necessary. By the end of the century, there were a total of 16 termini. Several of them – particularly St Pancras, King's Cross, Euston, Charing Cross, Paddington, Waterloo and Victoria – attracted grand hotels and shopping precincts to their areas, encouraging an influx of shoppers and overseas visitors. Victoria Street was filled with shops, newly fashionable luxury flats and the Grosvenor Hotel. Paddington boasted the Great Western Royal Hotel, there was the Midland at St Pancras and the Great Northern at King's Cross. Few survived the 20th century.

During the Second World War the railway companies were controlled by the government, and nationalised in 1947. Over the next half century, the sums invested in rail transport fell far short of what the operators felt they required and British Rail was widely criticised for running a less efficient service than elsewhere in western Europe. In the early 1990s, the process of re-privatisation began and there have been noticeable improvements, since independent companies have taken over the networks.

London's Railway Boom

- Pre1855 railway
- 1855–65
- 1865–75
- 1875–1900

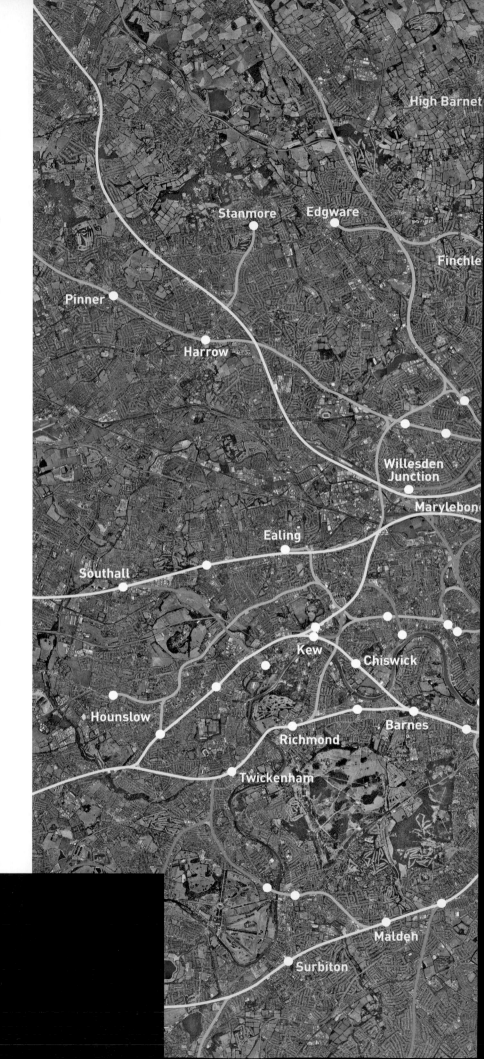

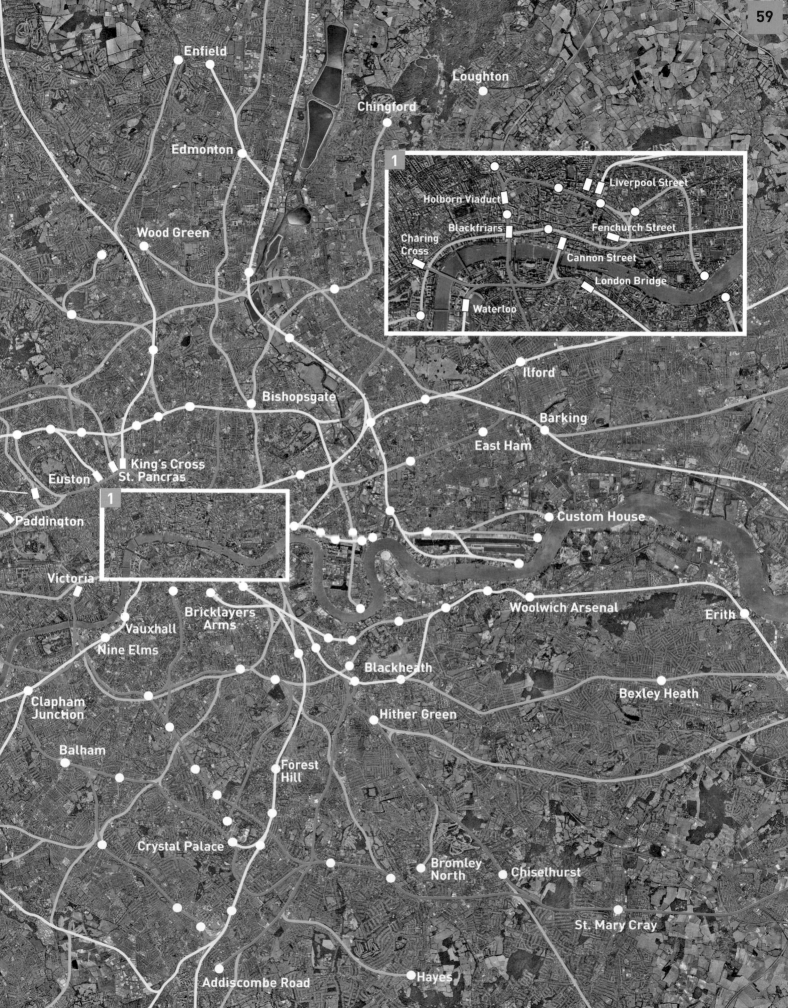

1

Holborn Viaduct

Liverpool Street

Blackfriars

Fenchurch Street

Charing Cross

Cannon Street

London Bridge

Waterloo

Enfield

Loughton

Chingford

Edmonton

Wood Green

Ilford

Bishopsgate

Barking

East Ham

King's Cross St. Pancras

Euston

Custom House

Paddington

1

Victoria

Woolwich Arsenal

Erith

Bricklayers Arms

Vauxhall

Nine Elms

Bexley Heath

Blackheath

Clapham Junction

Hither Green

Balham

Forest Hill

Crystal Palace

Bromley North

Chiselhurst

St. Mary Cray

Addiscombe Road

Hayes

Victoria Station
Christ Church
Elephant and Castle
Bricklayers Arms
Vauxhall Station
Camberwell Gate
Chelsea – Bridge
Kennington Gate
Battersea Park Station
Camberwell Green
Camber Town H
Stockwell
Denmark Hill Station
Princes Head
Wandsworth Road Station
Loughborough Junction
Clapham Station
Brixton Station
Clapham Junction
Plough Clapham
East Dulwich Station
Herne Hill Station
Dulwich Library
Tulse Hill Station
Streatham Hill Station
West Norwood
Fare section
Terminal Points

South London tram routes
(unless stated all routes below ran week days and Sundays)

2: Wimbledon via to Victoria Embankment
14: Wimbledon via Wandsworth High Street and Battersea to London Bridge Station (week days only)
10: Tooting Broadway via Streatham Brixton and Westminster to the City
31: Wandsworth High Street via Battersea and central London to Hackney Station
32: Plough Clapham to Chelsea Bridge
33: West Norwood via Brixton and central London to Manor House (north London)
78: West Norwood via Brixton to Victoria Station
80: West Norwood via Elephant and Castle to Victoria Embankment
35: Forest Hill via central London to Highgate (north London)
66: Forest Hill via Dulwich to Bloomsbury (week days only)
48: Brixton via Elephant and Castle to the City (week days only)

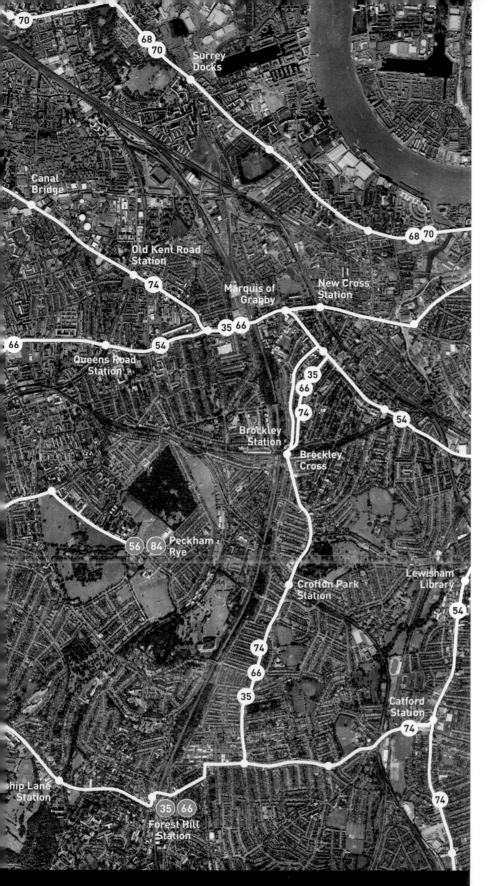

HANSOM-CABS, TAXIS AND TRAMS

Before the invention of public transport in the 19th century, people got around the city on foot, on horseback, or (if they were rich) in cabriolets – light, two-wheeled carriages drawn by a horse. In 1834, Joseph Hansom, designed and patented a four-wheeled, more comfortable version for public conveyance. Called the hansom-cab, the driver was separated from the carriage. It was much altered and improved by other coach builders over the next 70 years, and Hansom is reported to have earned nothing from his invention – but his name survives. By the end of the 19th century, more than 10,000 cabs of various styles were operating, and even the newly widened roads were constantly jammed.

Taxicabs, their successors, have a curious history too (the word is derived from taximeter cab, a cab with an instrument attached to record the distance covered and the fare due). In 1897, an engineer called Walter Bersey designed an electrically powered cab, and produced 70 of them to operate in London. They had a range of 30 miles, and a top speed of 9 miles per hour, but the cost of the batteries was excessive, and his company closed down two years later. Several further attempts to create successful electrical cabs also failed over the following century.

In 1903, the French company Prunel introduced the first motor-driven cab to be licensed in London, with a body similar to the hansom-cab and driven by a 12-horsepower engine. By 1907 the taxicab boom had begun. Humber Ltd led it with a fleet of 40 taxis, followed by other competing companies, including Unic, Austin, Napier and Morris. During the 20th century, new and improved taxi models were introduced every few years. The leading manufacturer today is London Taxis International, which has produced over 100,000 of their TX1 model. But the most familiar London taxi is the Austin FX-4, introduced in 1959 and in production until 1997.

Trams have a rather shorter history in London, and were confined mainly to outer areas. Horse-drawn trams were introduced in the 1870s, linking areas such as Holloway, Stamford Hill and Camberwell with the outer edges of the City. Electrical versions appeared at the beginning of the 20th century, but were excluded from the City and West End, which remained the preserve of cabs and buses. The tram lines eventually closed down in 1952. Today there are plans to reintroduce them in limited areas, for example, from Uxbridge to Shepherd's Bush, and from Brixton and Peckham across Waterloo Bridge to Camden Town.

54: Grove Park Station via Lewisham to Victoria Station
56: Peckham Rye via Camberwell Green to Victoria Embankment (week days only)
84: Peckham Rye via Camberwell Green to Victoria Embankment
68: Greenwich via Elephant and Castle to Waterloo Station
70: Greenwich via Southwark to London Bridge Station
74: Southend Village via Catford and Bricklayers Arms to Victoria Embankment

THE CIRCLE LINE

The Circle Line, coloured yellow on the tube map, is one of London's oldest tube lines. It was begun in 1868, five years after the world's first underground train had been opened by the Metropolitan Railway Company. Running from Bishop's Bridge Road in Paddington to Farringdon Street, this line is now known as the Metropolitan and District line. It was an immediate success, and other companies immediately put forward proposals for further developments. In 1864, the government authorised the development of an 'inner circuit', which would connect both ends of Metropolitan Railway line with mainline stations in the south of the city – Cannon Street, Blackfriars, Charing Cross and Victoria. To raise the capital required to achieve this, a new company was formed called Metropolitan and District Railway (MDR).

The Metropolitan Railway and District Railway Companies separately began work on the project, with Metropolitan extending its line eastwards to Mark Lane, and from Paddington to South Kensington. The District developed the line from South Kensington to Mansion House, but by the 1870s it was in financial trouble. Under pressure from City businesses and the government, Metropolitan was forced to complete the line from Mansion House to Tower Hill. The inner circuit was finally opened in 1884, with the separate District and Circle lines using the same tracks in competition with each other, each with their separate ticket office at every Circle Line station. They only began to co-operate after the trains were electrified in 1905, when MDR's profits substantially improved.

Even then, there was a last-minute crisis. The new electric tube trains were due to open on 1 July, but it was discovered at the last minute that Metropolitan had used narrower collector shoes and more accurately placed conductor rails than had District. Their trains had to be contained on the northern side of the line until modified.

Mark Lane station was closed in 1967 and replaced by the nearby Tower Hill, but tube travellers between Tower Hill and Monument can still glimpse its platforms as they pass. On the road above, the original stairways down to the station can be seen next to the All Bar One wine bar. The line has run unaltered through its twenty-seven stations ever since.

SECOND WORLD WAR BOMBING

On 19 September 1940, a bomb hit the tunnel roof between Euston Square and Great Portland Street, killing two railwaymen and injuring several passengers. Service was resumed a week later.

On 16 October 1940, a 1000kg bomb destroyed the tunnels between King's Cross and Farringdon. Services on this line were suspended until the following March.

At Sloane Square on 12 November 1940, a bomb hit a crowded train, causing 79 casualties, and totally destroying the newly built escalators. Train service resumed within two weeks.

During the fire bomb raid on 29 December 1940, the Aldersgate–Moorgate area was set alight, and Moorgate station totally engulfed. Farringdon, Mark Lane, Blackfriars, Whitechapel and Aldersgate stations were all closed because of damage, but re-opened within 24 hours.

On 9 March 1941, the platforms and station roof at King's Cross were badly damaged, killing two railwaymen and injuring three.

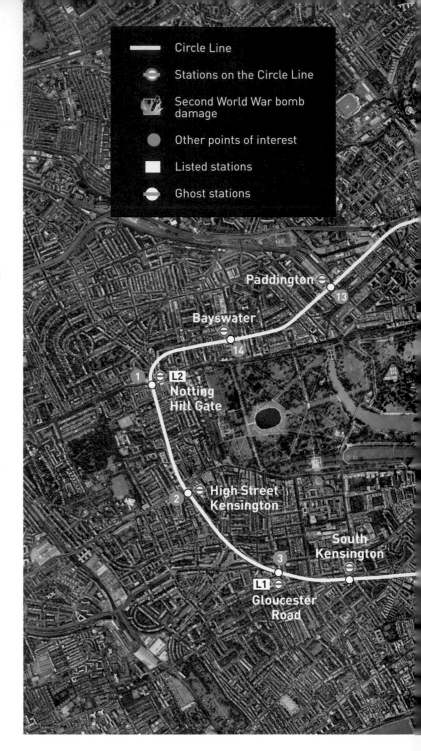

OTHER POINTS OF INTEREST

At Notting Hill Gate (1), there had been separate stations for the Central and Metropolitan lines since the tube line opened. A new station, beneath the widened A40, was constructed and opened in March 1959, with a central underground ticket hall and new stairways to the different lines.

The shopping arcade at High Street Kensington (2) was restyled in 1987, providing one of the most attractive malls in London's underground.

In the last twenty years, hoardings and panelling on the walls of many Circle Line stations have been removed to restore the original Victorian brickwork, together with new signs and lighting. These include Gloucester Road (3), Notting Hill Gate (1), Bayswater (14), Paddington (13), Great Portland Street (12), Euston Square (11), and Barbican (9). Other improvements at Gloucester Road include shopping arcades and luxury flats, completed in 1993.

King's Cross
St. Pancras

Euston
Square

10

L3
Baker Street

12

11

L4

Great
Portland Street

Barbican

L5
Farringdon

9

Liverpool
Street

7

L6

8

6

Moorgate

Mansion
House

Aldgate

Temple

Monument

Blackfriars

5

Cannon
Street

Tower
Hill

Mark
Lane

Embankment

Westminster

4

St. James's
Park

L7

Victoria

Sloane
Square

Grade 1 listed stations:
L1: Gloucester Road (Sir John Fowler, 1868)
L2: Notting Hill Gate (Sir John Fowler, 1868)
L3: Baker Street (Sir John Fowler, 1863; and Charles Clark, 1929)
L4: Great Portland Street (Sir John Fowler, 1863; and Charles Clark, 1930)
L5: Farringdon (Sir John Fowler, 1865; and Charles Clark, 1923)
L6: Moorgate (Thomas Phillips Figgis, 1900)
L7: St James's Park (Charles Holden, 1929)

The entrance to Bank station at the corner of the Bank of England is also Grade 1 listed.

In 1999 there were fears that vast crowds gathering to celebrate the millennium might cause damage to the tube lines beneath Parliament Square in Westminster (4). A hidden load-bearing platform was constructed over the Circle and District lines in the middle of the square, without interrupting traffic.

Mansion House (5) was closed for over a year in 1989 and refurbished with white wall tiles and mottled brown terrazzo flooring.

Aldgate East station (6) opened in October 1884 on the north side of Whitechapel High Street and the corner of Goulston Street. An entirely new station was opened in 1938 to accommodate the extra cars, a few hundred yards to the east. A defunct section of tunnel can still be seen at the south end of the Circle Line platform at Aldgate East.

The shopping arcade at Liverpool Street (7) was badly damaged by the IRA bombing of Bishopsgate in 1993, but was restored in 1994.

After being badly damaged in the second world war bombing, Moorgate (8) was finally rebuilt in 1970, supported by a huge property redevelopment scheme, including a shopping piazza above the station.

When the Barbican (9) development scheme began in the 1960s, the line between Aldersgate and Moorgate stations was straightened, and Aldersgate was renamed Barbican in 1968. That year Sir John Betjeman wrote a poem entitled 'Monody on the death of Aldersgate Street station'.

A fire broke out at King's Cross underground station (10) in November 1987, and 31 people died. Smoking has been prohibited on all trains ever since.

Between January and March 1996, Bayswater (14) station was closed for major reconstruction, including a new footbridge across the tracks, a wider street entrance and additional ticket gates.

Old Spitalfields Market

BISHOPSGATE

Brick Lane

Annie Chapman
Found at the rear of
29 Hanbury Street, 8
September.

Mary Jane Kelly
Found at 9 Miller's Court,
Dorset Street (now Field
Street), Spitalfields,
9 November.

Catherine Eddowes
Found at 30 (southwest corner)
Mitre Square (off Mitre Street),
just north of Aldgate,
30 September.

Commercial Street

Whitechapel High Street

ALDGATE HIGH STREET

THE WHITECHAPEL MURDERS, 1888

No London murders are more famous than those committed by Jack the Ripper in 1888, when at least five female victims were brutally killed and dissected with a knife, all within half a mile of Whitechapel High Street, between 31 August and 9 November. The murderer has never been identified, although dozens of theories and hundreds of books have been written on the subject. The lives of the victims shed a grim light on working-class life in Victorian London.

The first victim was Mary Ann Nichols, the 42-year-old daughter of a south London blacksmith called Edward Walker, known to her friends as Polly. She had married young and had five children, but she separated from her husband several times, finally in 1881 after he discovered she was working as a prostitute. She then lived in Lambeth Workhouse, and was occasionally allowed home by her father, at one point getting a job as a servant to a middle class couple in Wandsworth, which she only managed to hold on to for two months. By 1888 she was living in lodgings in Whitechapel, sharing a room with three other women, in a street described at the time as 'perhaps the foulest and most dangerous street in the whole metropolis'. In the early hours of 31 August she was out in the street, prostituting, and immediately spending her earnings on drink. Her brutally stabbed body was found at about 3.45 a.m. in Buck's Row.

Annie Chapman's life was not dissimilar. Born in June 1841, the daughter of a soldier in the Life Guards, she married a coachman, and had three children. The eldest died of meningitis aged 12, the second joined a circus in France and the third was born so crippled that he was sent to a home. She was separated in 1884, and her husband died two years later. After that she took to prostitution. She was murdered at around 6.30 a.m. on 8 September and was found near Hanbury Street.

The next victim, Elizabeth Stride, was born in Sweden in 1846, and was married for several years to a carpenter from Sheerness who later owned a coffee room in Poplar. He died in October 1884, but by 1882 she too was living in the same lodging house as Mary Ann Nichols. She later moved in with a docklands labourer called Michael Kidney, with whom she had a 'stormy' relationship, and was several times arrested on 'drunk and disorderly' charges. Her body was found at about 12.40 a.m. on 30 September in the backyard of a working men's club in Berner Street. She had been slit across her throat.

Catherine Eddowes was murdered on the same night and was found in Mitre Square. Also known as Kate Conway, though not married to her partner Thomas Conway with whom she had three children, Catherine was born in April 1842, the daughter of a tin plate worker from Wolverhampton called George Eddowes. She later had another partner called John Kelly, an Irish porter. She had been arrested for drunkenness and released by the police on the very evening she was murdered.

The last victim officially attributed to Jack the Ripper was the much younger Mary Jane (Marie Jeanette) Kelly, born in Ireland in 1865, but brought up in Wales. She left her family and moved to London in 1884, where she found work in a brothel in the West End. In April 1887 she met Joseph Barnett, a dock labourer, and moved in with him the next day. After a year, in early September 1888, he lost his job, she resumed prostitution, and they broke up. On 9 November her body, sliced brutally to pieces by the murderer, was found in her room in Spitalfields.

Commercial Road

Mary Ann Nichols
(also called Polly)
Found at Buck's Row (now Durward Street), 31 August.

Elizabeth Stride
Found at the rear of the International Working Mens' Club, 40 Berner Street, (now Henriques Street), 30 September.

CITY SLAUGHTERS

Murders in London have been frightful throughout its history, whether or not they're as famous as the Jack the Ripper killings, and represent part of its spirit. The list is endless. One of the oddest unsolved murders was that of Sir Edmund Berry Godfrey, a 57-year-old London magistrate whose body was found stabbed and mutilated on Greenberry Hill on 17 October 1678. He had been killed to conceal a Catholic plot to kill Charles II, which had apparently been leaked to him by Titus Oates, the anti-Catholic agitator. In due course three Catholic men, servants of Queen Catherine at Somerset House, were arrested and executed. Their names were Green, Berry and Hill. Today, Greenberry Hill is called Primrose Hill. The real murderers were never found.

More conventional was the execution of Catherine Hayes at Tyburn by fire and strangulation, in May 1726. She had murdered her husband, cut off his head and thrown it into the Thames, where it was found by the Horse Ferry (where Lambeth Bridge now stands). The rest of his body was discovered in a pond in a field in Marylebone.

The Ratcliffe Highway murders in 1811 inspired Thomas de Quincey to write his striking essay 'Murder Considered as One of the Fine Arts'.

Several victims were slaughtered in the docklands between Wapping and Shadwell. The murderer, John Williams, hanged himself the night before he was due to be arrested. He was buried at the junction of Cannon Street Road and Commercial Road, half a mile north of where the murders occurred, with a stake driven through his heart. His remains were uncovered 100 years later, and his skull donated to the owner of a pub that still stands on the crossroads.

In July 1910, the American Dr Hawley Harvey Crippen and his wife Cora had been living for five years at 39 Hilldrop Crescent, in Kentish Town, with their housekeeper, Ethel Le Neve. Cora, who had unsuccessfully aspired to become a vaudeville singer under the name of Belle Elmore, mysteriously disappeared, and when questioned Dr Crippen explained that she had eloped with a lover. The police left, but when they returned the next day, Crippen and Le Neve had vanished. They searched the house, and discovered Cora's headless corpse buried beneath the coal cellar. Crippen and Le Neve were arrested on a ship heading for Montreal, and in November he was convicted and hanged at Pentonville Prison.

One of the most celebrated mass murderers in London's history was Reginald Christie, who lived at 10 Rillington Place in Notting Hill. He was convicted in 1953 of murdering, over a period of ten years, two of his neighbours, three prostitutes and his own wife. He too was hanged at Pentonville. Not long after, the house in which these gruesome killings took place was pulled down, and the name of the street changed. It is now Ruston Mews, just off Ladbroke Grove.

Dennis Nilsen, born in 1945, murdered at least 15 young men over several years, in his flats at 195 Melrose Avenue, Noel Park (near Wood Green Station) and 23 Cranley Gardens in Muswell Hill. In 1983 he was sentenced to life imprisonment, not eligible for parole for 25 years. He has been in prison ever since, although he may emerge in 2008.

1: Primrose Hill (Greenberry Hill) – Murder of Sir Edmund Berry, 1678
2: 10 Rillington Place (now Ruston Mews, off Ladbroke Grove) – Christie murders, 1940s–53
3: Tyburn (Marble Arch) – Site of London gallows, 1571–1783
4: 39 Hilldrop Crescent, Kentish Town – Dr Crippen murder, 1910
5: Ratcliffe Lane (E1) – Ratcliffe Highway murders, 1811
6: 195 Melrose Avenue, Noel Park – Nilsen murders, 1970s–1983
7: 23 Cranley Gardens, Muswell Hill – Nilsen murders, 1970s–1983

PRISONS AND POLICE

In ancient and medieval London, it was traditional that responsibility for securing law and order was given to individuals appointed within their communities. In Saxon England, all citizens were divided into groups of ten, called 'tythings', each represented by a tything-man, and into larger groups of ten tythings, represented by a hundred-man who reported to the sheriff of the county. In 1285, a public 'watch' system was introduced: all householders were required to serve as part of the watch from time to time, reporting to a constable, under the rules of 'hue and cry'. As time went on, they would delegate this task to an employee, who was usually incompetent.

As the population grew, the system's shortcomings became more serious, and in 1749 Henry Fielding was appointed Bow Street magistrate and employed a group of mobile 'thief-takers'. In 1754 he was succeeded by his half-brother John Fielding, who extended the system of Bow Street runners. In 1829, under the new Home Secretary Sir Robert Peel, an Act of Parliament established the metropolitan police force, and ten years later the separate City of London police force was set up.

The Metropolitan Police occupied a house in Whitehall Place, with a courtyard behind known as Scotland Yard. Space had run out by 1890, and the headquarters was moved to a new building on the Victoria Embankment, designed by Richard Norman Shaw, called New Scotland Yard. It moved again in 1967, to Broadway, off Victoria Street.

London has had more prisons than any other city in Europe. The oldest was in the Tower of London. Fleet Prison was built alongside the Fleet river in 1197, one of the first buildings in the city made of stone. It was rebuilt after the Great Fire of 1666, and again after destruction in the Gordon Riots (1780), and was finally demolished in 1846. Newgate Gaol was originally in a London Wall gate built in the 12th century, and was also rebuilt twice, before closing in 1902 and being replaced by the Old Bailey, the central criminal court off Newgate Street. The Clink, in Clink Street, dates back at least to 1509, and was demolished in 1745. The Tun in Cornhill was built at the end of the 13th century, and demolished in the 19th. Clerkenwell Gaol, founded in the 17th century and rebuilt several times, soon became the largest remand prison in London, with over 10,000 inmates. Demolished in 1890, its underground cells and perimeter wall survive, and are now a tourist attraction (Clerkenwell Close, EC1). There were dozens of others.

Today, London has seven prisons: Belmarsh Prison in Greenwich, Brixton, Feltham near Hounslow, Holloway, Pentonville in Caledonian Road, Wandsworth, and Wormwood Scrubs in North Kensington.

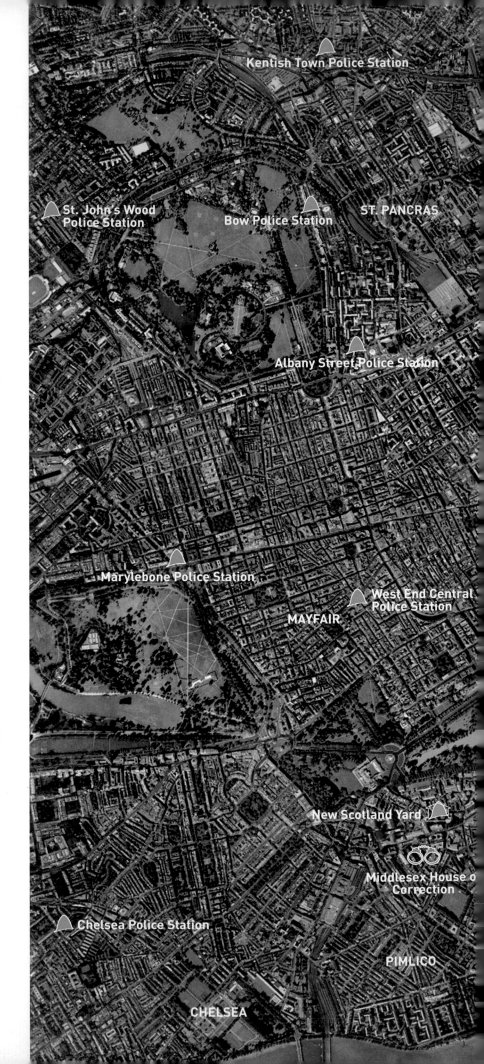

Prisons

Police stations

Other buildings

Pentonville

CLERKENWELL

SHOREDITCH

Fleet Prison

House of Correction

Middlesex House of Detention

Clerkenwell Bridewell House of Detention

BETHNAL GREEN

Holborn Police Station

JOMSBURY

Whitecross Street Prison

Brick Lane Police Station

Newgate Prison

The Tun

Bridewell Prison

Charing Cross Police Station

Tower Prison

The Clink

New Scotland Yard, now Norman Shaw Building

Walworth Police Station

Queen's Bench Prison

Rotherhithe Police Station

Strong Room, House of Common

Surrey County Gaol

Bridewell House of Occupation

llbank Prison

SOUTHWARK

Vauxhall Police Station

THE STORY OF HYDE PARK CORNER

When John Rocque began his *Exact Survey of London* in 1737, Hyde Park Corner was the entrance to London from the west, with a tollgate ('turnpike') across the road where the tube station now stands, and a few buildings on either side. Beyond them were fields to the south, and the royal Hyde Park to the north-west. In one of the buildings, Rocque opened his print shop, where he sold his magnificent map of London, along with other products. Tyburn Lane (now Park Lane) ran north up the edge of the park. The Grosvenor family had begun in 1720 to build up their immense 100-acre estate, centred around Grosvenor Square, in what is now Mayfair, but a lot of it on either side of Curzon Street was open land. Much of Green Park to the east was wooded, with grand houses going up along the north side of Piccadilly.

On the west side, in 1719, Viscount Lanesborough built himself a large but plain red brick mansion facing Hyde Park. Fourteen years later he rented the building to the governors of a new hospital, St George's. In 1827, it was hugely expanded, to a design by William Wilkins, and the hospital remained there until it was moved to Tooting in 1980. The building is now the luxurious and expensive Lanesborough Hotel.

Henry Bathurst was Lord Chancellor in the 1770s and had married the daughter of Sir Allen Apsley. He acquired land at the corner of the park and commissioned the architect Robert Adam to design Apsley House. Twenty years later, he sold it to the Marquess of Wellesley, Governor-General of India and the future Duke of Wellington's oldest brother. Wellington bought it from his brother in 1818 for £42,000, and 12 years later spent the same huge sum renovating it, facing the brick walls with Bath stone, and adding a Corinthian portico. The 7th Duke of Wellington presented it to the nation in 1947, and it is now the Wellington Museum (and popularly known as number one London).

When George IV was upgrading Buckingham Palace in the 1820s, Decimus Burton's Constitution Arch was erected close to Apsley House, topped by a colossal bronze statue of the Duke of Wellington on horseback. Sir Richard Westmacott's bronze of Achilles, cast from the metal of captured French guns, was erected in the park on the other side of the house. In 1882 the whole area of Hyde Park corner was redesigned to allow through more traffic, the arch was moved to the top of Constitution Hill, and the statue on top was transported to Aldershot and eventually replaced by the present Quadriga by Adrian Jones (1912). Burton also designed the Hyde Park Screen, beside Apsley House, with its carvings by John Herring. Further traffic improvements were made in the 1960s, including a road tunnel and pedestrian underpasses.

Where South Carriage Drive meets Park Lane, new and rather brash gates, made of stainless steel, were installed in 1993 behind Burton's Screen, in honour of Queen Elizabeth the Queen Mother (d. 2002).

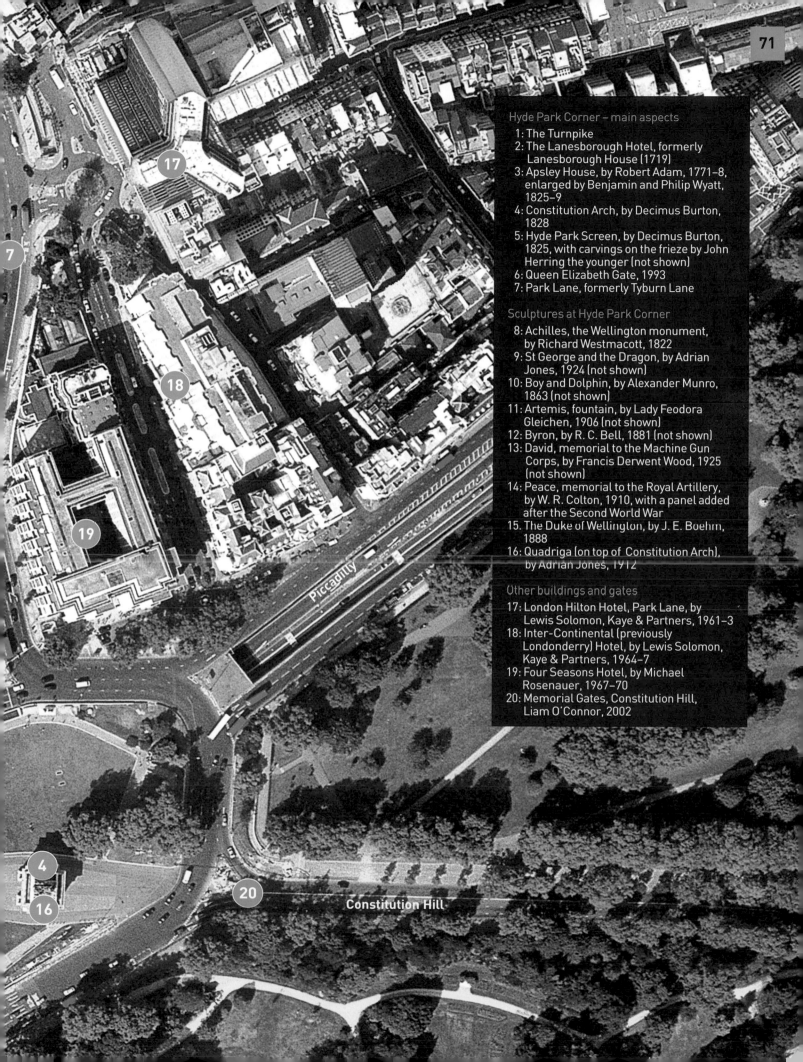

Hyde Park Corner – main aspects

1: The Turnpike
2: The Lanesborough Hotel, formerly Lanesborough House (1719)
3: Apsley House, by Robert Adam, 1771–8, enlarged by Benjamin and Philip Wyatt, 1825–9
4: Constitution Arch, by Decimus Burton, 1828
5: Hyde Park Screen, by Decimus Burton, 1825, with carvings on the frieze by John Herring the younger (not shown)
6: Queen Elizabeth Gate, 1993
7: Park Lane, formerly Tyburn Lane

Sculptures at Hyde Park Corner

8: Achilles, the Wellington monument, by Richard Westmacott, 1822
9: St George and the Dragon, by Adrian Jones, 1924 (not shown)
10: Boy and Dolphin, by Alexander Munro, 1863 (not shown)
11: Artemis, fountain, by Lady Feodora Gleichen, 1906 (not shown)
12: Byron, by R. C. Bell, 1881 (not shown)
13: David, memorial to the Machine Gun Corps, by Francis Derwent Wood, 1925 (not shown)
14: Peace, memorial to the Royal Artillery, by W. R. Colton, 1910, with a panel added after the Second World War
15: The Duke of Wellington, by J. E. Boehm, 1888
16: Quadriga (on top of Constitution Arch), by Adrian Jones, 1912

Other buildings and gates

17: London Hilton Hotel, Park Lane, by Lewis Solomon, Kaye & Partners, 1961–3
18: Inter-Continental (previously Londonderry) Hotel, by Lewis Solomon, Kaye & Partners, 1964–7
19: Four Seasons Hotel, by Michael Rosenauer, 1967–70
20: Memorial Gates, Constitution Hill, Liam O'Connor, 2002

Piccadilly

Constitution Hill

DICKENS'S LONDON

No writer conveys the harsh realities of life in Victorian London more vividly than Charles Dickens (1812–70), who had a passion for portraying the grim and crowded areas of London in his novels. The map shows his London homes, and a selection of the hundreds of references in his works to specific London areas.

Dickens lived as a boy at 16 Bayham Street, Camden Town (50) It is described in *Dombey and Son*, and the Cratchets *(A Christmas Carol)* and the Micawbers *(David Copperfield)* lived here. In his teenage years Dickens worked at Warren's blacking factory, and he frequently crossed the Blackfriars Bridge (5) to meet his family at Marshalsea Prison in Southwark, where his father was imprisoned for debt in 1824, and where Dickens's Little Dorrit is born. Jo in *Bleak House* stops on the bridge to gaze at St Paul's Cathedral.

Dickens began his writing career in 1831 as a reporter on the *Morning Chronicle*, and until 1834 he lodged in the Adelphi (1) (demolished in 1938), just north of Hungerford Bridge. He married Kate Hogarth at St Luke's Church (51) , in Sydney Street, Chelsea. In *Bleak House*, Richard Carstone studies law nearby.

From 1834–7 Dickens lived in Furnival's Inn (52) in Holborn, one of the Inns of Chancery which was closed in 1817 and replaced with a block of

flats. The site is now part of the huge premises of the Prudential Insurance Company. *Pickwick Papers* was begun here, and after he began publishing the monthly instalments, the young Charles and Kate Dickens moved to 48 Doughty Street (53) in 1837. Here he completed the later chapters of *Pickwick Papers*, and wrote *Oliver Twist* and *Nicholas Nickleby*. It is now the Charles Dickens Museum.

For a short time in 1839 Dickens rented a house in Petersham, just south of Richmond, before moving to Devonshire Terrace. He wrote a large part of *Nicholas Nickleby* here. And from 1839 to 1851 the family lived at 1 Devonshire Terrace (54), south of Regent's Park. The whole terrace was demolished in 1960, and replaced by Ferguson House. Among the many works he wrote while living here are *The Old Curiosity Shop, Barnaby Rudge, Martin Chuzzlewit, A Christmas Carol, Dombey and Son*, and *David Copperfield*. Five of his children were born here.

From 1851 Dickens lived in Woburn Place, off Tavistock Square (55), in part of the old Tavistock House (rebuilt in 1938 by Edwin Lutyens and now the headquarters of the British Medical Association, *Bleak House, Little Dorrit, Hard Times, A Tale of Two Cities* and part of *Great Expectations* were written here.

LONDON LOCATIONS IN DICKENS'S NOVELS

Adelphi, WC2 (1): David Copperfield lodges in Mrs Crupp's house here. Pickwick and Wardle frequently attend the hotel bar (*Pickwick Papers*).

Bedlam, Shoreditch, E1 (2): *Christmas Carol*: Scrooge says: 'I'll retire to Bedlam'.

Belgrave Square, SW1 (3): The Wititterlys (*Nicholas Nickleby*) live near here.

Bishopsgate, EC2 (4): Brogley, 'sword broker and appraiser' (*Dombey and Son*), kept a second-hand furniture shop here.

Blackfriars Bridge, EC4 (5): Hugh (*Barnaby Rudge*) broke open the toll houses here during the Gordon Riots. Jo (*Bleak House*) stops here to gaze at St. Paul's Cathedral.

Bleeding Heart Yard, EC1 (6): The Plornish family (*Little Dorrit*) live here, as is Daniel Doyce's factory.

Bond Street, W1 (7): Mrs Billickin (*The Mystery of Edwin Drood*) refers to it as smart and fashionable area.

Bow Street, WC2 (8): The Artful Dodger (*Oliver Twist*), and Barnaby (*Barnaby Rudge*) were taken to the police station.

Bridewell Place, EC4 (9): Miss Miggs (*Barnaby Rudge*) was chosen to be Female Turnkey at the workhouse here.

British Museum, WC1 (10): David and Steerforth (*David Copperfield*) visit the museum.

Cavendish Square, W1 (11): Madame Mantalini (*Nicholas Nickleby*) had her dressmaking shop here, and the Merdles (*Little Dorrit*) live here.

Chancery Lane, WC2 (12): *Bleak House*: Kenge and Carboys offices are in Lincoln's Inn, and the Jarndyce and Jarndyce case was heard at Lincoln's Inn Hall (and later at Westminster Hall). Mr Tulkinghorn lives in Lincoln's Inn Fields. Miss Flite, Gridley, Nemo (Captain Hawdon), and Tony Jobling (Weevle) live in Cursitor Street. Mrs Jellyby lived in Thavie's Inn (off Holborn), moving after her bankruptcy to Hatton Garden.

Charing Cross, SW1 (13): David (*David Copperfield*) stays in the Golden Cross Hotel here.

Cheapside, EC2 (14): The undertaker Mould (*Martin Chuzzlewit*) lives here; and Pickwick (*Pickwick Papers*) is taken to meet Tony Weller at an inn here.

Clare Market, WC2 (15): Site of the Old Curiosity Shop, and gin shops.

Clerkenwell, EC1 (16): Gabriel Varden's locksmith shop, the Golden Key (*Barnaby Rudge*), is in Clerkenwell. Jarvis Lorry, clerk at Tellson's bank (*A Tale of Two Cities*), lives here.

Cornhill, EC3 (17): Dodson and Fogg (*Pickwick Papers*) have offices here.

Covent Garden, WC2 (18): David Copperfield watches *Julius Caesar* at the theatre here, and buys flowers for Dora in the market. Arthur Clennam (*Little Dorrit*) lodges here; and Job Trotter (*Pickwick Papers*) spends the night in a vegetable basket here.

Drury Lane, WC2 (19): Miss Petowker of the Crummles Company performed in the theatre (*Nicholas Nickleby*). Dick Swiveler lives over a tobacconist here (*The Old Curiosity Shop*).

Fetter Lane, EC4 (20): David Copperfield orders beef at Johnson's Beef House here.

Fleet Prison, off Farringdon Road, EC1, (now Caronne House) (21): Pickwick (*Pickwick Papers*) was imprisoned here.

Golden Square, W1 (22): Ralph Nickleby (*Nicholas Nickleby*) lives here. Mr. Peggotty and Martha find Little Emily nearby (*David Copperfield*).

Gray's Inn, WC1 (23): Mr. Phunky (*Pickwick Papers*) has chambers here, and Traddles (*David Copperfield*) lives at 2 Holborn Court, nearby.

Grosvenor Square, W1 (24): Lord Rockingham's house is blockaded against the Gordon Rioters (*Barnaby Rudge*).

Holborn, EC1 (25): Fagin (*Oliver Twist*) runs his den of thieves at Saffron Hill. Rosa Bud (*Edwin Drood*) stays in rooms at Furnival's Inn (now Prudential Insurance) on Holborn. Mrs. Gamp lives at Kingsgate Street, High Holborn (*Martin Chuzzlewit*). Traddles (*David Copperfield*) lives in Castle Street, Holborn.

29 Knightrider Street, EC4 (26): Horn Coffee House, where Pickwick (*Pickwick Papers*) sent for a few bottles of wine, while in Fleet Prison, to celebrate Mr Winkle's visit.

Lambeth Palace, SE1 (27): Attacked by the Gordon Rioters (*Barnaby Rudge*).

Leadenhall Street, EC3 (28): Tim Linkinwater (*Nicholas Nickleby*) recommends buying eggs in the market here. The offices of Dombey & Son are here.

London Bridge, EC4 (29): David (*David Copperfield*) liked to sit on the bridge and watch people go by. The prostitute Nancy (*Oliver Twist*) is spotted by Noah Claypole on the bridge, and subsequently murdered.

Lower Thames Street, EC3 (30): Mrs Clennam (*Little Dorrit*) lives here, and Ralph (*Nicholas Nickleby*) lodges Mrs Nickleby and Kate in 'an old and gloomy' empty house here.

Newgate Prison (now the Old Bailey), EC1 (31): Oliver (*Oliver Twist*) visits Fagin here, and later witnesses his hanging. Hugh, Dennis and Barnaby (*Barnaby Rudge*) are imprisoned here. Wemmick and Pip (*Great Expectations*) visit the prison.

Oxford Street, W1 (32): John Jarndyce, Esther, Richard, and Ada (*Bleak House*) have 'cheerful lodging over an upholsterer's shop' near Oxford Street.

Piccadilly, W1 (33): Mr Micawber (*David Copperfield*) imagines living in a spacious flat above a respectible business here.

Regent Street, W1 (34): Lord Frederick Verisopht (*Nicholas Nickleby*) lives in 'a handsome suite of private apartments in Regent Street'.

St. Bartholomew's Hospital, EC1 (35): Bob Hopkins (*Pickwick Papers*) is a doctor here, and Betsy Prig, friend of Mrs Gamp (*Martin Chuzzlewit*), is a nurse. John Baptist Cavalletto (*Little Dorrit*) is taken here after being hit by a mail coach.

St Mary Axe, EC3 (36): Here is the roof garden (*Our Mutual Friend*) where Lizzie and Jenny Wren sat, above the premises of Pubsey & Co.

St. Paul's Cathedral, EC4 (37): David (*David Copperfield*) takes Peggotty to the top of the tower.

Scotland Yard (now Whitehall Place), SW1 (38): Described in *Sketches by Boz*.

Smithfield, EC1 (39): Oliver and Sikes (*Oliver Twist*) pass through the market on their way to burgle Mr Brownlow. Pip (*Great Expectations*) goes there while waiting for Mr Jaggers.

Southwark Bridge, EC4 (40): John Chivery (*Litte Dorrit*) proposed to Amy Dorrit on the bridge.

The Strand, WC2 (41): Mr Haredale (*Barnaby Rudge*) walks along the street after his house is burned down. David (*David Copperfield*) finds a good shop to buy pudding. The Nicklebys (*Nicholas Nickleby*) lodge there in the home of Miss La Creevy.

The Temple, EC4 (42): Pip (*Great Expectations*) has chambers here, where he is visited by Magwitch; as do Sir John Chester (*Barnaby Rudge*), and Stryver, the lawyer who defends Charles Darnay (*A Tale of Two Cities*).

Tower Hill, EC3 (43): Mr and Mrs Daniel Quilp (*The Old Curiosity Shop*) live here. David (*David Copperfield*) takes Peggotty sightseeing at the Tower. Pip, Herbert and Startop (*Great Expectations*) row past it while trying to help Magwitch escape the country.

Tottenham Court Road, W1 (44): Peggotty (*David Copperfield*) helps Traddles recover his property from a broker's shop here.

Waterloo Bridge, WC2 (45): Sam Weller (*Pickwick Papers*) tells Pickwick that he 'once had unfurnished lodgin's for a fortnight' under the arches of the bridge.

Westminster Abbey, SW1 (46): Pip and Herbert Pocket (*Great Expectations*) attend services here. The undertaker Mould (*Martin Chuzzlewit*) tells Mrs Gamp that it's possible to buy a gentleman a tomb here if he chooses to invest in such a purchase.

Westminster Bridge, SW1 (47): David (*David Copperfield*) crosses the bridge with his mother on their return to London after hiding in the country.

Whitechapel, E1 (48): Pickwick, Sam Weller, his father and Peter Magnus (*Pickwick Papers*) leave the Bull Inn here on their journey to Ipswich.

Windsor Terrace, off City Road, N1 (49): Mr Micawber (*David Copperfield*) lives here.

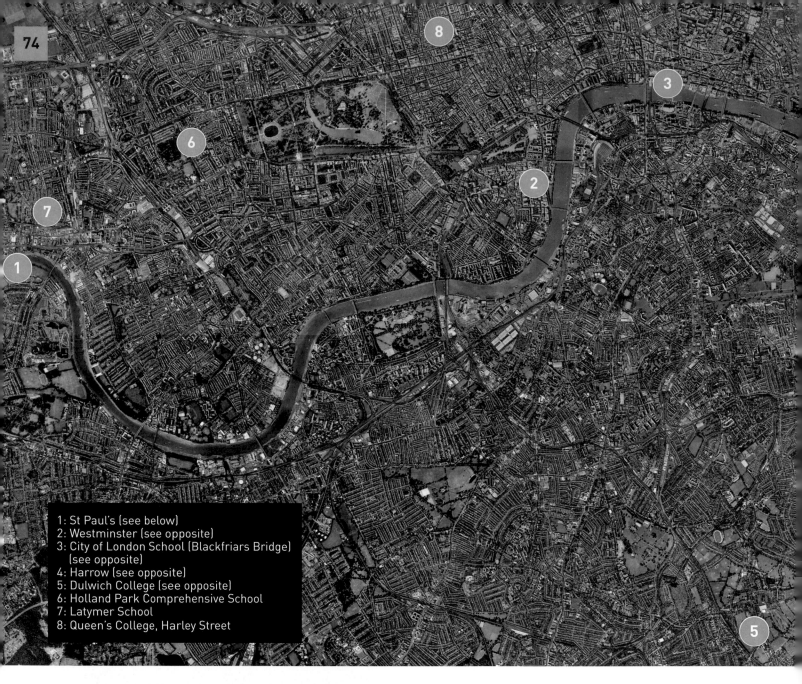

1: St Paul's (see below)
2: Westminster (see opposite)
3: City of London School (Blackfriars Bridge)
   (see opposite)
4: Harrow (see opposite)
5: Dulwich College (see opposite)
6: Holland Park Comprehensive School
7: Latymer School
8: Queen's College, Harley Street

SCHOOLS

Until 1870, when compulsory schooling was finally introduced in Britain, there was no national system of education. Public schools had been in existence since the 14th century, catering for the sons (and much later the daughters) of the middle and upper classes, and sometimes offering limited free places to the poor.

Westminster School began as a school for the clerks of the Benedictine abbey, but when the monastery was dissolved by Henry VIII in 1540, the school continued, and was re-founded by Elizabeth I in 1560.

St Paul's School was founded in 1509, the largest in England, and provided free education for up to 153 boys, who were to be 'of all nations and countries indifferently'. Its building, situated next to the cathedral, burned down in 1666, was rebuilt in 1670 and again in 1822. The school moved to Hammersmith in 1884, and then to Barnes in 1968.

Other ancient private schools include Merchant Taylor's School, founded in 1561 in Suffolk Lane, which moved to Charterhouse Square in 1875 and then to Northwood in Middlesex; Harrow, founded in 1572; Charterhouse (1611), which moved to Godalming in 1872; Dulwich College (1616); and Latymer School (1624) in Hammersmith. City of London School was opened in 1837 in Cheapside, moving to Victoria Embankment in 1883 and to Paul's Walk near Blackfriars Bridge in 1986. Queen's College in Harley Street (1848) was the pioneer of higher education for girls. Many more were founded in the 20th century.

In 1818, a Portsmouth shoemaker called John Pounds developed the so called 'ragged schools', providing the poorest children with a basic education and practical skills. The Ragged School Union, under the patronage of Lord Shaftesbury, united the movement, and by 1852

London contained 132 ragged schools catering for 26,000 children. When the 1870 Education Act was passed, making education to the age of 12 free and compulsory, there were 250 of these schools, which were then brought under the aegis of local elected school boards. In the 1870s and 1880s a mass of new school buildings were erected all over London, most of which, with their distinctive red brick architecture, are still with us today.

School boards were abolished in 1902, with control being transferred to new local education authorities. In 1918 education became compulsory to the age of 14, rising to 15 by 1947 and to 16 by 1973. Universal free secondary education was not formalised until the Education Act of 1944, which also linked church schools with the state-maintained sector, while retaining their religious affiliations.

London college and universities
1: Birkbeck College
2: Courtauld Institute of Art
3: Goldsmiths' College
4: Heythrop College
5: Imperial College of Science, Technology and Medicine
6: Charing Cross & Westminster Medical School
7: Charing Cross & Westminster Medical School
8: Charing Cross & Westminster Medical School
9: Charing Cross & Westminster Medical School
10: St Mary's Hospital Medical School
11: Kennedy Institute of Rheumatology
12: Institute of Education
13: King's College London
14: Institute of Psychiatry
15: GKT School of Medicine, Guy's Hospital
16: London Business School
17: London School of Economics and Political Science
18: London School of Hygiene and Tropical Medicine
19: Queen Mary College
20: Royal Academy of Music
21: Royal Veterinary College
22: School of Oriental and African Studies

23: School of Pharmacy
24: University College London
25: City University
26: London Metropolitan University
27: Middlesex University
28: South Bank University
29: Thames Valley University
30: Wolfson Institute of Health and Human Sciences
31: University of East London, Stratford
32: University of East London, Docklands
33: University of Greenwich
34: University of Surrey Roehampton
35: Roehampton, Whitelands College
36: Westminster University
37: Guildhall School of Music and Drama
38: London Institute, Camberwell College of Art
39: London Institute, Central St Martin's College of Art
40: London Institute, Chelsea College of Art
41: London Institute, College of Fashion
42: London Institute, College of Printing
43: Royal College of Art
44: Royal College of Music
45: Trinity College of Music

COLLEGES AND UNIVERSITIES

Although several attempts were made in the 16th and 17th centuries to establish universities in parts of England other than Oxford and Cambridge, the country was monopolised by these two ancient institutions until well into the 19th century. In 1826 University College London was founded in Gower Street to provide education for non-Anglicans, who were excluded from Oxford and Cambridge. Two years later, a rival, sponsored by the Church of England and the Duke of Wellington, was set up in the Strand under the name of King's College London. Ten years later, in 1836, the government under Lord Melbourne founded the University of London, with the task of uniting the existing colleges (by 1908 they had been amalgamated) and providing examinations for students, regardless of their religion.

The university started in rooms in Somerset House, moving in 1853 to Burlington House. A new site was created in 1936 in Malet Street, next to University College London, which was taken over during the war by the Ministry of Information but returned in 1945 for use as the main university offices, lecture halls and library. It is the largest university in Britain, with around 100,000 internal students, about 30,000 external students, and many thousands more on extramural and short courses. It comprises 18 colleges and other institutions, some of which, such as the Royal Veterinary College (1791) and Birkbeck College (1823), predate its own existence. Some best-known components are Imperial College (1907), the London School of Economics (1895), the Royal Academy of Music (1823), Royal Holloway College (1886), which in 1985 merged with Bedford College (1849), Goldsmiths' College (1891), and St George's Hospital Medical School (1834).

Throughout the 19th and 20th centuries various specialist academic institutions were founded in London. Medical schools were among the most prolific, mostly attached to the main hospitals. Polytechnics, providing a more practical and technical education than universities, were created mainly in the second half of the 20th century. However, this distinction was removed by the Higher and Further Education Act (1992), with the result that most of them are now universities. Westminster University, for example, was formerly the Polytechnic of Central London. Other universities include Brunel (1957), London Metropolitan (2002), and City (1966), formerly Northampton Polytechnic (1896). Among many other distinguished colleges are the Royal College of Art, founded in 1837 as a school of industrial design, and the Royal College of Music, founded by the Prince of Wales in 1882.

The University of London's colleges and institutes

Other university

Independent colleges

The tree-lined Malet Street, directly north of the British Museum, is dominated by departments of London University. At the northern end on the east side is the busy students' union building, opposite the elegant College Hall built in 1931. Other institutions include Birkbeck College (4), the RADA theatre (5), the London School of Hygiene and Tropical Medicine (6) and the Senate House and university library (7).

Great Russell Street (2) and Museum Street are awash with shops selling rare and second-hand books and art. The independent publishing firm Souvenir Press is based at 43 Great Russell Street, and George du Maurier, the illustrator of several Thomas Hardy novels (and grandfather of the novelist Daphne du Maurier), lived at number 91. The elegant 18th-century terraced houses at the southern end of Bloomsbury Street contain several hotels, such as The Morgan (3) and The Gresham.

To the north and west of Russell Square (8) (which is currently being restored), many other London University institutions are housed, including the School of Slavonic and East European Studies, the School of Oriental and African Studies, the Institute of Education, and the Brunei Gallery.

THE BRITISH MUSEUM

Every major European city set up a national museum in the 18th century and the British Museum in Montagu House, Bloomsbury, opened to the public in January 1759, was among the first. For centuries the rich and aristocratic classes had assembled collections of antiquities and works of art, and by 1700 it was becoming fashionable to present them to the nation on patriotic grounds. The money to acquire Montagu House was raised by public lottery and, soon after the museum opened, its collections began to expand dramatically by purchases and gifts of every sort. In 1757 George II donated the Royal Library comprising 10,000 volumes, which had been collected by British monarchs since the time of Henry VIII. In 1816 the famous Elgin marbles from the Parthenon were acquired. By 1823, the museum's possessions were far greater than Montagu House had space for, and the architect Robert Smirke was employed to design major extensions. In 1842, Montagu House itself was demolished, and replaced with the imposing classical façade and portico which we see today. In 1857 the courtyard behind was converted into the Reading Room, beneath a huge copper dome, where (until it was moved to purpose-built premises in St Pancras) generations of scholars and writers, from Thomas Carlyle to Karl Marx, made use of the ever growing library.

Even the new building was soon overcrowded and its congestion has been alleviated several times. In 1881 the natural history collections were moved to the Natural History Museum in South Kensington (see pages 122–5); in 1905 a newspaper library was built in Colindale; additional galleries were created in 1914 and between the First and Second World Wars; and an extension was built in Museum Street in 1980. The new Great Court was opened by the Queen in 2000.

Although several times in the Museum's history attempts have been made to introduce admission charges, entry remains free and an average of 20,000 people visit the museum every day. There are 94 permanent and temporary exhibition galleries.

Heading north from the museum for one mile, the whole area is today dominated by the University of London, with its great library in the Senate House on Gower Street, the faculties and departments in individual terraced houses, and various of its colleges. For example, the School of Oriental and African Studies, founded in 1916, stands at the north of Russell Square, with its new Brunei Gallery opened in 1995. University College Hospital, founded in 1834 when medical degrees could only be obtained at Oxford and Cambridge, is still at the northern end, opposite University College London.

St George's Church (Bloomsbury Way) (1) was designed by Nicholas Hawksmoor and completed in 1730. On top of the extraordinary steeple is a statue of George I in Roman dress. The design of the church has been much criticised over the centuries and is today in a crumbling state – although restoration is under way.

CLERKENWELL
SHOREDITCH
Gray's Inn Fields
HOLBORN
Moorfields
Spitalfields
MILE END
SMITHFIELD
Lincoln's Inn Fields
Goodman's Fields
CHEAPSIDE
BILLINGSGATE
Tower
St. Katherine Docks
ST. JAMES
Lambeth Marsh
Wapping Docks
SOUTHWARK
LAMBETH
St. George's Fields
WESTMINSTER
KENNINGTON

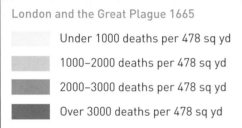

London and the Great Plague 1665

Under 1000 deaths per 478 sq yd

1000–2000 deaths per 478 sq yd

2000–3000 deaths per 478 sq yd

Over 3000 deaths per 478 sq yd

PLAGUE

London was constantly assaulted by bubonic plague throughout the Middle Ages, with some epidemics more severe than others. Much the worst was the Black Death, which originated in the East, and ravaged Europe throughout the 14th century. It reached England in 1347, and London was in its grip by November 1348. Within a few months of a cold and wet winter the Plague had wiped out around 40 per cent of the entire population. Many of the dead were buried outside the Wall, in the open space then known as Smythe Fyeld behind the Charterhouse. The 'red plague', as Shakespeare called it, regularly returned at least 23 times over the next 300 years, killing tens of thousands. In 1603 it was so severe that 2,798 died in one week in the City alone; and another 35,000 died in an

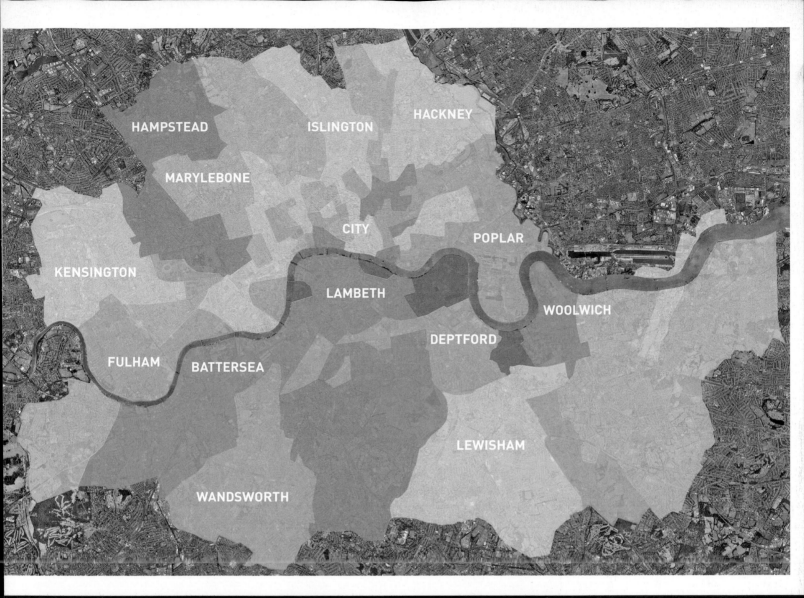

HAMPSTEAD

ISLINGTON

HACKNEY

MARYLEBONE

CITY

POPLAR

KENSINGTON

LAMBETH

WOOLWICH

DEPTFORD

FULHAM

BATTERSEA

LEWISHAM

WANDSWORTH

earth, in areas like Mount Mills, off Gosford Road, which still today is a waste ground used as a car park.

There have been other epidemics in London's history, though no recurrences of the plague. Cholera was endemic in India, and as trade with that continent expanded in the 19th century it spread west. In February 1832 the disease broke out in Rotherhithe and Limehouse, and it attacked London twice more, in 1848–9 and again in 1854. It was particularly bad in areas close to the river, such as Southwark and Vauxhall. Dr John Snow, the Queen's obstetrician, deduced over these three pandemics that the disease was water-borne, with the result that eventually major improvements were made to London's water supplies and sanitation (see page 52). Cholera is now extremely rare in Britain.

The so-called Spanish influenza epidemic struck Britain in 1918, 16 days before the armistice was signed ending the First World War. At its height, in the week following 27 October, 2,200 people died in London. The world-wide AIDS and HIV epidemic has affected many Londoners since the 1980s.

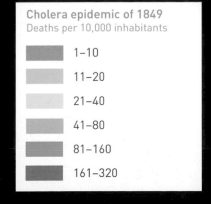

Cholera epidemic of 1849
Deaths per 10,000 inhabitants

	1–10
	11–20
	21–40
	41–80
	81–160
	161–320

Air quality in London in 2001

Although pollution has continuously fallen over recent years, two pollutants, Nitrogen dioxide (NO_2) and Fine particles (PM10) are currently running above the targets set by the authorities. Both are largely caused by petrol vehicles, and the use of gas in buildings; so they tend to be high in built-up areas and close to busy roads.

The Air Quality Network has monitors placed at over 100 sites throughout London, which record pollution levels every day. The levels reported over the twelve months of 2001 are shown here, in relation to the targets, for the two pollutants mentioned above.

For PM10 (Fine particles), two different targets have been set for different areas.

Nitrogen dioxide — Target: 40

1: Barking & Dagenham (Rush Green)	36
2: Barnet (Tally Ho Corner)	57
3: Barnet (Finchley)	40
4: Barnet (Strawberry Vale)	40
5: Bexley (Slade Green)	37
6: Bexley (Belvedere)	36
7: Bexley (Bedonwell)	34
8: Bloomsbury	47
9: Brent (Kingsbury)	37
10: Bromley (Central)	60
11: Camden (Swiss Cottage)	64
12: Camden (Marylebone Road – Baker Street)	82
13: Camden (Shaftesbury Avenue)	72
14: Croydon (Purley Way)	44
15: Croydon (George Street)	56
16: Croydon (Norbury)	67
17: Croydon (Euston Road)	39
18: Crystal Palace (Crystal Palace Parade)	48
19: Ealing (Ealing Town Hall)	40
20: Ealing (Acton Town Hall)	52
21: Enfield (Church Street)	42
22: Enfield (Salisbury School Ponders End)	36
23: Enfield (Derby Road, Upper Edmonton)	48
24: Greenwich (Eltham)	35
25: Greenwich (Trafalgar Road)	55
26: Greenwich Bexley (A2 Falconwood)	48
27: Hackney (Clapton)	46
28: Hammersmith & Fulham (Hammersmith Broadway)	68
29: Harringay (Town Hall)	46
30: Harringay (Priory Park)	38
31: Harrow (Stanmore)	30
32: Havering (Rainham)	42
33: Havering (Romford)	41
34: Heathrow Airport	51
35: Hillingdon (South Ruislip)	44
36: Hounslow (Brentford)	52
37: Hounslow (Cranford)	41
38: Hounslow (Chiswick High Road)	53
39: Islington (Upper Street)	47
40: Islington (Holloway Road)	65
41: Kensington & Chelsea (North Kensington)	41
42: Kensington & Chelsea (Cromwell Road)	73
43: Kensington & Chelsea (Knightsbridge)	81
44: Kensington & Chelsea (King's Road)	84
45: Lambeth (Christchurch Road)	57
46: Redbridge (Perth Terrace)	39
47: Redbridge (Ilford Broadway)	119
48: Redbridge (Fullwell Cross)	63
49: Redbridge (Gardner Close)	46
50: Richmond (Castelnau)	44
51: Southwark (Elephant and Castle)	48
52: Southwark (Old Kent Road)	63
53: Sutton (Town Centre)	43
54: Sutton (North Cheam)	40
55: Teddington	30
56: Tower Hamlets (Poplar)	43
57: Tower Hamlets (Mile End Road)	70
58: Tower Hamlets (Bethnal Green)	45
59: Waltham Forest (Dawlish Road)	42
60: Wandsworth (Town Hall)	47
61: Wandsworth (High Street)	51
62: West London	47

Fine Particles (1) — Target: 10

5: Bexley (Slade Green	18
8: Bloomsbury	6
9: Brent (Kingsbury)	21
12: Camden (Marylebone Road – Baker Street)	0
64: Croydon (Thornton Heath)	14
19: Ealing (Ealing Town Hall)	3
22: Enfield (Salisbury School Ponders End)	25
24: Greenwich (Eltham)	14
27: Hackney (Clapton)	0
30: Haringey (Priory Park)	20
35: Hillingdon (South Ruislip)	4
37: Hounslow (Cranford)	15
41: Kensington & Chelsea (North Kensington)	12
65: Kingston (Chessington)	28
46: Redbridge (Perth Terrace)	17
51: Southwark (Elephant and Castle)	7
55: Teddington	30
56: Tower Hamlets (Poplar)	16
60: Wandsworth (Town Hall)	10

Legend:
- Nitrogen dioxide
- Fine particles (1)
- Fine particles (2)
- – – – Target

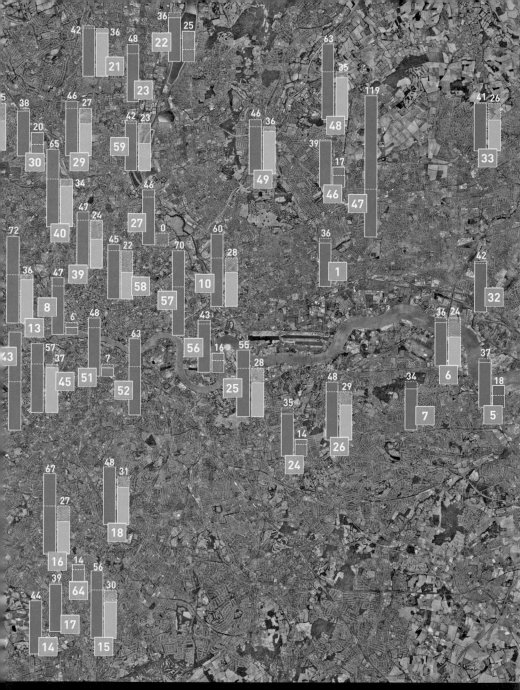

POLLUTION

Fog, which Dickens in *Bleak House* calls 'a London particular', seems to have oppressed the area from ancient times. Tacitus refers to it in his account of the Roman invasion; Elizabeth I found it aggravating; and John Evelyn in 1661 described 'that hellish and dismal cloud of sea-coal' which harmed the lungs of Londoners. Even the inner walls of grand houses were marked with soot. It was the burning of coal that caused it, and as London's industries grew in the 18th century it got worse.

On 27 December 1813 a fog descended which was so thick that the Prince Regent was unable to get into the city past Kentish Town, and had to return to Hatfield House. It lasted for eight days. Later in the century, the fogs sometimes lasted weeks on end, usually in November. The opening chapter of *Bleak House* has a vivid description of fog-strewn London; and fog is equally a leading character in novels by Arthur Conan Doyle, Robert Louis Stevenson and many others. In 1899 and 1901 Monet came over from Paris to paint the fogs.

The phenomenon gradually declined during the 20th century, and the Clean Air Act of 1956 (updated several times, most recently in 1993), among other things, allowed local councils to declare 'smokeless zones' in which housekeepers were prohibited from burning coal in their fireplaces. Nonetheless, the fogs continued for several years, inflicting death and injury. The Lewisham rail disaster in 1957, in which 87 people died, was caused by fog. I vividly recall the last great London fog, which appropriately covered the West End on the evening of the London premiere of Benjamin Britten's 'War Requiem', performed in Westminster Abbey on 6 December 1962.

Over the last 40 years, most Londoners have switched to gas or electric heating, or adopted smokeless solid fuels, whether they lived in a smokeless zone or not. London's air is much cleaner, and its river is certainly healthier, attracting fish that haven't been seen in it for hundreds of years. But pollution still exists, albeit invisible, in different forms, much of it caused by the vast increase in traffic. The environmental research group at King's College runs a website (www.erg.kcl.ac.uk), on which Londoners can check the levels of the seven main pollutants in their area.

Fine Particles (2)	Target: 40		Target: 40
66: Barking & Dagenham (Scrattons Farm)	25	31: Harrow (Stanmore)	22
3: Barnet (Finchley)	23	33: Havering (Romford)	26
4: Barnet (Strawberry Vale)	25	34: Heathrow Airport	28
6: Bexley (Belvedere)	24	69: Hillingdon (Hillingdon Hospital)	25
67: Bexley (Thamesmead)	24	70: Hillingdon (AURN)	28
68: Brent (Ikea)	40	36: Hounslow (Brentford)	36
10: Bromley (Central)	28	38: Hounslow (Chiswick High Road)	32
11: Camden (Swiss Cottage)	33	39: Islington (Upper Street)	24
13: Camden (Shaftesbury Avenue)	36	40: Islington (Holloway Road)	34
15: Croydon (George Street)	30	42: Kensington & Chelsea (Cromwell Road)	35
16: Croydon (Norbury)	27	45: Lambeth (Christchurch Road)	37
18: Crystal Palace (Crystal Palace Parade)	31	12: Camden (Marylebone Road – Baker Street)	43
20: Ealing (Acton Town Hall)	30	48: Redbridge (Fullwell Cross)	35
21: Enfield (Church Street)	36	49: Redbridge (Gardner Close)	36
25: Greenwich (Trafalgar Road)	28	50: Richmond (Castelnau)	26
26: Greenwich Bexley (A2 Falconwood)	29	53: Sutton (Town Centre)	26
		58: Tower Hamlets (Bethnal Green)	22
28: Hammersmith & Fulham (Hammersmith Broadway)	35	59: Waltham Forest (Dawlish Road)	23
29: Harringay (Town Hall)	27	61: Wandsworth (High Street)	28

DEAD AND BURIED

As the city's population expanded in the 17th century, it became impossible to find any more burial space in the small local churchyards, and indeed their hugely overcrowded graveyards had become a public scandal. So the parishes began to establish burial grounds on the outer edges of the city, which remained in use until they too became scandalously overcrowded in the 19th century, and were closed down. From 1850 onwards much larger cemeteries were opened by local authorities and other public bodies, most of which are still open today.

Almost all of the 17th- and 18th-century burial grounds have now been built over, but some survive as public gardens. The best known is Bunhill Fields, beside City Road, which had been a graveyard since at least the 14th century. It was known as a nonconformist and puritan cemetery, and although it was built at the time of the Great Plague, none of its victims appear to have been buried there. It was closed in 1852, but is still a striking site, including monuments to John Bunyan (d.1688), Daniel Defoe (d.1731) and William Blake (d.1827). The Huguenot Burial Ground off East Hill, Wandsworth, was opened in 1687 by the French church, and was enlarged twice before being closed in 1854. It is now a public garden. The tiny Jewish burial ground in Queen's Elm Square, off the Fulham Road, was opened in 1815 and some 300 people were buried there, with gravestones marked in Hebrew, before it closed in 1885. It is now inaccessible, behind high brick walls. Another Jewish cemetery, in Brady Street, Whitechapel, was acquired by a group of Jewish traders in 1761, and extended in 1795. It was soon full, and earth was brought in to raise it by several feet so that a second cemetery could be created on top of the first one. It closed in 1858, but the large, flat-topped mound is still visible.

All over London there are nearly 100 of the larger, commercial cemeteries that opened in the 19th century. The Brompton Cemetery is the most central, and one of the most striking, with its octagonal chapel and miles of Victorian gravestones. The suffragette Emmeline Pankhurst was buried there in 1928. Among the best known are Highgate Cemetery, opened in 1829. Karl Marx was buried there in 1883. Kensal Green (1833) is still owned by the company that founded it, and is the burial place of such figures as Sydney Smith (d.1845), Isambard Kingdom Brunel (d.1859), Thackeray (d.1863), Trollope (d.1882) and Wilkie Collins (d.1889). West Norwood Cemetery, opened in 1837, is widely regarded as containing the finest collection of sepulchral monuments in London. Mrs Beeton, of cookbook fame, was buried there in 1865.

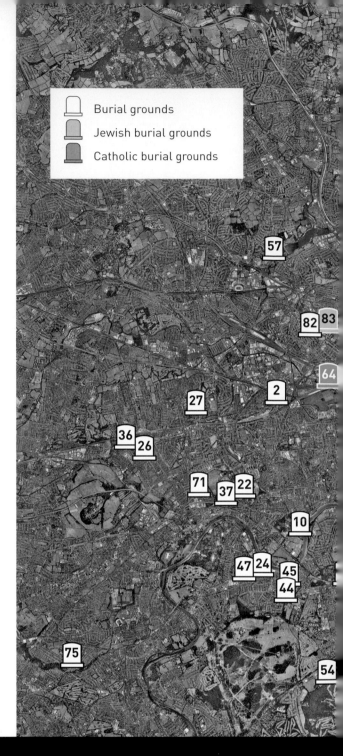

Burial grounds

Jewish burial grounds

Catholic burial grounds

London burial grounds and cemeteries

1: Abney Park Cemetery 1840, now a park
2: Acton Cemetery 1895
3: Brockley Cemetery 1858, closed 1966
4: Brompton Cemetery 1840, closed 1930s
5: Brook Street Cemetery 1894
6: Bunhill Fields 1665, closed 1854
7: Camberwell Old Cemetery 1856
8: Camberwell New Cemetery 1927
9: Charlton Cemetery 1864
10: Chiswick Old Cemetery 1888
11: City of London Cemetery 1856
12: East Finchley Cemetery 1885
13: East London Cemetery 1874
14: East Greenwich Pleasaunce 1857
15: Edmonton Cemetery 1884

16: Enfield Southgate Cemetery c.1880
17: Erith Cemetery 1894
18: Fulham Cemetery 1865
19: Gibraltar Row Burial Ground 1793
20: Golders Green 1902
21: Greenwich Cemetery 1856
22: Gunnersbury Cemetery 1929
23: Hammersmith Cemetery 1869
24: Hammersmith New Cemetery 1926
25: Hampstead Cemetery 1878
26: Hanwell Cemetery 1854
27: Harlington Burial Ground 1871
28: Hendon Cemetery 1899
29: Highgate Cemetery 1839, enlarged 1857
30: Hither Green Cemetery 1873
31: Huguenot Burial Ground 1687, closed 1854
32: Jewish Burial Ground 1815

closed 1885
33: Jewish Cemetery 1761, closed 1858
34: Plashet Jewish Cemetery 1896
35: Kensal Green Cemetery 1833
36: Kensington & Chelsea Cemetery 1855
37: Kensington Cemetery 1929
38: Lambeth Parish Burial Ground 1703, closed 1853
39: Ladywell Cemetery 1858
40: Long Lane Quaker Burial Ground 1697, closed 1895
41: Manor Park Cemetery 1874
42: Mill Hill Cemetery 1937
43: Moravian Burial Ground 1751
44: Morden Burial Ground 1883
45: Mortlake Old Cemetery 1839
46: New Southgate, formerly Great Northern, Cemetery 1861
47: Fulham (North Sheen) Cemetery 1909

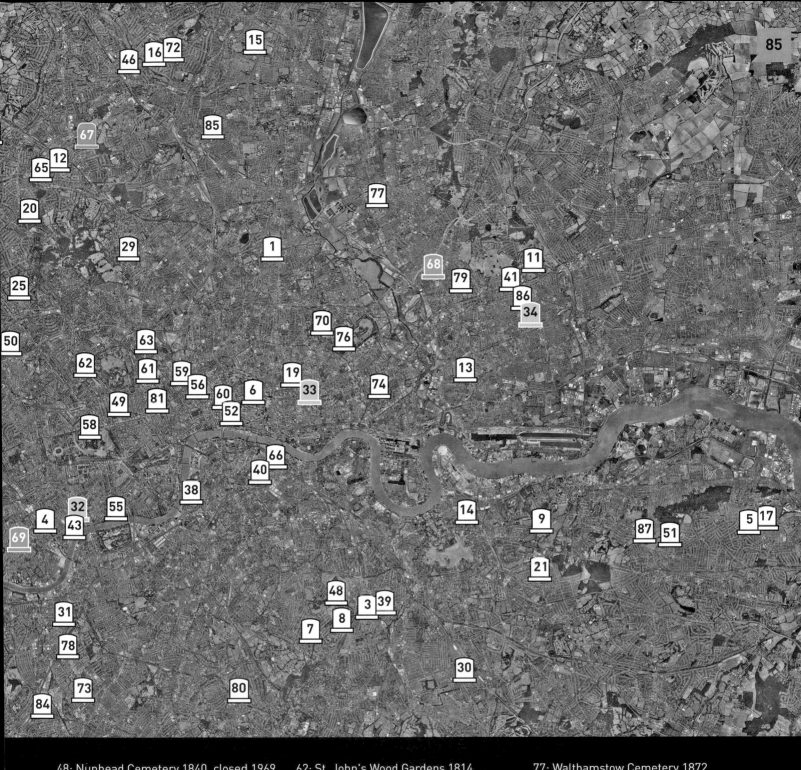

48: Nunhead Cemetery 1840, closed 1969
49: Paddington Gardens 1733, public
    garden after 1886
50: Paddington Old Cemetery 1855
51: Plumstead Cemetery 1890
52: Postman's Park, former churchyards,
    park after 1880
53: Putney Lower Common Cemetery 1855
54: Putney Vale Cemetery 1891
55: Royal Hospital Burial Ground 1692
56: St. Andrew's Gardens 1754,
    closed 1885
57: St. Andrew's Old Church 1932
58: St. George's Fields 1725
59: St. George's Gardens 1715, public
    space after 1885
60: St. John Clerkenwell 1744, garden
61: St. James's Gardens 1793, public
    garden after 1887

62: St. John's Wood Gardens 1814,
    on site of Plague pit
63: St. Martin's Gardens 1805, public
    garden after 1889
64: St. Mary's Cemetery 1858
65: St. Marylebone Cemetery 1855
66: St. Olave's Estate 1586, closed 1853,
    public recreation ground 1888
67: St. Pancras & Islington 1853
68: St. Patrick's Cemetery 1861
69: St. Thomas's Church 1848
70: St. Thomas's Square 1837
71: South Ealing Cemetery 1861
72: Southgate Cemetery c.1880
73: Streatham Cemetery 1893
74: Tower Hamlets Cemetery 1841,
    closed 1966, now a public park
75: Twickenham Cemetery 1868
76: Victoria Park Cemetery 1853

77: Walthamstow Cemetery 1872
78: Wandsworth Cemetery 1878
79: West Ham Cemetery 1854
80: West Norwood 1837, Greek
    cemetery added 1842
81: Whitefields Ground 1756 to 1853,
    public space from 1895
82: Willesden New Cemetery 1893
83: Jewish Cemetery 1873
84: Wimbledon Cemetery 1876
85: Wood Green Cemetery 1856
86: Woodgrange Park Cemetery c.1880,
    closed 1974
87: Woolwich Cemetery 1856,
    extended 1885

Ancient hospitals (with dates of foundation)
1: Bethlehem Royal Hospital (1247)
2: British Lying-in Hospital (1749)
3: Charing Cross Hospital (1818)
4: General Lying-in Hospital (1765)
5: Guy's Hospital (1721)
6: London Hospital (1740)
7: Middlesex Hospital (1745)
8: Queen Charlotte's Hospital (1739)
9: Royal Free Hospital (1828)
10: Royal Hospital for Children and Women (1816)
11: Royal Westminster Ophthalmic Hospital (1816, united with Moorfields, 1946)
12: St. Bartholomew's Hospital (1123)
13: St. Giles-in-the-Fields (1101, closed 1539)
14: St. George's Hospital (1733)
15: St. James's Hospital (closed 1531, now St James's Palace)
16: St. Thomas's (1207)
17: St. Thomas's Hospital, Southwark (1106, destroyed 1212, rebuilt on Borough High Street, moved 1871 to Lambeth Palace Road by Westminster Bridge)
18: University College Hospital (1834, now united with 7 others)
19: Westminster Hospital (1720)

Modern hospitals
20: Athlone House
21: Bethnal Green Hospital
22: Bolingbrooke Hospital
23: British Home and Hospital for incurables
24: Brompton Hospital
25: Brook General Hospital
26: Central Clinic
27: Chelsea and Westminster Hospital
28: Dental Hospital and School (King's College Hospital)
29: Dental Hospital
30: Devonshire Hospital
31: Dispensaire Francais
32: Eastman Dental Hospital
33: Edenhall (Marie Curie Memorial Foundation)
34: Fitzroy Nuffield Hospital (Nuffield Nursing Homes Trust)
35: Goldie Leigh Hospital
36: Gordon Hospital
37: Hammersmith Hospital
38: Harley Street Clinic
39: Hospital for Sick Children
40: Hospital for Tropical Diseases
41: Hospital for Women
42: Hospital of St. John and St. Elizabeth
43: Humana Hospital Wellington
44: Inverforth House Hospital
45: Islington Chest Clinic
46: King Edward VII's Hospital for Officers (Sister Agnes)
47: Lister Hospital
48: London Chest Hospital
49: The London Clinic
50: London Clinic of Psycho-analysis
51: London Foot Hospital and School of Podiatric Medicine
52: London Hospital (Mile End)
53: London Hospital (Whitechapel)
54: Maida Vale Hospital for Nervous Diseases
55: Maudsley Hospital

56: Medical Rehabilitation Centre
57: Metropolitan Ear, Nose and Throat Hospital
58: Middlesex Hospital
59: National Hospitals College of Speech Sciences
60: National Temperance Hospital
61: The National Hospital
62: Plaistow Hospital
63: Portman Clinic
64: Princess Grace Hospital
65: Royal Ear Hospital

66: Royal Marsden Hospital
67: Royal National Throat, Nose and Ear Hospital (Golden Square)
68: St. Charles Hospital

HOSPITALS AND DOCTORS

St. Bartholomew's, the oldest surviving London hospital, was founded in 1123 on a strip of land in Smithfield, just outside the city wall. It still stands there today. But there were older ones: St. James's Hospital may have been in existence before the Norman Conquest, and survived until Henry VIII bought it from Eton College, and built St. James's Palace on the site. St. Giles was founded by Henry I's wife Queen Matilda in 1101, alongside where the church of St. Giles-in-the-Fields now stands, as a refuge for lepers expelled from the city. Henry VIII closed it in 1539.

Among other medieval hospitals, St. Thomas's (now by Westminster Bridge) was originally part of the priory of St. Mary Overie in Southwark, where it burned down at the beginning of the 13th century. It was rebuilt in Borough High Street on a site donated by the Bishop of Winchester (now London Bridge Station). In 1721 Guy's Hospital went up next door to it. The Bethlehem Royal Hospital was founded as part of the Priory of St. Mary Bethlehem outside Bishopsgate in 1247, and became a lunatic asylum in 1547. Londoners called it Bedlam. In 1676 it was moved to a new building in Moorfields, and in 1815 the wretched patients (or victims) were transferred to Lambeth. There, new blocks were added to accommodate criminal lunatics, who were moved to Broadmoor in 1864. Finally, the hospital moved out of London altogether, and in 1936 the building became the Imperial War Museum.

Quite a few of today's hospitals have their roots in the 18th century. Westminster Hospital was founded in 1720 on the site next to the Abbey where the Queen Elizabeth II conference centre now stands (in 1998 it combined with Chelsea and moved to the Fulham Road). St. George's at Hyde Park Corner was a project undertaken by the Westminster governors, who bought Lanesborough House for the purpose. It moved to Tooting in 1980. Queen Charlotte's Maternity Hospital in Goldhawk Road began in 1752 as the General Lying-In Hospital, aiming 'to afford an asylum for indigent females during the awful period of childbirth'. Moorfields Eye Hospital now stands in the City Road, where London Hospital opened in 1740. Middlesex Hospital opened in 1745, in Windmill Street a few hundred yards from its present location, to assist 'the sick and lame of Soho'.

Harley Street, synonymous with doctors, is home to hundreds of medical specialists. But they didn't move in until the mid-19th century. Wimpole Street is now equally medical, with the Royal Society of Medicine located at no. 1 (designed by John Belcher in 112). Elizabeth Barrett lived at no. 50 until she eloped with Robert Browning in 1846.

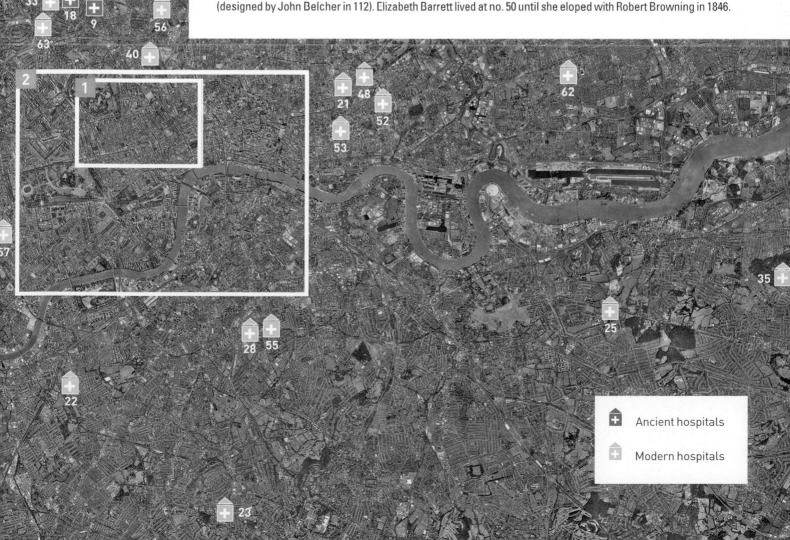

Ancient hospitals

Modern hospitals

Markets founded before 1800
1: Billingsgate Market (Fish), Lower Thames Street, EC3, moved to Isle of Dogs, 1982
2: Borough Market (Fruit & veg.), Southwark, SE1
3: Carnaby Street (Clothing), Carnaby Street, W1
4: Covent Garden (Fruit & veg.), WC2, moved to Nine Elms, 1974
5: Leadenhall Market (General), Gracechurch Street, EC2
6: Petticoat Lane Market (General), Petticoat Lane, E1
7: Shepherd Market (General), W1
8: Smithfield Market (Meat), EC1
9: Spitalfields (Vegetables), Commercial Street, E1, moved to Waltham Forest, 1991
10: Whitechapel Market (General), Whitechapel Road, E1
11: Bartholomew Fair (Cloth), Smithfield, EC1
12: Bermondsey Market (Leather), Leathermarket Street, SE1
13: Berwick Street Market (General), Berwick Street, W1
14: Bread Street Market (Bread), Bread Street, EC4
15: Cheapside (General), Cheapside, EC2
16: Clare Market (Food), Clare Market, WC2
17: Garlickhythe (Garlic), Garlick Hill, EC4
18: Fish Street Market (Fish), Fish Street Hill, EC3
19: Fleet Market (Meat & veg.), Farringdon Street, EC4
20: Haymarket (Hay & straw), Haymarket, SW1
21: Honey Lane Market (Meat), Cheapside, EC2
22: Hungerford Market (Food), Charing Cross, SW1
23: Mortimer Market (General), Capper Street, WC1
24: New Exchange (General), 54–64 Strand, WC2
25: Newgate Market (Corn, meat), Newgate Street, E4
26: Newport Market (General), Little Newport Street, WC2
27: Oxford Market (Food), Great Portland Street, W1
28: Queenhithe Market (General), Queenhithe, Upper Thames Street, EC4
29: St James's Market (General), Waterloo Place, SW1
30: Shambles (Meat), Newgate Street, E4
31: Southampton Market (General), Southampton Row, WC1
32: Southwark Fair (General), Borough High Street, SE1
33: Spital Yard (Fruit & veg.), Spital Square, E1
34: Stocks Market (Fish & meat), Mansion House, EC2
35: Strutton Ground Market (General), Strutton Ground, SW1

Markets founded after 1800
36: Bayswater Road Art (Paintings), Bayswater Road, W2
37: Bermondsey Market (Antiques), Bermondsey Square, SE1
38: Brick Lane Market (General), Brick Lane, E1
39: Brixton Market (General), Coldharbour Lane, SW9
40: Camden Lock Market (General), Camden Lock, NW1
41: Chapel Market (General), Chapel Street, N1
42: Charing Cross Collectors' Fair, Villiers Street, WC2
43: Chelsea Antiques Market, 245–53 King's Road, SW3
44: Columbia Road Flower Market, Columbia Road, E2
45: Church Street Market (General), Bell Street, NW8
46: East Street Market (General), East Street, SE1
47: Leather Lane Market (General), Leather Lane, EC1
48: London Farmers' Market (Food), Notting Hill Gate, W11
49: Northcote Road Antiques Market, Northcote Road, SW11
50: North End Road Market (General), North End Road, SW6
51: Portobello Road Antiques Market, Portobello Road, W11
52: Roman Road Market (General), Roman Road, E2
53: Rupert Street Market (General), Rupert Street, W1
54: Shepherd's Bush Market (General), Goldhawk Road, W12
55: Whitecross Street Market (General), Old Street, EC1

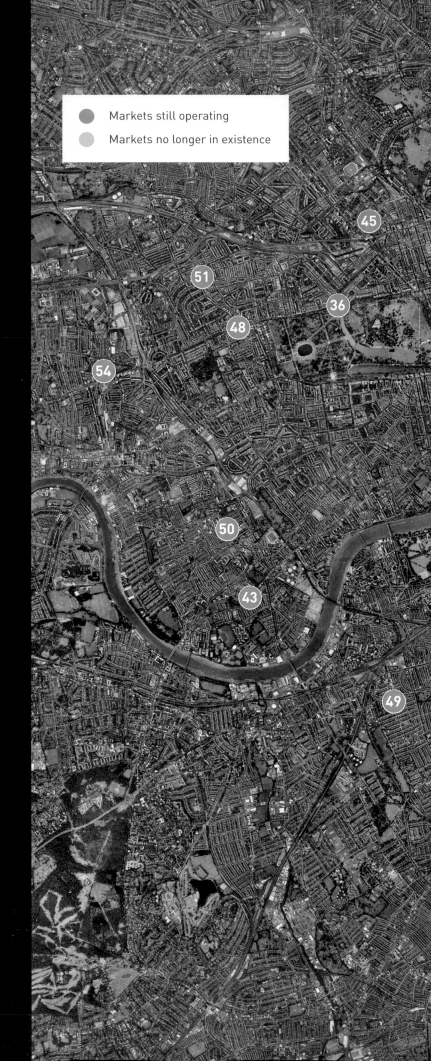

● Markets still operating
● Markets no longer in existence

MARKETS

Billingsgate is perhaps the most ancient of London's markets, dating back as far as the Dark Ages. It was certainly thriving in 1016, from which date the first toll regulations survive. Corn, coal, iron, wine, salt and pottery were on sale there – and fish, with which trade it became exclusively associated in the 16th century. Traders operated in the open or under wooden stalls until 1850, when the first proper market building went up. The one that survives by the north side of London Bridge was erected in 1873. The market moved to the Isle of Dogs in 1982, where it still flourishes.

Smithfield Market's history is not quite so long, but in the 11th century the 'smooth field' just outside the city wall was where you could go to buy horses, cattle, sheep or pigs, alive or dead. It was also a public execution site for over 400 years. The cattle market was granted a royal charter in 1638, and the first buildings on the present site went up in 1851–66. In 1990 the City Corporation raised £70 million to refurbish the buildings.

For vegetables and fruit, Borough Market was the place to go from at least 1276. The site has moved around a bit over the centuries in the area south of London Bridge, and its present building next to Southwark Cathedral was built in 1851. Poulterers and cheesemongers formed Leadenhall Market in the 14th century; today's beautiful buildings were designed by Horace Jones in 1881. Covent Garden market began in the mid-17th century, trading in fruit and vegetables as well as other products, not long after Inigo Jones had developed the square for its owner, the 4th Earl of Bedford. By the end of the 19th century most of the present buildings in the area had gone up. The market moved to Nine Elms in 1974. Petticoat Lane, just south of the old Spitalfields Market (1682), is perhaps the best-known – and oldest – of London's street markets, flourishing today as it did in the 15th century. Bermondsey Antiques Market was reportedly started by Prince Albert in 1855. One hundred years later Brixton launched its Afro-Caribbean markets over several areas in the borough.

MONEY

Although the late Iron Age British rulers began minting coins in the first century BC, London's connection with money began with the Roman conquest. The Anglo-Saxon monarchs minted their own individual coins in different parts of Britain, and the Royal Mint in London was founded in AD 825 under the rule of King Egbert of Wessex. In 1300 a site was built for it at the Tower, where it remained until it was moved at the beginning of the 19th century to Little Tower Hill. In 1968 it moved again, to Wales.

The City's reputation as a financial centre grew from the successful international trading activities of Londoners in the 18th century, supported by its position as England's capital and by the eclipsing of Edinburgh and Dublin after the acts of union. The City Livery Companies, or craft guilds (some of which had been established as early as the 12th century), represented the interests of a large variety of commercial activities, and today there are 97 of them, many housed in elegant buildings around the City. The Royal Exchange, founded in 1568, was designed to provide civilised headquarters for commercial activities, and continued to perform this function until 1939. The grand building designed by Sir William Tite in 1844 still dominates the corner between Threadneedle Street and Cornhill.

Banking and investment are at the root of the City's monetary history. The Bank of England was founded in 1694, mainly to help William III's government to finance its war against France. Brokers in stocks and shares had been operating since the 16th century, but the Stock Exchange was formally created in 1773 when a group of them bought a building in Threadneedle Street. Today's building, with its 23,000-square-foot trading floor, went up in 1972.

Private banks were established in the 18th century, and by 1793 there were 280 throughout Britain. Over the next century they began to merge together and today's leading clearing banks are their conglomerations. Merchant banks, specialising in corporate and government finance, evolved in the 18th century too. Baring Brothers, for example (destroyed at the end of the 20th century by the rogue trader Nicholas Leeson), reached the height of its reputation in the 1820s.

Another major institution is Lloyds of London, founded in Edward Lloyd's coffee shop in Tower Street in the 1680s. Today it is the world's largest insurance market, housed in an elegant building designed by Richard Rogers at 1 Lime Street.

Major financial institutions
1: Royal Exchange (1568), Threadneedle Street
2: Bank of England (1694), Threadneedle Street
3: The Stock Exchange (1773), Old Broad Street
4: Lloyds of London (1680s), Tower Street (until 1691)/Lime Street

City livery company halls
5: Woodmongers' Hall
6: Blacksmiths' Hall
7: Painter-Stainers' Hall
8: Innholders' Hall
9: Fruiterers' Hall
10: Dyers' Hall
11: Plumbers' Hall
12: Vintners' Hall
13: Parish Clerks' Hall

14: Joiners' Hall
15: Skinners' Hall
16: Tallow Chandlers' Hall
17: Cutlers' Hall
18: Fishmongers' Hall
19: Pewterers' Hall
20: Ironmongers' Hall
21: Clothworkers' Hall
22: Bricklayers' and Tilers' Hall
23: Leathersellers' Hall

City livery company halls

Surviving company halls

Major financial institutions

24: Fletchers' Hall
25: Waterbearers' Hall
26: Carpenters' Hall
27: Drapers' Hall
28: Armourers'/Brasiers' Hall
29: Founders' Hall
30: Masons' Hall
31: Weavers' Hall
32: Girdlers' Hall
33: Coopers' Hall

34: Brewers' Hall
35: Curriers' Hall
36: Plaisterers' Hall
37: Bowyers'Hall
38: Barber-Surgeons' Hall
39: Cooks' Hall
40: Goldsmiths' Hall
41: Butchers' Hall
42: Stationers' Hall
43: Cordwainers' Hall

44: Salters' Hall
45: Merchant Taylors' Hall
46: Grocers' Hall
47: Mercers' Hall
48: Waxchandlers' Hall
49: Embroiderers' Hall
50: Saddlers' Hall
51: Apothecaries' Hall
52: Haberdashers' Hall
53: Bakers' Hall

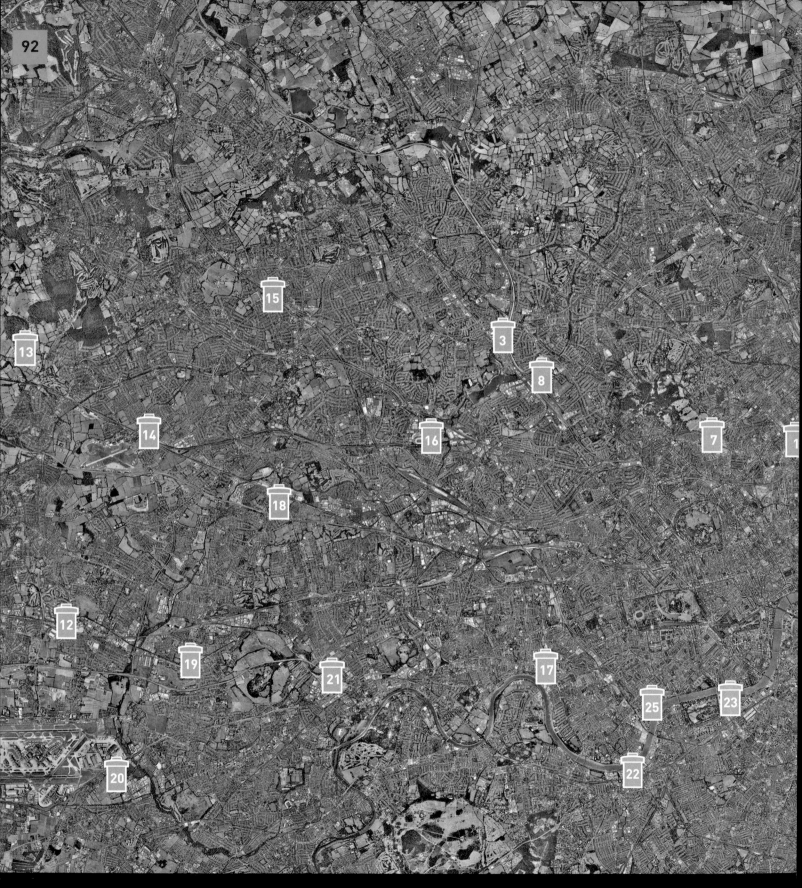

Waste transfer stations and civic amenity sites

North London waste authority
1: Ashburton Grove, N7
2: Edmonton Solid Waste Incineration
   Plant, N18 (London Waste Ltd)
3: Hendon Rail Transfer Station
4: Carterhatch Lane, Enfield

5: Barrowell Green, N21
6: South Access Road, E17
7: Regis Road, NW5
8: Brent Terrace, NW2 (Shanks
   Waste Solutions)

East London waste authority
9: Frizlands Lane, Dagenham
10: Jenkins Lane, Barking

11: Chigwell Road, Woodford, E18

West London waste authority
12: Rigby Lane, Hayes
13: Newyears Green Lane, Harefield
14: Victoria Road, South Ruislip
15: Forward Drive, Wealdstone
16: First Way, Wembley
17: Stirling Road, Acton

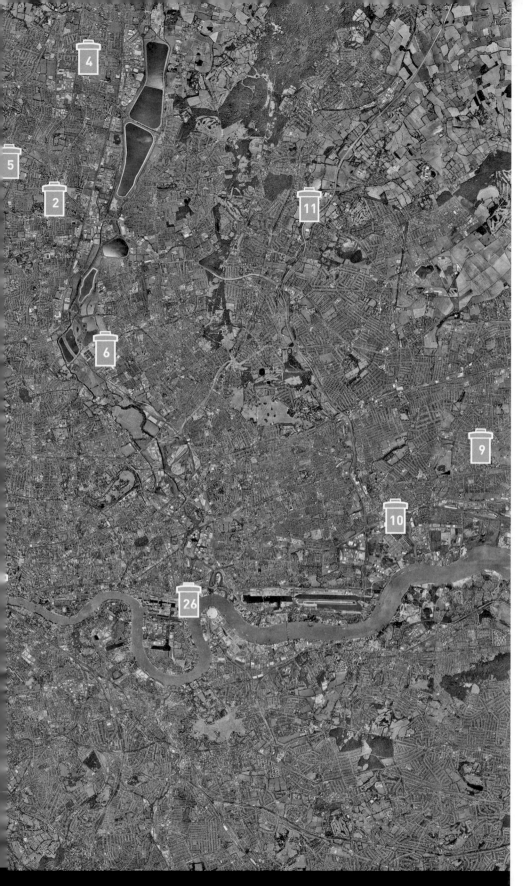

RUBBISH

The city has for centuries disgorged endless tons of rubbish and excrement. Its cleanest period was probably in Roman times, when highly disciplined systems of public baths and latrines were in place amidst a modest population. In the Dark Ages these standards collapsed, and were scarcely improved until cleansing regulations were introduced in the 13th century, as well as the first public lavatories – called privies. Citizens of London have continued through the centuries to 'chuck their muck' into the streets and rivers, and most of the city today is built over rubbish dumps.

By the 18th century, a market for refuse developed: manure was valuable for agriculture, and household cinders were used in brick making. Gradually improvements were made. Rubbish 'mounts' were created in areas such as Battlebridge Lane in Southwark, and the Whitechapel Mount off Bath Street. By the 19th century, street-sweepers, bone-pickers, mud larks, toshers, sweeps, dustmen and rag-finders were scouring the streets to make a living. Eventually, motivated by the 'great stink' of 1858, there was a 'sewage revolution'. The Metropolitan Board of Works began to construct new chains of cement-built sewers, many of them constructed along the edge of the river under what is now the embankment, directing the sewage to outfalls at Barking and Crossness. This sewage system is still in use today, though it has been much expanded.

In the 20th century, the mounts and open ash-pits were removed, and huge incineration plants were set up in places like Beckton, Wandsworth and Edmonton, under the control of four 'waste authorities'. Nowadays local councils provide rubbish collection for all households at least once a week, as well as 'mini recycling centres'. In Kensington and Chelsea, for example, there are 24 of these centres, many of them close to shopping malls. The waste authorities, with the help of private companies, recycle and incinerate, and also transport a lot of London rubbish to so-called landfill sites in East Anglia and Kent. A number of 'civic amenity sites' are dotted around London.

London's rubbish grows by the day, ten million tonnes of it, including half a million tonnes of paper alone.

AFFLUENCE AND POVERTY IN 1890

Charles Booth (1840–1916), the rich founder of a Liverpool shipping line, moved to London in 1878 and embarked on the most detailed study of London's living conditions ever produced. Employing a team of investigators, over 19 years he studied every corner of the city, assessing the inhabitants of every street and reporting the results in a huge 17-volume publication called *Life and Labour of the People of London* (1903). Accompanying it was his 'poverty map' covering the whole of central London, with different colours showing eight categories, from the poorest (in black) to the wealthiest (in yellow). Overall, the East End is as always where the poorest live, and the residential West End is home to the well-to-do.

If we look closely at the area from Marylebone Road down to Piccadilly, with Regent Street to the west and Charing Cross Road to the east, his map reveals the whole variety of living conditions. Union Street (now Riding House Street), just north of Middlesex Hospital, was home to the 'very poor, casual', with 'chronic want'. So too were Rathbone Street and the area to the west of Great Windmill Street and other areas to the east of Regent Street. Soho as a whole, from Carnaby Street along Broadwick Street to Wardour Street, was a mixed area, 'fairly comfortable', with moderate sized families living on 18 shillings (90p) a week or more.

To the west of Regent Street the pattern is radically different. Here are the red and yellow areas, where the well-to-do and wealthy upper classes live. The middle classes dominate both sides of Oxford Street, Regent Street and Piccadilly. John Nash's plan to separate Mayfair from Soho, completed in 1823 (see pages 134–5), had clearly worked.

By the time Booth had completed his study, he was aware that conditions were constantly changing, the worst slums had been pulled down, their inhabitants moved to new council estates, and sanitation and general urban hygiene had improved. But several surveys in the 20th century continued to report that between five and 15 per cent of Londoners live below the poverty line. The highest counts in recent surveys were in Tower Hamlets, Southwark, Hackney and Lambeth – exactly the same places inhabited by the poor in the 18th and 19th centuries. The poor, even if their definition changes, still exist, and London still needs them, for cheap and casual labour.

Booth's research concluded that over 30 per cent of Londoners were living in the four lower categories – in other words, in poverty – and 70 per cent in comfort. The worst regions, with fewest inhabitants in the upper categories, were in East End areas such as Shadwell, Whitechapel and Limehouse, but there were many blue and black streets around the eastern side of Lincoln's Inn, in St. Pancras, Pimlico, and parts of Lambeth and Camberwell. Any Londoner who wants to know something about the social history of his street or neighbourhood a hundred years ago can study Booth's remarkable poverty map on the internet, at the London School of Economics website (booth.lse.ac.uk); and his detailed records are stored in the archives of the British Library of Political and Economic Science. Among his other achievements in the field of social reform, Booth was a pioneer of the old age pension.

Charles Booth's categories

- Lowest class. Vicious semi criminals.
- Very poor, casual. Chronic want.
- Poor. 18–21s a week for a moderate family.
- Mixed. Some comfortable, others poor.
- Fairly comfortable. Good ordinary earnings.
- Well-to-do. Middle class.
- Upper-middle and upper classes. Wealthy.

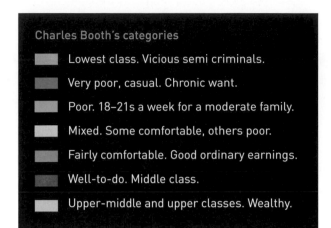

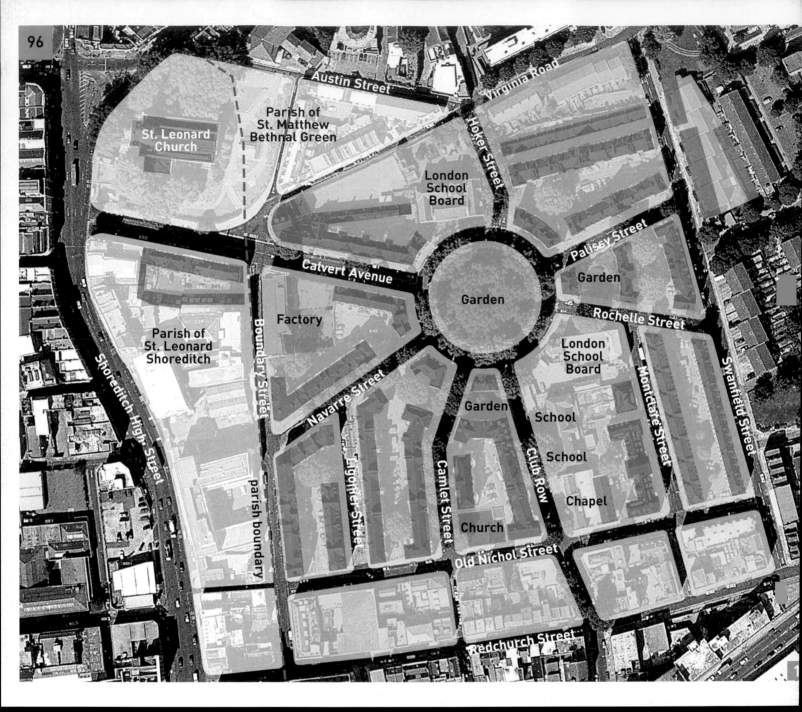

St. Leonard Church

Parish of St. Matthew Bethnal Green

Austin Street

Virginia Road

Hoker Street

London School Board

Palissy Street

Garden

Calvert Avenue

Factory

Garden

Rochelle Street

Boundary Street

Parish of St. Leonard Shoreditch

Garden

London School Board

Navarre Street

School

MontClare Street

Swanfield Street

Shoreditch High Street

parish boundary

Elgoffer Street

Camlet Street

Garden

School

Club Row

Chapel

Church

Old Nichol Street

Redchurch Street

The redevelopment of the Boundary Street Estate, Bethnal Green, c.1900

1: Modern street names/buildings
2: Streets which disappeared in the re-development

VICTORIAN HOUSING DEVELOPMENT

The removal of the gallows from Tyburn (Marble Arch) in 1825 allowed respectability to make its way towards Paddington. The bishops of London owned the land, and began rapidly developing it. Further west, the area around the Hippodrome Racecourse on the Ladbroke estate was turned into elegant middle-class housing in the 1840s, with crescents following the old lines of the racetracks, and spacious gardens between them. South of Hyde Park and to the east of Sloane Street, the Grosvenor family owned the land and developed Belgravia and Pimlico – so successfully that in 1874 they were awarded the dukedom of Westminster. No property developer has been so richly rewarded before or since. Not all these areas maintained their respectability for long: by the end of the century both Pimlico and Bayswater

St. Leonard's Church

Parish of St. Matthew Bethnal Green

New Castle Street

Calvert Street

Jacob's Street

Fournier Street

Parish of St. Leonard's Shoreditch

Mead Street

Shoreditch High Street

parish boundary

Half Nichol Street

Turnville Street

Mount Street

New Nichol Street

Old Nichol Street

Church Street

had become seedy slums. The Victorian middle classes were becoming more and more attracted to villas in suburbs such as St John's Wood.

Meanwhile, progress was being made in improving the living conditions of the underprivileged. In the 1840s, various agencies were formed to develop 'model dwellings' for the poor, at rental rates they could afford. An increasing number of charitable organisations, such as the Peabody Trust in the 1860s, and the Four Per Cent Industrial Dwellings Company, founded by Lord Rothschild in 1885, constructed economical blocks of flats all over London which, by 1900, housed nearly 80,000 people. From 1855, the Metropolitan Board of Works, succeeded in 1888 by the London County Council (LCC), began to clear the slums and to develop public housing. Under the 1890 Housing Act, the LCC initiated large-scale housing developments all over London, from Bermondsey

example is in Bethnal Green, where a maze of narrow streets to the east of Shoreditch High Street (see above) was converted to the Boundary Street Estate, a handsome complex of blocks of flats facing onto a central garden (see above left). Today, it is in serious need of refurbishment.

Many of the new council blocks, particularly in the East End and Docklands, although rentable at much lower rates than commercial properties, proved hard to let and remained empty or only half full for years. The rates were still too much for the lowly-paid dockers. Only skilled workers and their families could afford these new homes.

Despite the efforts of the LCC, there was an increasing demand towards the end of the century for its powers to be balanced by the creation of local authorities. In 1899 the district boards were replaced by 28 new metropolitan borough councils, which would play a key part

GENTRIFICATION

The years following the end of the Second World War have seen radical changes in London. The population declined from 8.6 million in 1946 to 6.5 million by 1990 – although it is now rising again and has reached 7 million. Londoners have moved out to the suburbs and new towns; manufacturing has declined; the docks have closed, with the loss of 25,000 jobs; and increasingly the city's economy has become dependent on services, employing white collar workers, around 670,000 of whom commute in to work every day.

By the 1960s, many residential areas built in Victorian and Edwardian times were in a serious state of disrepair, and the number of new homes built in London was rapidly declining. But over recent decades the older houses have been gradually and steadily rescued by private investment. This process of 'gentrification' has dramatically changed large areas of the city, particularly in the inner suburbs, such as Islington, Camden, North Kensington, Hammersmith, Wandsworth, Lewisham and Greenwich. Not just houses and streets, but whole neighbourhoods, have been transformed by the arrival of the increasingly affluent middle classes.

An example is the area north of Kensington Gardens, from Paddington to Ladbroke Grove (encompassing Notting Hill), which had been developed in the 1840s and became a neighbourhood of middle-class respectability (see pages 96–7), with a few pockets of poverty. By the middle of the 20th century it had drastically declined. Immigrants from the Caribbean were attracted to Notting Hill after 1948 because it was relatively central and the housing was cheap. Hundreds of them were assaulted by gangs of white youths in the horrific race riots that took place there in 1958. It was in this area that Peter Rachman, the famous racketeer landlord, operated in the 1950s, buying up cheap houses, violently evicting their tenants, and re-renting them at extortionate rates to the homeless West Indians.

In 1960 you could buy an elegant but run-down 19th-century four-bedroom house in Northumberland Place for £10,000. Thirty years later, the same house would sell for half a million, and at least twice as much as that today. Property prices rose again after the international success of the film *Notting Hill*. All Saints Road, which in the 1970s was a notorious drug-dealing headquarters, is today lined with elegant shops and restaurants, catering for the new, rich professionals who dominate the neighbourhood.

THE MOST EXPENSIVE AREAS

House prices are highest in central London, and in western areas such as Richmond and Wandsworth. The top five boroughs' prices are more than twice as high as the bottom five.

CHANGES IN THE LAST EIGHT YEARS

The highest price rises in the last eight years have mainly been in outer London: Waltham Forest, Harringay, Kingston-upon-Thames, Brent, Enfield, Harrow and Redbridge. But they have also risen substantially in Lambeth, Hackney and Lewisham. A year ago, the pattern was different. The main increases were in inner areas like Kensington & Chelsea, Tower Hamlets, Newham and Hammersmith & Fulham. So gentrification is moving outwards.

CHANGES IN THE LAST TWELVE MONTHS

In the last year, house prices over the whole of London have fallen slightly (by just under 1%). But there are vast differences around the city. In central areas like Westminster, Kensington & Chelsea and Hammersmith they have fallen dramatically, by as much as 17%. But in outer areas they have risen even more – by nearly 24% in Enfield, and in Kingston (17%), Waltham Forest (15%), Hillingdon (15%), Harrow (14%), Croydon (14%) and Barking (13%). The exception is a large fall in Hounslow (-14%), possibly caused by plans to extend Heathrow Airport.

BEST BUYS

Considering that Lewisham and Greenwich are as close to London's centre as Hammersmith and Wandsworth, and average house prices in these boroughs are well below the city's average, they are likely to become targets for gentrification over the next few years.

Average house prices in London boroughs between 1995 and 2003

	1995 £	2003 £	Ranked in order of increase	% increase
1. Kensington & Chelsea	218,500	524,400	23	139.9
2. Westminster	181,500	387,700	31	113.6
3. Richmond	143,150	341,400	25	138.5
4. Camden	148,000	335,800	27	126.3
5. City of London		311,000		
6. Hammersmith	133,500	301,500	28	125.9
7. Wandsworth	110,600	285,000	13	157.7
8. Barnet	108,250	264,400	22	144.3
9. Kingston	94,275	263,900	5	179.9
11. Merton	94,000	245,800	12	161.5
12. Harringay	85,400	240,600	4	181.7
13. Harrow	88,600	238,600	8	169.3
14. Lambeth	76,850	228,500	2	197.3
15. Ealing	93,600	224,100	24	139.5
16. Bromley	96,220	216,000	29	124.5
17. Southwark	84,150	213,300	16	153.5
18. Brent	77,650	210,200	6	170.7
19. Hackney	71,055	209,900	3	195.4
20. Enfield	76,629	206,900	7	170.0
21. Hillingdon	83,050	205,000	20	146.9
22. Tower Hamlets	76,175	195,000	14 (joint)	156.0
23. Redbridge	73,875	193,700	10	162.2
24. Sutton	78,721	193,100	21	145.3
25. Croydon	72,100	190,200	11	163.8
26. Hounslow	88,650	180,500	32	103.6
27. Greenwich	70,665	177,400	17	151.0
28. Havering	74,239	170,600	26	129.8
29. Waltham Forest	56,465	170,300	1	201.6
30. Bexley	66,184	164,400	18	148.4
31. Newham	52,813	135,200	14 (joint)	156.0
32. Lewisham	50,750	135,200	9	166.4
33. Barking	50,383	125,000	19	148.1
Greater London	98,296	230,800		134.8

1: Kensington Park
   Gardens
2: Eaton Square
3: South Audley Street
4: Albany

THE GRANDEST HOMES IN LONDON

It is estimated that over 23,000 houses in London today are worth more than a million pounds. But value is not quite the same as grandeur. The very rich are attracted to various areas for different reasons, such as seclusion, security, fashion, tradition, and fine architecture.

If you want to live in the centre of the West End, and still have all these qualities and benefits, there is no better choice than a flat at the Albany. This remarkable building is only 200 yards away from Piccadilly Circus, tucked away behind a courtyard opposite Fortnum & Mason, the luxury department store that first opened in 1707. The Albany began as Melbourne House in 1770. The house, divided into separate apartments upstairs with communal rooms on the ground floor, stands at the front of the property. Behind, leading north to Vigo Street, is a long covered walkway, with entrances to the flats in the two large blocks on either side. They were originally designed for bachelors, but this rule no longer prevails. Residents since the Albany was completed in 1802 include Lord Palmerston, Lord Byron, J. B. Priestley, Aldous Huxley, Graham Greene, Isaiah Berlin, Harold Nicholson, Edward Heath and Terence Stamp.

The most expensive house ever put up for sale in London is in Kensington Park Gardens, a street running parallel to the western side of Kensington Gardens. The asking price, in 2001, was £85 million. This long avenue lined with grand houses was developed after 1843, when the kitchen gardens attached to Kensington Palace were sold. The houses were originally bought by the great industrialists and bankers of the 19th century, and the street was soon known as Millionaire's Row. Today, most of the buildings are embassies – including the Russian, Finnish, Lebanese, Czech and Slovak – but some are still owned by the Crown Estate and a few privately. In the Second World War, no. 8 was used to detain senior Nazi prisoners, and was known as 'the Cage'. There are security posts at each end of the tree-lined road, but pedestrians are allowed through.

The Grosvenor Estate in Mayfair, begun in 1720, was completed in the 1770s. Although some areas were designed for smaller houses and shops, the basic plan was to attract the rich and famous, and they have been lodging there ever since. Around South Audley Street many of the original 18th-century houses survive, but they rarely come up for sale. Today, one of the elegant Georgian houses in Chesterfield Street, with five bedrooms and four reception rooms, would cost a buyer something in the region of £5 million.

The Grosvenors developed their Belgravia estate (see pages 70–1) in the mid-19th century, and Eaton Square and its neighbourhood has hundreds of equally fine properties. The owner of the first completed house in Eaton Square was the brewer, W. H. Whitbread.

Strip clubs and pubs
 1: Carnival Theatre Club, Old Compton Street
 2: Churchill's, 52 Piccadilly
 3: Penny Farthing, Kingsland Road
 4: Raymond Review Bar, Brewer Street
 5: Sunset Strip, Dean Street
 6: Stringfellows, Covent Garden
 7: The Cottage, 1 Duck Lane
 8: Brown's, 1 Hackney Road
 9: Crown & Shuttle, 223 Shoreditch High Street
10: Commercial Tavern, Commercial Street
11: Flying Scotsman, 4 Caledonian Road
12: Griffin, 125 Clerkenwell Road
13: Images, 482 Hackney Rd
14: Lord Nelson, 17 Mora Street
15: Nag's Head, 17/19 Whitechapel Road
16: Norfolk Village, 220 Shoreditch High Street
17: Rainbow Sport Bar, 72 Shoreditch High Street
18: The Seven Stars, 49 Brick Lane
19: Spread Eagle, 1–3 Kingsland Road
20: Ten Bells, 84 Commercial Street
21: Traders, 222 Shoreditch High Street
22: White Horse, 66 Shoreditch High Street
23: Ye Old Axe, 69 Hackney Road
24: Club Cherokee, 43–45 East Smithfield

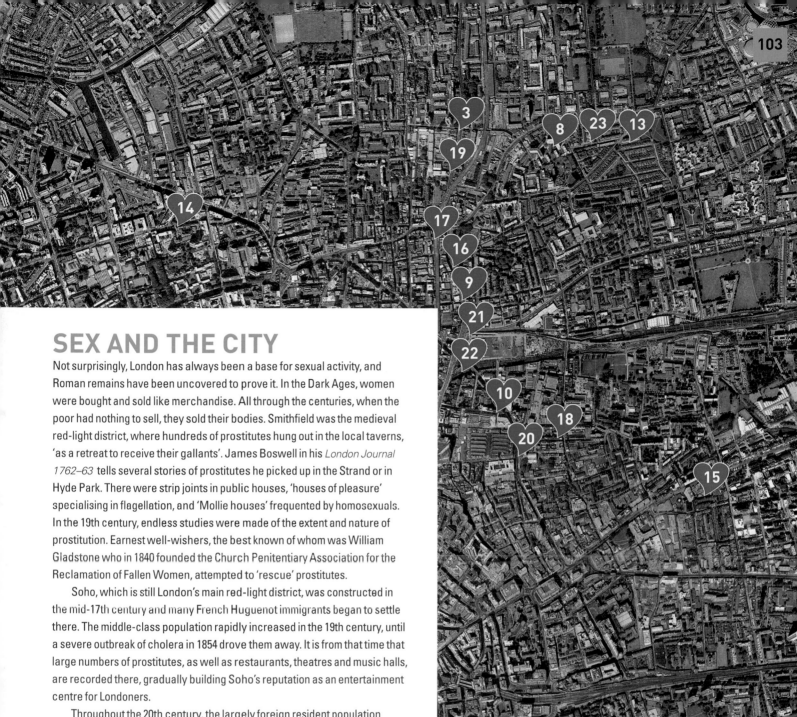

SEX AND THE CITY

Not surprisingly, London has always been a base for sexual activity, and Roman remains have been uncovered to prove it. In the Dark Ages, women were bought and sold like merchandise. All through the centuries, when the poor had nothing to sell, they sold their bodies. Smithfield was the medieval red-light district, where hundreds of prostitutes hung out in the local taverns, 'as a retreat to receive their gallants'. James Boswell in his *London Journal 1762–63* tells several stories of prostitutes he picked up in the Strand or in Hyde Park. There were strip joints in public houses, 'houses of pleasure' specialising in flagellation, and 'Mollie houses' frequented by homosexuals. In the 19th century, endless studies were made of the extent and nature of prostitution. Earnest well-wishers, the best known of whom was William Gladstone who in 1840 founded the Church Penitentiary Association for the Reclamation of Fallen Women, attempted to 'rescue' prostitutes.

Soho, which is still London's main red-light district, was constructed in the mid-17th century and many French Huguenot immigrants began to settle there. The middle-class population rapidly increased in the 19th century, until a severe outbreak of cholera in 1854 drove them away. It is from that time that large numbers of prostitutes, as well as restaurants, theatres and music halls, are recorded there, gradually building Soho's reputation as an entertainment centre for Londoners.

Throughout the 20th century, the largely foreign resident population declined, but the streets remained crowded at night, and the sex establishments increased rapidly from the mid-1960s, with strip-tease shows and sex shops opening all around Old Compton Street. The Soho Society was formed in 1972 to try to stem this proliferation of the sex industry, with some success. The local authority today licenses some 32 sex premises in Soho.

There are many other brothels and massage parlours and strip joints in other parts of London. Perhaps the headquarters in recent years is Shoreditch, where there are some ten pubs within a few hundred yards of each other, all of which show topless dancers through the evening. Cynthia Payne's famous brothel, for which she was jailed for six months in 1978, was at 32 Ambleside Avenue in Streatham. Brothels in Soho, like The Cottage at 1 Duck Lane, can be contacted on the internet. More expensive strip shows can be found at the Windmill Theatre in Great Windmill Street, the Carnival Theatre Club in Old Compton Street, Stringfellows in Covent Garden, and the Raymond Review Bar in Brewer Street. If you're looking for an inexpensive prostitute, wander around Chinatown and look for doorways marked 'Model'.

THE STORY OF ISLINGTON

In Saxon times King Aethelbert granted Islington to the canons of St. Paul's (hence the name Canonbury). Throughout the Middle Ages it was an area of hunting and sport, where 'citizens played ball, exercised on horseback and took delight in birds'.

Islington enjoyed this rural tranquillity well into the 19th century. In Thomas Starling's 'Plan of Islington Parish' printed in 1831, there are open fields all the way from Lower Street (now Essex Road) to Newington Green. The village high street winds past Camden Passage (then called Pullens Row), divides at the Green (as it still does), and wanders north through meadows and market gardens. London's first bypass, the New Road from Paddington to the famous Angel Inn, just south of the village, was constructed in 1756, and extended down City Road five years later. Traffic hurled by towards the City, but Islington remained a quiet backwater.

Charles Lamb moved here, to Colebrook Cottage (just off Islington Green) in 1823, and much enjoyed the rural life and the convivial local hostelries. But as London crept northwards, building works started all around. In the 1830s the Northampton estate built cheap tenements on its land south of the village, and the Packington Estate followed suit fifteen years later (Packington Square, 16). By the 1860s the whole area was built up, with closely packed streets and terraces, populated by poorly-paid clerks who worked in the City. The more affluent inhabitants moved away.

Into the 20th century, Islington itself became poor, virtually a slum in inner London. From the 1930s London County Council attempted to redeem it by building council-house estates and tower blocks, pulling down rows of Victorian and Georgian terraces to make space for them. But before they were able to destroy the entire neighbourhood, the 1960s arrived and Islington became a target for the gentrifiers (see pages 98–9). Middle-class families, encouraged by 'improvement grants' from the borough council, began to purchase and restore the remaining houses in places like Union Square (17) and Arlington Square (18), and wherever else they could. Islington today, like many other former villages, is a hugely broad mixture of cultures and incomes. Along both sides of Upper Street there are now more restaurants and bars than anywhere else in London, restoring its age-old reputation for hospitality and geniality.

ANGEL ISLINGTON

The Angel Inn (1) stood on the west corner of Pentonville Road and Upper Street, where the Cooperative Bank now stands. In the Islington Business Centre next door, there is a modern version with the old name.

Two hundred yards to the west, down Pentonville Road, the Independent Chapel (2) is now the gallery of the Crafts Council, established in 1971 to promote contemporary craftsmanship.

On the south corner of Islington Green, where Watch House once stood, is the old Elizabethan statue of Sir Hugh Myddleton

(3). Myddleton Hall in Almeida Street, where he lived, was rebuilt in 1891. It now houses the Almeida Restaurant (19).

The Islington Literary and Scientific Institution (4) building in Almeida Street was completed in 1837, providing reading rooms and a lecture hall. It was later converted to a music hall, and a Salvation Army headquarters. Today it is the highly successful Almeida Theatre, which reopened in May 2003.

The London Fever Hospital (5) was built in the 1830s and later became the Royal Free Hospital. It is now a quietly pleasant residential estate in Old Free Hospital Square.

The vast Agricultural Hall (6), built in the late 1850s, was used for popular activities like indoor racing and fairs. It was converted into the Business Design Centre in 1986.

Finnemore House (7) now stands where the clothworkers' houses were at the end of Britannia Row. Council estates surround the area.

St Mary's Church (8) on Upper Street still stands, with its churchyard now a small park lined with old gravestones. The Vestry is still the vicarage. The Little Angel Theatre stands behind it in Dagmar Passage.

The Islington Workhouse (9) where the poor and homeless were housed in the mid-19th century, is now the Barnsbury Housing Association estate on Moreland Mews.

A glimpse of Mr Laycock's Yard (10), with its cattle sheds spread along Highbury Station Road, is still to be seen in Laycock Street Park, off the northern end of Upper Street.

New River (11) used to flow all the way through the eastern part of Islington. It was mostly covered over in the 1870s, but part of it can still be seen, along a narrow garden beside the Marquis Tavern on Douglas Road.

Frog Lane (12) used to run all the way north from City Road to where Rotherfield Street meets Essex Road. It was mostly built over when the Packington estate was constructed in the 1840s, although Devonia Road and Raleigh Street still follow its line. The church of St Peter's in Devonia Street has now been converted to a block of flats.

The Tower (13) on Canonbury Place was built in 1532 by Prior Bolton of St Bartholomew's in Smithfield and used to be known as the Queen Elizabeth Tower. After the dissolution it was acquired by the earls of Northampton. They still own the building and the elegant 18th-century houses surrounding it. For many years it was used as the Tower Theatre, which closed in 2003. Local residents are worried about what the present Earl will do with it next.

St Matthew School (15) in Ecclesbourne Road, renamed Norfolk Street in the 19th century, is now one of Islington's many unprepossessing council housing estates built in the 1930s.

The Roman Catholic Chapel (14) in Duncan Terrace, and its school, is today the Catholic church of St John the Evangelist, and remains associated with the neighbouring primary school.

Upper Street

Essex Road

Regent's Canal

London theatres with date of foundation

 1: Adelphi, 1806
 2: Albery, 1903
 3: Aldwych, 1905
 4: Apollo, 1901
 5: Arts, 1927
 6: Barbican, 1982
 7: Bridewell, 1994
 8: Cambridge, 1930
 9: Cochrane, 1963
10: Comedy, 1881
11: Criterion, 1874
12: Dominion, 1929
13: Donmar Warehouse, 1992
14: Drill Hall, 1981
15: Duchess, 1929
16: Duke of York's, 1892
17: Fortune, 1924
18: Garrick, 1889

19: Gielgud, 1906 (formerly Globe)
20: Globe, 1997
21: Her Majesty's, 1705
22: ICA, 1947
23: London Coliseum. 1904
24: London Palladium, 1910
25: Lyceum, 1771
26: Lyric, 1888
27: New Ambassadors, 1913
28: New London, 1973
29: Old Vic, 1818
30: Palace, 1891
31: Peacock, 1960
32: Phoenix, 1930
33: Piccadilly, 1928
34: Players, 1927
35: Playhouse, 1882
36: Prince Edward, 1930
37: Prince of Wales, 1884
38: Queen's, 1907

39: Royal National, 1976
40: Royal Opera House, 1732
41: St Martin's, 1916
42: Savoy, 1881
43: Shaftesbury, 1911 (formerly Prince's)
44: Soho, 2000
45: Southwark Playhouse, 1933
46: Strand, 1905
47: Theatre Royal Drury Lane, 1663
48: Theatre Royal Haymarket, 1720
49: Theatre Underground
50: Union, 2000
51: The Venue
52: Vaudeville, 1870
53: Whitehall, 1930
54: Wyndhams, 1899
55: Young Vic, 1970
56: Theatre Museum, 1963

THEATRELAND

A Roman theatre is thought to have existed off Victoria Embankment, 50 yards east of the recently closed Mermaid Theatre in Puddle Dock. Plays in the Middle Ages were performed on church steps or in inn yards. The first two purpose-built theatres, the Theatre (1576) and the Curtain (1578), went up in Shoreditch a few hundred yards apart. The City puritans were hostile to entertainment, so the early theatres had to be established outside their jurisdiction – and the choice was Bankside in Southwark. Here the Rose went up in 1587, the Swan in 1595, Shakespeare's famous Globe in 1599, on the site where Anchor Terrace now stands, and the Hope in 1614.

Elizabethan drama was of course hugely popular among ordinary Londoners, and the lively crowd who attended the plays tended to scare the upper classes. When the Puritans came into power in the 1640s they banned all public stage plays, and all London's theatres were closed for twenty years. After that, Lincoln's Inn Fields Theatre was the first to open (1660). Its first production was of *Hamlet*, produced by Sir William D'Avenant (once rumoured to be Shakespeare's illegitimate son). Two years later, the Theatre Royal opened in Drury Lane. Popular theatre audiences went on being accused of violence and coarseness well into the 19th century.

The first theatre to be built in Shaftesbury Avenue, the centre of today's West End theatre district, was the Shaftesbury, opening in 1888 with a performance of *As You Like It* with Sir Johnston Forbes-Robertson playing Orlando. It was bombed to the ground in 1941, and the former Prince's Theatre, founded in 1911, took over its name in 1962. There are now four other theatres in Shaftesbury Avenue, and 40 more in the West End.

London's theatres are far from confined to this area. There are at least as many dotted all over the city. The best known is the Old Vic in Waterloo Road, founded in 1818 under the name Royal Coburg in honour of its main patrons, Prince Leopold and Princess Charlotte. The Young Vic nearby was invented in 1970 by Frank Dunlop. The Royal Court Theatre in Sloane Square went up in 1870, the Theatre Royal Stratford East in 1884, and the Lyric Hammersmith in 1890.

In the 20th century a number of new theatres opened which have subsequently proved successful. The Aldwych, opened in 1905 when the crescent link between Kingsway and the Strand was created, built its reputation from the 1960s when it was the London home of the Royal Shakespeare Company. The Barbican opened after the vast residential and cultural centre was created there in the 1970s. Recent successes include the Tricycle (1980), the Almeida (1990), the Donmar Warehouse (1992), the Soho (2000) – and of course the reconstruction of Shakespeare's Globe (1997).

PUBLIC HOUSES

Londoners have been drinking alcohol for 4,000 years – mead made by fermenting honey and water with added spices is one of the earliest examples. Already in the 13th century the city was famous for its inhabitants' immoderate drinking, and in the early 14th century some 350 taverns and over 1,300 breweries were recorded. When John Stow conducted his survey in 1598, he reported that drunkenness was so widespread that 200 London alehouses were closed down.

The most drunken period in London's history is said to have occurred in the 18th century, when different varieties of drink called 'brown ale', 'bitter beer', 'pale ale' and 'stout' became fashionable. Thousands of public houses were opened all around the city, catering for labouring people as much as landlords and tradesmen. Gin, originally made in Holland and called 'geneva', also became enormously popular, and by the middle of the century there were reported to be some 17,000 'geneva shops' located in cellars or workshops, mostly on the eastern side of the city. William Hogarth's famous painting of *Gin Lane* portrays the horrific misery that gin was believed to inflict on its addicts.

Although the gin fever declined, visitors to London in the 19th century reported that drunkenness was just as prevalent then too, and 25,000 citizens annually were arrested for it. The well-off drank just as freely as the poor. More and more public houses opened as the city and its population expanded, and they introduced new segregations: saloons, lounges and private bars to attract the middle classes. By 1870 there were 20,000 public houses and beer-shops in London.

Quite a few of them have survived, some with ancient histories, and many designed to convey a sense of that history and tradition. But there have also been innovations: pubs with theatres upstairs, pubs that are also strip-joints (see page 103), pubs with live music and dancing, and pubs with top-class restaurants attached to them. There are also gay pubs, and pubs for transvestites.

The contemporary pubs shown on this page have been chosen on various grounds: their exceptional service, the quality of the beers and other drinks they offer, their excellent food, and their popularity. In 2002 three of them were awarded stars by The Good Pub Guide as among the very best pubs in Britain: the George Inn in Southwark, which is London's only surviving coaching inn, restored after a devastating fire in 1676; the Lamb in Bloomsbury, built in the 1720s but 'improved' in the 19th century; and Jerusalem Tavern off Clerkenwell Road, also originating in the 1720s, and famous for its St Peters Brewery ales brewed in Suffolk.

Good pubs in London

1: The Admiral Codrington, 17 Mossop Street
2: The Albert, Victoria Street
3: Archery Tavern, 4 Bathurst Street
4: Argyll Arms, Argyll Street
5: The Bishops Finger, 9–10 West Smithfield
6: The Black Friar, 174 Queen Victoria Street
7: The Cittie of Yorke, 22 High Holborn
8: The Cross Keys, 31 Endell Street
9: The Dog & Duck, 18 Bateman Street
10: The Eagle, 159 Farringdon Road
11: The Fox, Paul Street
12: The Grapes, Shepherd Market

13: The Grenadier, 18 Wilton Row
14: The Guinea, 30 Bruton Place
15: Jerusalem Tavern, 55 Britton Street
16: The Lamb, 94 Lamb's Conduit Street
17: The Lamb & Flag, 33 Rose Street
18: Lord Moon of the Mall, 16–18 Whitehall
19: The Moon Under Water, 105–7 Charing Cross Road
20: Museum Tavern, 49 Great Russell Street
21: The Nags Head, 53 Kinnerton Street
22: O'Hanlons, 8 Tysoe Street
23: Old Bank of England, 194 Fleet Street
24: The Red Lion, 2 Duke of York Street
25: The Red Lion, 1 Waverton Street

26: The Seven Stars, 53 Carey Street
27: Star Tavern, 6 Belgrave Mews West
28: Westminster Arms, 9 Storey's Gate
29: Ye Olde Cheshire Cheese, Wine Office Court, off 145 Fleet Street
30: Ye Olde Mitre, Ely Court, 9 Ely Place
31: The Grapes, 76 Narrow Street
32: Prospect of Whitby, 57 Wapping Wall
33: The Chapel, Chapel Street
34: The Compton Arms, 4 Compton Avenue
35: Duke of Cambridge, 30 St Peters Street
36: Waterside, York Way
37: The Alma, 499 Old York Road
38: The Anchor, 34 Park Street, Bankside
39: The Bull's Head, 373 Lonsdale Road

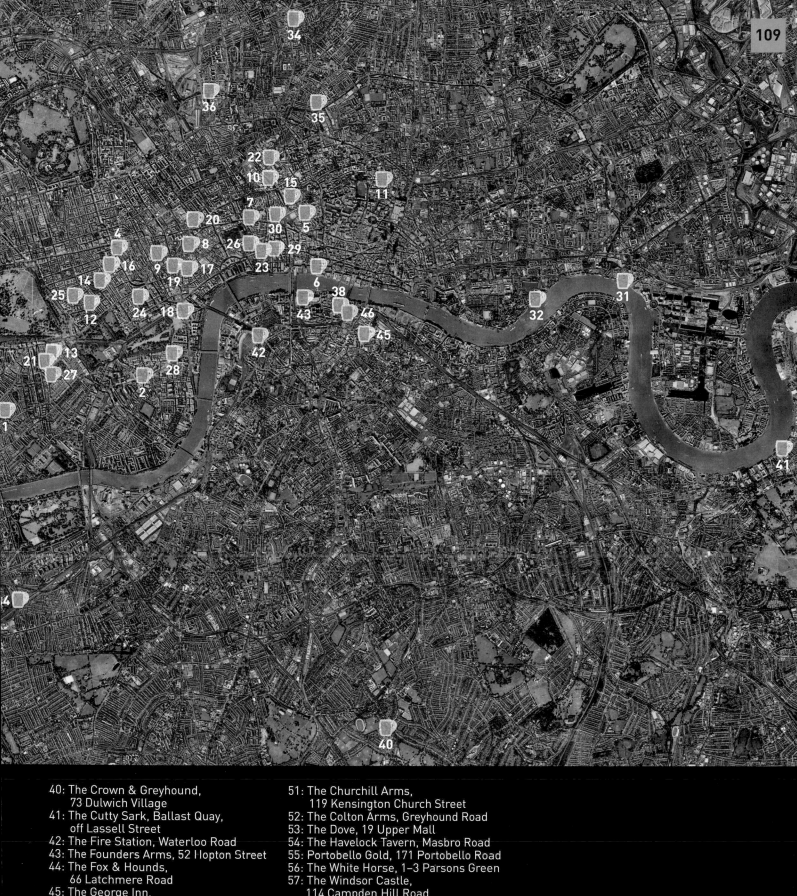

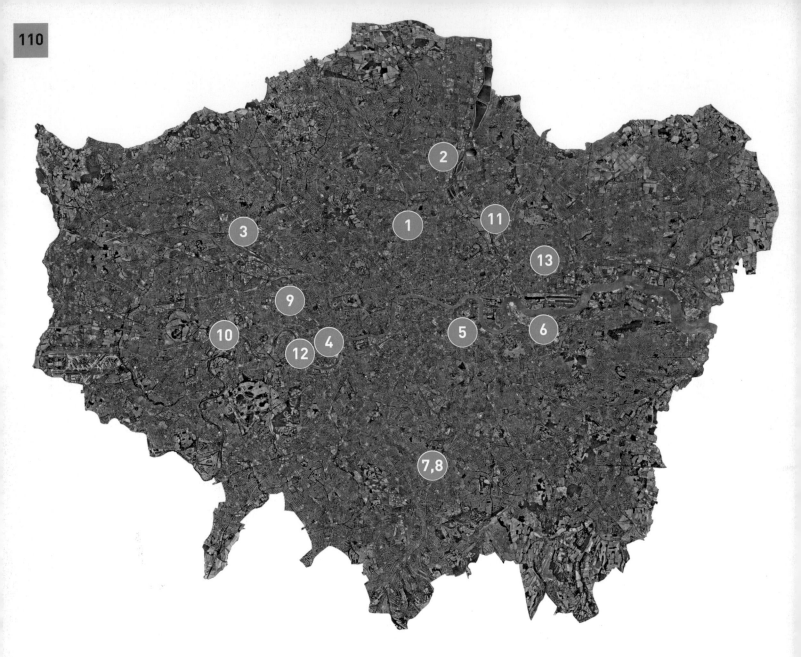

FOOTBALL

Londoners have evidently played football since earliest times, though the evolution of its rules was gradual and most clubs and grounds were formed in the 19th century. William Fitz-Stephen, Thomas à Becket's friend and biographer, wrote an account of life in London in the 12th century in which he describes how 'after lunch all the youth of the city go out into the fields to take part in a ball game. The students of each school have their own ball; the workers from each city craft are also carrying their balls. Older citizens, fathers, and wealthy citizens come on horseback to watch their juniors competing, and to relive their own youth vicariously: you can see their inner passions aroused as they watch the action and get caught up in the fun being had by the carefree adolescents'. In 1314 a law was introduced banning football in city streets because of its violence; but it was generally ignored.

London has eight principal football clubs with 19th-century origins, and four others founded in the 20th century. Fulham began in 1879 as the football club of St Andrew's of West Kensington and became a professional club in 1898. Arsenal was formed by a group of workers at an armament factory in Woolwich in 1886, who called themselves the

Dial Square Football Club. Brentford, Leyton Orient and Millwall date from similar times. Tottenham Hotspur are still based in White Hart Lane, where they played their first professional match against Notts County in September 1899, and beat them 4–1. The land was rented from a local brewer and publican, George Beckwith, who had previously used it for growing vegetables.

Chelsea came into existence in 1905. The team rented Stamford Bridge stadium, which had previously been the grounds of the London Athletic Club. A neighbouring market garden was annexed to make space for Chelsea's 100,000-fan football stadium, designed by Archibald Leitch. Crystal Palace was also formed in 1905.

Arsenal moved to Highbury in 1913, but it was not until the 1930s that their supremacy in English football began to develop. Since then they have won the football league twelve times and the FA cup eight times. The next most successful London team is Tottenham Hotspur, who first won the FA Cup in 1901 and have achieved the same honour six times since. Wimbledon (1889), West Ham United (1900) and Charlton Athletic (1905) have attained similar but much more occasional triumphs. Queen's Park Rangers (1885) have won the League Cup once, in 1967.

Principal London stadiums
 1: Arsenal – Highbury, Avenell Road
 2: Tottenham Hotspur – White Hart Lane, High Road
 3: Wembley – Empire Way, Wembley
 4: Chelsea – Stamford Bridge, Fulham Road
 5: Millwall – The New Den, Zampa Road
 6: Charlton Athletic, Charlton Lane, nr Woolwich Road
 7: Crystal Palace – Selhurst Park, Holmedene Road
 8: Wimbledon – Temporarily based at Selhurst Park
    (may move to Milton Keynes)
 9: Queen's Park Rangers – Loftus Road,
10: Brentford Griffin Park, Braemar Road
11: Leyton Orient – Matchroom Stadium, Brisbae Road
12: Fulham – Craven Cottage, Stevenage Road
13: West Ham – Upton Park, Green Street

OTHER SPORTS

Football may be the most popular sport, but it is by no means the only one for which London is renowned. Cricket is certainly as old, and like football it was once illegal. The first fully documented cricket match, Kent versus All England, took place at Finsbury in June 1744. Lord's Cricket Ground, founded along with Marylebone Cricket Club by a Yorkshireman called Thomas Lord, was originally on the site of Dorset Square, off Marylebone Road. The club moved to its present St John's Wood site in 1816. By the mid-19th century the Marylebone Cricket Club, or 'MCC', had become accepted as the supreme authority on the rules of the game. The Middlesex county cricket club moved there in the 1870s.

Meanwhile, down in Kennington, the Surrey county cricket club had established its headquarters at the Oval in 1845, renting what had been a market garden from its owner the Duchy of Cornwall. In its early years the Oval was used for many other sports, including football and rugby.

The game of rugby probably evolved as football did, from the same 12th-century 'ball game', and forms of it were played in the 18th century at public schools such as Eton and Winchester. The rugby variation was formalised at the school of that name in the 1820s, and by 1871 the Rugby Football Union was founded, with its headquarters at 'Billy Williams's Cabbage Patch', as the famous stadium at Twickenham was then called. Today there are ten principal rugby clubs in the city. The oldest is Blackheath, founded in 1858 by former students at Blackheath Preparatory School. It is still based there. Richmond was next in 1861, and in 1996 was the first club to establish the game as professional rather than amateur. It was unsuccessful, and has reverted to its amateur status, but hopes to climb back into the league before long. The three Premiership clubs of London are London Wasps (formed in 1867), Saracens (1876) and London Irish (1898).

Numerous other sports are traditional in London life, from athletics and boxing to archery and skateboarding. Every public park has a corner devoted to tennis, and there are dozens of tennis clubs with private courts all over the metropolis. Among London's most famous annual sporting events are the Boat Race between the universities of Oxford and Cambridge in April, the London Marathon begun in 1981 and currently attracting over 45,000 runners each year, and the Wimbledon tennis championships in June.

Cricket

1: ▮▮'s Cricket Ground, St. John's Wood Road
2: The Oval (cricket), Kennington

Rugby

3: Athletic Ground, Richmond
4: Blackheath Rugby Club (1858), Blackheath
5: Harlequins (1866), Twickenham
6: London Scottish (1878), Richmond
7: London Wasps (1867), Sunbury

8: Metropolitan Police RFC (1923), East Molesey
9: Richmond (1861), Richmond Athletic Ground, Richmond
10: Rosslyn Park (1879), Richmond
11: Saracens (1876), Watford
12: Twickenham Rugby Stadium

Tennis Clubs

13: All England Lawn Tennis & Croquet Club, Wimbledon
14: Blackheath Wanderers, Etham Road

15: David Lloyd Sports and Fitness Club, Raynes Park
16: Queens Club (tennis), Hammersmith

Archery

17: London Archers, the Paddock, Kensington Palace Gardens

DIPLOMACY AND SPYING

Britain's security services date back to 1909, when the government was concerned about the danger posed to British naval ports by German espionage. Captain Vernon Kell ('K') of the South Staffordshire Regiment and Captain Mansfield Cumming ('M') of the Royal Navy jointly established the Secret Service Bureau. 'K' was responsible for counter-espionage in Britain (MI5), and 'M' took charge of gathering intelligence overseas (MI6). These are still their basic functions.

During the cold war, MI5's main activity was countering threats from the Soviet Union, and in the 1960s they identified some key Russian spies like George Blake, the Portland spy ring, and John Vassell, an employee at the Admiralty recruited by the KGB. In 1971, over a hundred Soviet personnel were thrown out of Britain because they were suspected of spying. In 1978 MI5 failed to prevent the murder on Waterloo Bridge of Georgi Markov, a leading Bulgarian anti-communist and journalist, who was stabbed in the leg with an umbrella containing ricin.

Terrorism, particularly involving the IRA, was also a key concern of MI5 in the latter part of the 20th century. A number of IRA attacks on London took place, but many were prevented. Today, MI5 is closely involved in Britain's commitment to preventing the spread of weapons of mass destruction, and also in countering serious crimes such as illegal drug importing, arms trafficking and illegal immigration rings. Their Director General from 1992 to 1996, Dame Stella Rimmington, played a key part in making more information about the security services available to the public. Her autobiography, *Open Secret*, was published in 2001.

MI6, also known as the Secret Intelligence Service (SIS), is less open about its activities overseas, but since the Intelligence Services Act was passed in 1997, a parliamentary committee is entitled to oversee both its administration and its policies – though not to reveal them to the public. Foreign embassies have traditionally been a base for intelligence activities, both covert and overt.

One hundred and fifty nations and states are represented in their embassies, high commissions and consulates around central London. The French have occupied their embassy at 1 Albert Gate since 1854, and recently extended it to 58 Knightsbridge next door. The American embassy in Grosvenor Square, designed by the American architect Eero Saarinen (1910–61), has been there since 1960. Canada House, though built in 1824, only became the country's high commission in 1925. Australia House, at the eastern end of the island created by Aldwych and the Strand, is their oldest diplomatic building abroad, and was opened in 1918.

Croatia
Mozambique
Latvia
Seychelles
Honduras
El Salvador
Maldives
Chile
Kenya
Sweden
China
Poland
Namibia
Lithuania
Sierra Leone
Switzerland
Macedonia
Antigua
Slovenia
Tonga
Barbados
Uzbekistan
Belize
Cuba
Botswana
Italy
Nicaragua
U.S.A.
Malawi
Sri Lanka
Brazil
Canada
Cyprus
India
Australia
Indonesia
Angola
Myanmar
Panama
Saudi Arabia
South Africa
Egypt
Bahamas
Malta
Tanzania
Afghanistan
Qatar
Papua New
New
United Arab Emirates
France
Guinea
Zealand
Tunisia
Mexico
Japan
Sudan
Nigeria
Thailand
7
Colombia
11
Malaysia
Ethiopia
Ecuador
13
Turkey
Iran
9
Ireland
Argentina
10
Jamaica
Trinidad
man
1
Norway
12
Bolivia
Peru
6
5
Swaziland
Kazakhstan
Denmark
Zaire
Belgium
Venezuela
Hungary
Albania
Iceland

A

B

C

Additional London embassies,
high commissions and consulates

1: Austria
2: Bangladesh   8: Netherlands
3: Brunei   9: Pakistan
4: Finland   10: Portugal
5: Germany   11: Singapore
6: Lesotho   12: Spain
7: Luxembourg   13: Syria

A: Waterloo Bridge (Georgi Markov
assassinated, 1978)

British intelligence services
B: MI5 (Thames House, Millbank)
C: MI6 (Albert Embankment,
Vauxhall Cross)

CELEBRITIES

There is a long tradition in London of valuing the homes of its most celebrated inhabitants, and this is best expressed by the 'blue plaques' first introduced on London buildings in 1867. They are erected in response to suggestions from the public, rather than providing an honours list of worthy people; so, curiously, there are no plaques for Sir Thomas More or Isaac Newton. Today the plaques are the responsibility of English Heritage.

There are 94 plaques in the borough of Kensington and Chelsea alone, of which more than a third celebrate the work of poets and writers, including G. K. Chesterton, T. S. Eliot, Henry James, James Joyce, A. A. Milne, William Makepeace Thackeray, Mark Twain and Oscar Wilde. The plaques record that one street in Chelsea, Cheyne Walk, was at different times home to Hilaire Belloc, George Elliot and Swinburne. The artists Walter Greaves, Dante Gabriel Rosetti, Philip Steer, John Tweed and James Whistler, and the suffragette Sylvia Pankhurst, also lived there, as did the Brunels, father and son. Although J. M. W. Turner and David Lloyd George both also lived there in their day, they have not yet been given plaques. Winston Churchill lived at 28 Hyde Park Gate, off Kensington Gore, and Andrew Bonar Law lived at 24 Onslow Gardens.

Some houses still hold the names of their famous inhabitants, often as museums. Dickens House was his home for a mere two years, but it is the only one that survives. Dr Johnson's House, in Gough Square off Fleet Street, was his home in the 1750s, and has been restored and furnished to its condition at that time. The American philosopher, scientist and statesman Benjamin Franklin rented 36 Craven Street, by Charing Cross, for several years in much the same period. The restored building will soon be open to the public. Thomas Carlyle's House at 24 Cheyne Row was Carlyle's home from 1834 to 1881, when he died there, and it survives much as it was then, full of his furniture, pictures and books. Keats House in Hampstead is another example, though Keats only lived there for two years. He wrote 'Ode to a Nightingale' in the garden there. The Freud Museum in Hampstead was Sigmund Freud's home from 1938, when he and his family fled from Nazi Austria, until his death the following year, and remained the family home until his youngest daughter, Anna Freud, died in 1982. His study survives unaltered, lined with his books. Finally, Sir John Soane (1753–1837) obtained an Act of Parliament to preserve his house in Lincoln's Inn Fields and its collection as a public museum. It is filled with the eccentric architect and collector's many paintings, statues, furniture, vases, manuscripts and other curiosities.

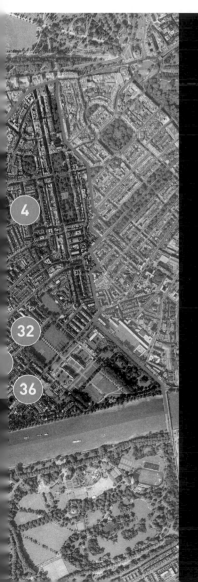

Blue plaques on the homes of writers

1: Sir Edwin Arnold, (1832–1904) Poet and journalist, 31 Bolton Gardens, SW5

2: Enid Bagnold (1889–1981) Novelist and playwright, 29 Hyde Park Gate, SW7

3: Hilaire Belloc (1870–1953) Poet, essayist and historian, 104 Cheyne Walk, SW10

4: Arnold Bennett (1867–1931) Novelist, 75 Cadogan Square, SW1

5: E. F. Benson (1867–1940) Writer, 25 Brompton Square, SW3

6: George Borrow (1803–1881) Author, 22 Hereford Square, SW7

7: G. K. Chesterton, (1874–1936) Poet, novelist and critic, 11 Warwick Gardens, W14

8: Dame Ivy Compton-Burnett (1884–1969) Novelist, 5 Braemar Mansions, Cornwall Gardens, SW7

9: Goldsworthy Lowes Dickinson (1862–1932) Author and humanist, 11 Edwardes Square, W8

10: Henry Austin Dobson (1840–1921) Poet and essayist, 10 Redcliffe Street, SW10

11: George Elliot (1819–1880) Novelist, 4 Cheyne Walk, SW3

12: T. S. Eliot, OM (1888–1965) Poet, 3 Kensington Court Gardens, W8

13: Ford Madox Ford (1873–1939) Novelist and critic, 80 Campden Hill Road, W8

14: Ugo Foscolo (1778–1827) Italian poet and patriot, 19 Edwardes Square, W8

15: George Gissing (1857–1903) Novelist, 33 Oakley Street, SW3

16: Kenneth Grahame (1859–1932) Author (Wind in the Willows) 16 Phillimore Place, W8

17: Radclyffe Hall (1880–1943) Novelist and poet, 37 Holland Street, W8

18: William Henry Hudson (1841–1922), Writer 40 St. Lukes Road, W11

19: Leigh James Henry Hunt (1784–1859) Essayist and poet, 22 Upper Cheyne Row, SW3

20: Henry James (1843–1916) Writer, 34 De Vere Gardens, W8

21: James Joyce (1882–1941) Author, 28 Campden Grove, W8

22: Charles Kingsley (1819–1875) Writer, 56 Old Church Street, SW3

23: Andrew Lang (1844–1912) Man of letters, 1 Marloes Road, W8

24: Stephane Mallarme (1842–1898), Poet 6 Brompton Square, SW3

25: George Meredith, OM (1828–1909) Poet and novelist, 7 Hobury Street, SW10

26: A. A. Milne (1882–1956) Author (Winnie the Pooh) 13 Mallord Street, SW3

27: Charles Morgan (1894–1958) Novelist and Critic, 16 Campden Hill Square, W8

28: Sir Henry Newbolt (1862–1938) Poet, 29 Campden Hill Road, W8

29: Mervyn Peake (1911–1968) Author and artist, 1 Drayton Gardens, SW10

30: Siegfried Sassoon (1886–1967) Writer, 23 Campden Hill Square, W8

31: Tobias Smollet (1721–1771) Novelist, 16 Lawrence Street, SW3

32: Bram Stoker (1847–1912) Author (Dracula) 18 St. Leonards Terrace, SW3

33: Algernon Charles Swinburne (1837–1909) Poet, 16 Cheyne Walk, SW3

34: William Makepeace Thackeray, (1811–1863) Novelist, 2 Palace Green, W8 and 16 Young Street, W8

35: Mark Twain (1835–1910) American writer, 23 Tedworth Square, SW3

36: Oscar O'Flahertie Wills Wilde (1854–1900) Dramatist and wit, 34 Tite Street, SW3

Blue plaques on the homes of the famous

Artists

1: Sir Max Beerbohm (1872–1956)
Artist and writer,
57 Palace Gardens Terrace, W8

2: Sir Edward Burne-Jones
(1833–1898) Artist,
41 Kensington Square, W8

3: Walter Crane (1845–1915)
Artist,
13 Holland Street, W8

4: Frank Dobson (1886–1963)
Sculptor,
14 Harley Gardens, SW10

5: Augustus John (1878–1961)
Artist, 28 Mallord Street, SW3

6: Sir John Lavery (1856–1941)
Painter, 5 Cromwell Place, SW7

7: Lord Frederick Leighton
(1830–1896) Painter,
Leighton House, 12 Holland
Park Road, W14

8: Percy Wyndham Lewis
(1882–1957), Painter
61 Palace Gardens Terrace, W8

9: Sir David Low (1891–1963)
Cartoonist,
33 Melbury Court, Kensington
High Street, W8

10: PhilMay (1864–1903)
Artist,
20 Holland Park Road, W14

11: Sir John Everett Millais, Bt PRA
(1829–1896) Painter,
2 Palace Gate, W8

12: Sir William Orpen (1878–1931)
Painter,
8 South Bolton Gardens, SW5

13: Samuel Palmer (1805–1881)
Artist, 6 Douro Place, W8

14: Charles Ricketts (1866–1931)
Artist, Lansdowne House, 80
Lansdowne Road, W11

Musicians

15: Bela Bartok (1881–1945)
Composer,
7 Sydney Place, SW7

16: Frank Bridg (1879–1941)
Composer and musician,
4 Bedford Gardens, W8

17: Muzio Clementi (1752–1832)
Composer, 128 Kensington
Church Street, W8

18: Percy Grainger (1882–1961)
Australian composer, folklorist,
pianist, 31 King's Road, SW3

19: John Ireland (1879–1962)
Composer,
14 Gunter Grove, SW3

20: Jenny Lind (1820–1887)
Singer,
189 Old Brompton Road, SW7

21: Sir Charles Hubert Parry
(1848–1918), Musician
17 Kensington Square, W8

22: Jean Sibelius (1865–1957)
Composer,
15 Gloucester Walk, W8

23: Stanford, Sir Charles
(1852–1924) Musician,
56 Hornton Street, W8

24: Peter, Philip Arnold Hesseltine
Warlock (1894–1930)
Composer, 30 Tite Street, SW3

Performing artists

25: Sir George Alexander
(1858–1918), Actor-manager
57 Pont Street, SW1

26: Princess Seraphine Astafieva
(1876–1934) Ballet dancer,
152 King's Road, SW3

27: Albert Chevalier (1861–1923)
Music hall comedian,
1 St Ann's Villas, W11

28: Sir W. S.Gilbert (1836–1911)
Dramatist,
39 Harrington Gardens, SW7

29: Dorothy Jordan (1762–1816)
Actress, 30 Cadogan Place, SW1

30: Lillie Langtry (1852–1929)
Actress, Cadogan Hotel, 22 Pont
Street, SW1

31: Sir Nigel Playfair (1874–1934)
Actor-manager,
26 Pelham Crescent, SW7

32: Dame Marie Rambert,
(1888–1982)
Founder of Ballet Rambert
19 Campden Hill Gardens, W8

33: Dame Ellen Terry (1847–1928)
Actress,
22 Barkston Gardens, SW5

34: Sir Herbert Beerbohm Tree,
(1853–1917), Actor-Manager
31 Rosary Gardens, SW7

● Artists
● Music
● Performing artists

13

2

Clerkenwell

12 14

3

1

Covent
Garden

30

6

21

28

St. George's Fields

16

18

20

5 23

29

32

Hyde Park

Spring
Gardens

22

26

11

4

1

9

36

25

35

8

19

37

31

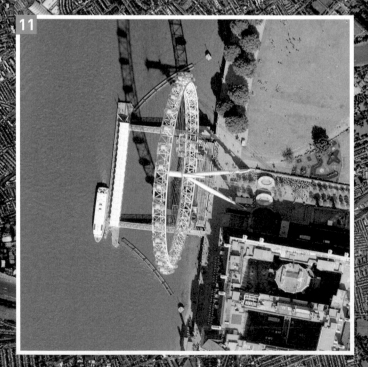

11

32

ENTERTAINMENT

Before the theatres went up along Bankside, this grassy parkland had for centuries been a louche area outside the jurisdiction of the City, home to brothels, and unconsecrated graveyards for the corpses of women who had worked in them. This was where you went to enjoy bear-baiting, bowling and gambling, crossing the river to Paris Garden Stairs, and wandering through the wooded gardens where conspirators and secret agents met at night. Through Moorgate, outside the Wall, where Finsbury Circus stands, there were open fields where people walked and practised archery, hung their clothes out to dry, and joined the Lord Mayor's Hunt. There were bullock hunts in Bethnal Green, and cock fighting and wrestling matches in Hyde Park and Clerkenwell. In Spring Gardens, at the end of the Mall, there was a bowling green, and butts for target practice. In the 1950s archery was still practised in St. George's Fields, off Bayswater Road, until the park was filled with new council housing.

Today's parks are more restful, though there is frantic roller-skating in Kensington Gardens, and London Archers still conduct their sessions in the Paddock. Skateboarders head for the South Bank, under Queen Elizabeth Hall. There is the daily changing of the guard outside Buckingham Palace, and window-shopping in Burlington Arcade, Covent Garden or Carnaby Street (made famous in the 1960s as the source of fashionable clothing for the young). Other entertainments and tourist attractions are more formalised.

When London Eye was erected in 2000, it was only granted a temporary licence because there was so much local complaint about its size, but most Londoners have grown to love it. Madame Tussaud's waxworks opened in Baker Street in 1835, and moved to its present site in 1884. It is still one of London's greatest tourist attractions. Next door to it, London Planetarium opened in the 1960s. The Tower of London attracts more than 2 million visitors a year, and London Zoo and St. Paul's Cathedral nearly a million. Traditional sights such as Westminster Abbey, Buckingham Palace, Big Ben and the Houses of Parliament are equally popular, followed by Hampton Court, Kensington Palace, the grisly London Dungeon, Kew Gardens, Shakespeare's Globe, and the Royal Academy at Burlington House.

Leading London tourist attractions
1: Big Ben
2: British Library Exhibition Galleries
3: British Museum
4: Buckingham Palace
5: Burlington Arcade
6: Carnaby Street
7: Finsbury Circus
8: Imperial War Museum
9: London Aquarium
10: The London Dungeon
11: London Eye
12: London Planetarium
13: London Zoo
14: Madame Tussaud's
15: Museum of London
16: National Gallery
17: National Maritime Museum
18: National Portrait Gallery
19: Natural History Museum
20: The Paddock, Kensngton Garden
21: Photographers Gallery
22: Queen Elizabeth Hall
23: Royal Academy
24: Royal Observatory
25: Science Museum
26: Serpentine Gallery
27: Shakespeare's Globe Exhibition
28: Somerset House
29: St. Martin-in-the-Fields
30: St. Paul's Cathedral
31: Tate Britain
32: Tate Modern
33: Tower Bridge
34: Tower of London
35: Victoria & Albert Museum
36: Westminster Abbey
37: Westminster Cathedral

Jewish Museum

London Canal Museum

Thomas Foundation for Children Art Gallery

Persival David Foundation of Chinese Art

University College Art Collections

Cricket Memorial Gallery

Madame Tussaud's

Planetarium

Potrait Museum of Egyptian Archaeology

Sherlock Holmes Museum

Pollock's Toy Museum

British Museum

John Soare's Museum

Wallace Collection

Library and Museum of Grand Lodge of Engalnd

Alexander Fleming Laboratory Museum

Royal Academy of Arts

National Potrait Gallery

Theatre Museum

London Toy and Model Museum

Michael Faraday's Laboratory and Museum

National Gallery

Kensington Palace, Court Dress Collection and State Apartments

Apsley House

Spencer House

ICA Gallery

Serpentine Gallery

Cabinet War Rooms

The Queen's Gallery

Guards Museum

Commonwealth Institute

Royal College of Music Potraits and Instruments

Donaldson Museum

Metropolitan Police Museum

London House

Science Museum

Westminster Abbey Museum

Natural History Museum

Victoria and Albert Museum

Geological Museum

Tate Britain

Royal Hospital Museum

Carlyle's House

National Army Museum

Chelséa Physic Garden

London Galleries and Museums

🏛 Art and Design

🏛 Science, Technology and Transport

🏛 History, Culture and Religion

🏛 Others

🏛 Entertainment and Leisure

🏛 Military

Museum of the Honerable
Artillery Company
Geffrye Museum

Dickens House
Museum

Inns of Court and City
Yeoman's Museum
Barbican
Art Gallery
John
Wesley's
House
Bethnal Green
Museum of
Childhood

Doctor Johnson's House

Museum of the
Order of St. John
Dennis Sever's
House

Public
Record
Office
Museum of
London
Clockmaker's
Company
Collection
Heritage Centre,
Spitalfields

St. Bride's
Crypt
Museum
Diocesar
Treasury
The Guildhall
Whitechapel
Art Gallery

Bank of England Musem

Telecom
Techmology
Showcase
Chartered Insurance
Institute Museum

Hunterian
Museum
Prince
Henry's
Room
Royal
Armouries

London Transport
Museum
All Hallows by the
Tower Undercroft
Museum

Bankside
Gallery
Shakespeare's
Globe Museum
Herald's
Museum,
Tower of
London

Hayward
Gallery
Tate Modern
London
Dungeon
Design
Museum

India Office Library

Banqueting
House
HMS
Belfast

Saatchi Gallery

Florence Nightingale Museum

Imperial War Museum

Museum of Garden History

Cuming Museum

MUSEUMS AND ART

The concept of a national collection of works of art took root in 1823 when the landscape painter and collector Sir George Beaumont undertook to donate his collection of paintings by Rembrandt, Rubens, Canaletto and others on condition that they should be suitably displayed to the public. King George IV supported the idea, and the government was persuaded to add to the collection and bought 38 masterpieces – including works by Raphael and Van Dyke – from the estate of a Russian-born merchant, J. J. Angerstein, who had died the year before. The works were first displayed in Angerstein's house in Pall Mall, until the National Gallery (1838) was built on the north side of Trafalgar Square – by which time both Georges had also died. During the next century, the gallery purchased a vast range of great works, and today it owns well over 2,000 pictures, dating from the 13th to the 19th century. First opened in 1859 in Great George Street, the National Portrait Gallery moved around the corner to St Martin's Place in 1895.

When the Tate Gallery was opened in 1897, the works of British painters, such as Hogarth, Gainsborough, Stubbs, Turner and Constable, were transferred from the National Gallery to its building on Millbank. It was designed to concentrate both on British and modern art; and today the two collections are divided between Tate Britain on Millbank and new Tate Modern gallery, which opened in 2000 and was constructed within what used to be the vast Bankside Power Station. It displays a magnificent collection of international 20th-century works, and has proved hugely popular, with both Londoners and tourists.

Other important public art collections in London include the Courtauld at Somerset House, which includes fine French Impressionist works as well as Old Masters. Dulwich Picture Gallery, founded in 1626, is England's oldest public picture gallery. Its present building in Dulwich was designed by Sir John Soane and opened in 1814. The Royal Academy of Arts opened in 1769, and moved to Burlington House 100 years later, after briefly sharing space with the National Gallery in Trafalgar Square. Its annual Summer Exhibition, which includes work by amateurs as well as professionals, has been going for more than two centuries and is a popular attraction. The Iveagh Bequest collection in Kenwood House is small but exquisite, with paintings by Rembrandt, Turner, Van Dyke, Gainsborough, and Sir Joshua Reynolds. The Wallace Collection in Manchester Square is perhaps the best of the family art collections now open to the public.

The Royal Geographical Society (4) is based in a building once called Lowther Lodge, on the corner of Exhibition Road and Kensington Gore. This was designed by Norman Shaw in 1874, and much expanded in 1930, to provide lecture rooms and a location for the society's important library.

MUSEUMLAND

The Great Exhibition, held in Joseph Paxton's Crystal Palace at the southern end of Hyde Park in 1851, was originally conceived by Sir Henry Cole, who at the time was assistant keeper of the Public Record Office. Despite pessimistic forecasts it was a triumphant success, and the profits made it possible for the commissioners, supported by Prince Albert, to purchase 87 acres of land stretching south from Kensington Gore to Cromwell Road, in order to create a centre dedicated to design and scientific research.

Queen Victoria opened the South Kensington Museum and School, which later became the Victoria & Albert Museum, in 1857. Sir Henry Cole was its first director, and its present huge building opened in 1909. In 1862, a vast International Exhibition building was erected along Cromwell Road, with the idea that exhibitions would be held every decade, but Prince Albert's death undermined the scheme, and the building was pulled down two years later. It was eventually replaced by Albert Waterhouse's Natural History Museum, which opened in 1881. Meanwhile, the Royal Albert Hall was completed in 1871, and the Albert Memorial went up in 1876.

Over the next half century there were other massive additions. The Royal College of Music was founded in 1882 and entered its present building in 1894. The Royal College of Organists, which had been based in Bloomsbury, moved next to the Albert Hall in 1904, but it has now moved to Holborn. The Royal College of Science, the Royal School of Mines and the City & Guilds College moved there at the end of the century, and in 1907 combined together to become the Imperial College of Science, Technology and Medicine, which now dominates the site south of the Albert Hall, and is part of the University of London. The Science Museum, an amalgam of various 19th century collections, opened in Exhibition Road in 1913 and has expanded several times since. The Geological Museum, now part of the Natural History Museum, moved there from Whitehall in 1935. The Imperial War Museum, now in the former Bethlehem Royal Hospital in Lambeth Road, was for a while in the 1920s housed alongside Imperial College.

The Royal College of Art, founded in 1837 in Somerset House, was originally intended to teach industrial design rather than fine art. It moved to different buildings, including Marlborough House and the South Kensington Museum in the 1850s, and to a new building in Queen's Gate in 1863. Today, it faces the Albert Hall on Kensington Gore, in a building designed by Sir Hugh Casson in 1961.

The Church of Jesus Christ of Latter-Day Saints (9) is the London base of the Mormon church, founded by the American Joseph Smith in 1838 on the basis that Jesus, after his resurrection, visited the American people, taught them his gospel, and formed his church among them.

Next to the Science Museum (10) is an entrance to one of the longest subways in London (8), leading all the way down to the South Kensington underground station.

The Goethe-Institut (7), promoting German art and culture in Britain, is based at 50 Exhibition Road. It owns Hugo's restaurant next door, noted for its organic food.

1: Albert Memorial
2: Royal College of Art
3: Royal Albert Hall
4: Royal Geographical Society
5: Royal College of Music
6: Imperial College of Science, Technology and Medicine
7: The Goethe-Institut
8: Subway from Science Museum to South Kensington Tube Station
9: The Church of Jesus Christ of Latter-Day Saints
10: Science Museum
11: Natural History Museum
12: Victoria & Albert Museum

CANALETTO'S LONDON

Canaletto's paintings of mid-18th-century London give a rich and succulent, if rather romanticised, view of the city at the time. Born in Venice in 1697, the son of a theatrical scene painter, he quickly rose to fame for his dramatic and picturesque views of the city. Some time in the early 1730s he became friends with Joseph Smith, an affluent local English merchant, who was appointed British Consul to Venice in 1744. Smith commissioned a number of works from Canaletto, which were later sold to George III and are part of the royal collection.

Canaletto came to London in 1746, living for several years at 41 Beak Street, off Regent Street. Among his first works were several views of the Thames, including Westminster Bridge which had just been built. In *Westminster Bridge from the North on Lord Mayor's Day*, the newly elected Lord Mayor, William Benn, is aboard a huge barge, surrounded by hundreds of skiffs and rowing boats, on his way to be sworn in at Westminster Hall to the right. Lambeth Palace can be seen in the distance on the south bank.

In the same year, he painted the even more lively *London: Seen through an Arch of Westminster Bridge*. This looks the other way, towards the City, with the newly-built St. Paul's Cathedral dominating the skyline. Along the south bank are rows of timber yards and wharfs, and Mr. Beaufoy's Vinegar Manufactory where the river swings round to the east. Directly ahead is Whitehall.

In his beautiful *Whitehall and the Privy Garden from Richmond House* (1747), alas nothing much has survived. Richmond House, which burned down in 1791, stood where Richmond Terrace now is, and we are looking north towards Parliament Street. Downing Street lies straight ahead in the distance. At the same time, and from the other side of Richmond House, he painted another splendid view of the river towards St. Paul's, with elegant ladies enjoying the sunshine in the courtyard below.

Two years later, in 1749, he produced several remarkable landscape views of Horse Guards Parade, of which one is reproduced opposite. Here too, none of the buildings survive, but the whole area still looks the same. The buildings on the right hand side were replaced in 1868 with today's Foreign Office (Downing Street is just beyond them to the right), and in the centre, William Kent's Horse Guards, which survives today, only began construction in 1750.

His view of Westminster Cathedral, on the other hand, is entirely recognisable. He was commissioned to paint this by the Dean of Westminster in 1749, to celebrate a ceremony for the Knights of the Order of the Bath. Northumberland House, built around 1600 on the site of a convent, was demolished in 1874 to make way for Northumberland Avenue. But the Percy Lion, at the top of the façade, can still be seen on top of Syon House in Isleworth.

1: Westminster Bridge from the North on Lord Mayor's Day
The celebrations accompanied the appointment of the new Lord Mayor of London. The largest City barge is shown taking the Mayor to Westminster Hall, by the abbey at the right, where he will be sworn in. Some barges are firing salutes to honour the Mayor. 1746. Oil on canvas. Yale Center for British Art, New Haven, Connecticut, USA

2: London: Seen through an Arch of Westminster Bridge
1746–7. Oil on canvas. Duke of Northumberland

3: Whitehall and the Privy Garden from Richmond House
1747. Oil on canvas. Trustees of Goodwood House, West Sussex

4: The Thames and the City of London from Richmond House
1747. Oil on canvas. Trustees of Goodwood House, West Sussex

5: Westminster Abbey, with a Procession of Knights of the Bath
The Order of the Bath is one of the oldest English chivalric orders, founded in 1399. Canaletto was commissioned to paint the picture by Joseph Wilcocks, Dean of Westminster. 1749. Oil on canvas. Dean and Chapter of Westminster Abbey

6: Horse Guards from St. James's Park
1749. Oil on canvas. Christie's Images, London/Bridgeman Art Library

7: Northumberland House
1752. Oil on canvas. Duke of Northumberland

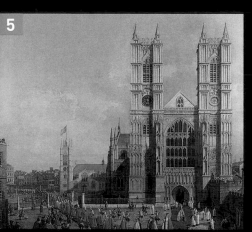

London Television Centre

Waterloo Bridge

Waterloo International Terminal

South Bank buildings
1: Old County Hall
2: Hungerford Bridge
3: Royal Festival Hall
4: Hayward Gallery
5: National Film Theatre
6: National Theatre
7: IMAX Cinema
8: Tate Modern
9: New Globe Theatre
10: Queen Elizabeth Hall and Purcell Room
11: London Eye
12: London Aquarium
13: Dali Universe
14: Saatchi Gallery
15: Oxo Tower Wharf

1951 South Bank Exhibition buildings
16: Dome of Discovery, now Jubilee Gardens
17: Skylon
18: Nelson Pier
19: Regatta Restaurant
20: Power and Production Pavilion
21: Transport Pavilion
22: The People of Britain Pavilion, now Shell Centre
23: Bankside Gallery

Blackfriars Bridge

Millennium Bridge

Bankside Gallery

15

23

8

9

THE SOUTH BANK

A century after the triumphant Great Exhibition of 1851 (see pages 124–5), in the grim years following the end of the Second World War, the idea emerged of celebrating Britain's cultural and technological strengths with a festival. The national economy was in a parlous state, but the post-war Labour government backed the scheme and Herbert Morrison, a long-standing member of the London County Council and now deputy Prime Minister, was appointed to oversee it. The objective was to provide 'a tonic to the nation' and to rekindle the belief that Britain was great. After long debates about where to hold the festival, the South Bank, the riverside stretch between County Hall and Waterloo Bridge, was chosen as the main exhibition site. It was in a derelict state after much wartime bombing.

Most of the striking buildings and displays were temporary, and today all that survives is the Royal Festival Hall (refurbished in the 1990s), and the river wall along the edge of the site. Under Waterloo Bridge, the exhibition included a pavilion called the Telekinema, which is where the National Film Theatre was constructed in 1956, and expanded more than once in the 1970s. The London Film Festival is held here annually. Two smaller concert halls next to the Festival Hall, Queen Elizabeth Hall and the Purcell Room, were opened by the Queen in 1967. In the following year the Hayward Gallery, which was designed by Ove Arup and Partners, opened next to them.

The National Theatre didn't arrive until 1976, in a building designed by Denys Lasdun and incorporating three separate theatres. It was originally planned in 1969 to provide this institution, which had been temporarily housed in the Old Vic since 1963, with a permanent home.

The arrival of the London Eye and Tate Modern (both in 2000) and the new Globe Theatre (1997) a little way down-river, have substantially increased the popular attraction of this whole riverside area to Londoners and tourists. The Hungerford footbridge has recently been rebuilt with bright lights and striking poles to attract more visitors across the river. The old County Hall (1922) is now home to three attractions, the London Aquarium, a permanent exhibition of works by the surrealist Salvador Dali, and the Saatchi Gallery.

Oxo Tower Wharf is another lively element in this area. A late Victorian power station, supplying electricity to the Post Office, was sold in the 1920s to a German meat extracting company which manufactured the bestselling Oxo cube. They employed the architect Albert Moore to develop the building, and he constructed windows on its tower spelling out OXO on all four sides. By the 1970s the building was decaying, and it was acquired by the local Coin Street Community Builders, who embarked on a massive £20 million refurbishment plan. Today it houses a highly popular restaurant (owned by Harvey Nichols) at the top of the tower which has stunning views across the river, 33 studios for contemporary retail designers, another restaurant and a bar below, and a gallery which stages art, design and photography exhibitions. And there are also 78 housing association flats available at low rents.

Several schemes for enlarging and improving the South Bank as an arts centre have been debated. In 1991 the architect Terry Farrell proposed one which involved much demolition and reconstruction, and another by Richard Rogers is currently under discussion.

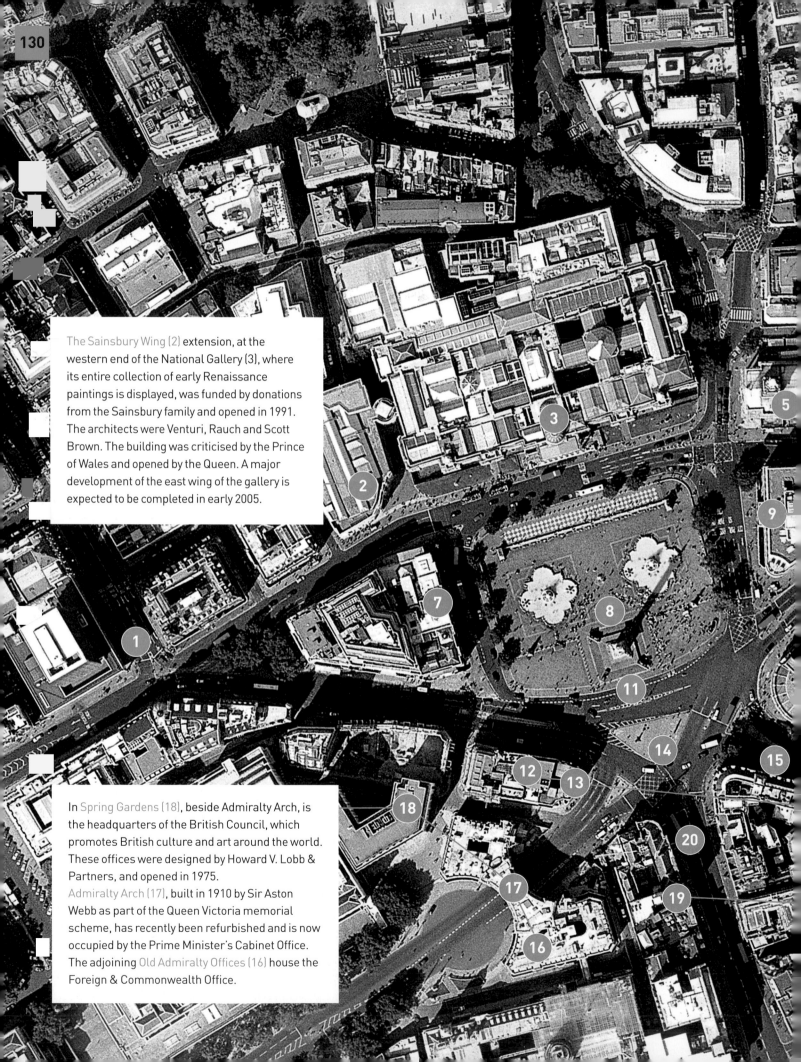

The Sainsbury Wing (2) extension, at the western end of the National Gallery (3), where its entire collection of early Renaissance paintings is displayed, was funded by donations from the Sainsbury family and opened in 1991. The architects were Venturi, Rauch and Scott Brown. The building was criticised by the Prince of Wales and opened by the Queen. A major development of the east wing of the gallery is expected to be completed in early 2005.

In Spring Gardens (18), beside Admiralty Arch, is the headquarters of the British Council, which promotes British culture and art around the world. These offices were designed by Howard V. Lobb & Partners, and opened in 1975.

Admiralty Arch (17), built in 1910 by Sir Aston Webb as part of the Queen Victoria memorial scheme, has recently been refurbished and is now occupied by the Prime Minister's Cabinet Office.

The adjoining Old Admiralty Offices (16) house the Foreign & Commonwealth Office.

The Coliseum (3) at the bottom of St. Martin's Lane, designed by Frank Matcham in 1904, is the home of the English National Opera. A major restoration and modernisation programme is currently under way, but it remains open to opera lovers.

On Cockspur Street, at the south end of Trafalgar Square, two other former British colonies set up their high commissions close to Canada House and South Africa House. Uganda House (12) is still the home of the Ugandan embassy, and shared with the republic of Rwanda. Next door at Malaysia House (13), travel to the far east is promoted by a company called Tourism Malaysia.

The Phoenix Theatre (19), at the northern end of Whitehall, was designed by Sir Giles Gilbert Scott and opened in 1930. Next to it is a pub called Lord Moon of the Mall, a favourite meeting place for civil servants.

THE STORY OF TRAFALGAR SQUARE

The church of St. Martin-in-the-Fields has stood in its present position since the 11th century, and the surrounding area remained leafy and semi-rural up until the end of the 16th century. A hundred years later, Charing Cross was a T-junction, running south down Whitehall, east up the Strand, and north-west up Haymarket. To the north of it was the spacious Mews Yard, where the king kept his horses, and on the corner of the Strand was the Duke of Northumberland's magnificent 1605 house (where Northumberland Avenue now runs). In the middle of the T-junction stood a statue of Charles I on horseback.

By 1805, when Admiral Nelson won — and was mortally wounded at — the battle of Trafalgar, not much had changed. Most of the houses facing the streets were rented by private individuals, and the buildings around King's Mews were used as a menagerie and a store for public records. Buckingham Palace now had its own royal mews. The Master of the Horse finally moved out of King's Mews in 1825. The next year, John Nash produced an ambitious improvement scheme for the Charing Cross area, which involved pulling down the Mews, and constructing an oblong-shaped Royal Academy of Arts along the north side of the new open space. This became the National Gallery, designed by William Wilkins and built in 1832–8 (it has much expanded since). This building set the pattern for the square in front.

The lower part of St. Martin's Lane was swept away, a total of 515 houses and other buildings, exposing the frontage of St Martin-in-the-Fields. An island on the eastern side was created for Morley's Hotel, where South Africa House (1921) now stands. On the western side today's Canada House, designed by Sir Robert Smirke, was built in 1824 to house the Union Club and the College of Physicians.

A Nelson Memorial Committee was formed in 1838 to raise money for a monument, and a competition for its design was won by William Railton: a 145-foot high fluted Corinthian column, with a 17-foot high stone statue of Nelson, sculpted by E. H. Baily, on top. It was erected by 1843, and the bronze bas-reliefs on the sides of the base, portraying his victories, were added six years later. It was not until 1867 that Sir Edwin Landseer's four bronze lions were placed around the foot of the column. The statue of Charles I still stands where it was erected in 1675.

Trafalgar Square is traditionally the focus point for rallies, demonstrations and public protests, and the whole northern area has been closed to traffic to make these events more accessible. A campaign is in hand to reduce the vast numbers of pigeons, with signs asking tourists not to feed them.

1: Haymarket
2: Sainsbury Wing
3: National Gallery
4: The Coliseum
5: St Martin-in-the-Fields
6: Strand
7: Canada House
8: Nelson's Column
9: South Africa House
10: Charing Cross
11: Landseer statues
12: Uganda House
13: Malaysia House
14: Statue of Charles I
15: Northumberland Avenue
16: Old Admiralty Offices
17: Admiralty Arch
18: Spring Gardens
19: The Phoenix Theatre
20: Whitehall

Statues in Trafalgar Square
Horatio Nelson (1758–1805), by William Railton, 1843
Charles I (1600–49), by Hubert Le Sueur, 1633
General Sir Charles Napier (1786–1860), by George Canon Adams, 1855
George IV (1762–1830), by Francis Chantrey, 1834
Major General Sir Henry Havelock, by William Behnes, 1861

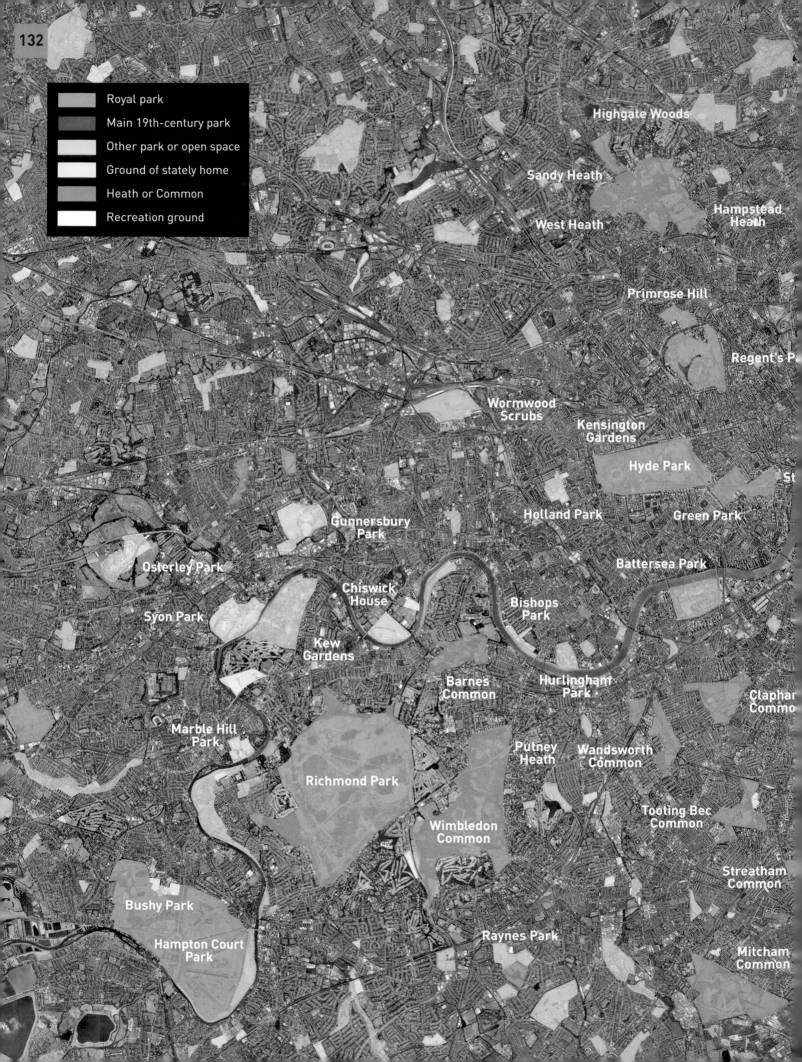

Royal park

Main 19th-century park

Other park or open space

Ground of stately home

Heath or Common

Recreation ground

Highgate Woods

Sandy Heath

West Heath

Hampstead Heath

Primrose Hill

Regent's P.

Wormwood Scrubs

Kensington Gardens

Hyde Park

St

Holland Park

Green Park

Gunnersbury Park

Osterley Park

Battersea Park

Chiswick House

Bishops Park

Syon Park

Hurlingham Park

Clapha Commo

Kew Gardens

Barnes Common

Marble Hill Park

Putney Heath

Wandsworth Common

Richmond Park

Tooting Bec Common

Wimbledon Common

Streatham Common

Bushy Park

Hampton Court Park

Raynes Park

Mitcham Common

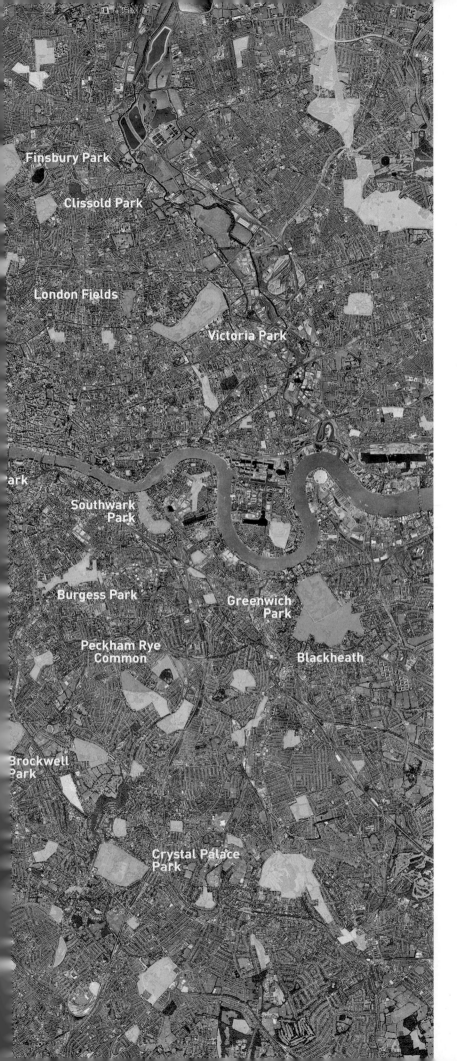

Finsbury Park

Clissold Park

London Fields

Victoria Park

...ark

Southwark Park

Burgess Park

Greenwich Park

Peckham Rye Common

Blackheath

Brockwell Park

Crystal Palace Park

GREEN LONDON

One of the delights and surprises of London is how much accessible open space there is in every area. Even in the congested City, there are around 400 green spaces. Overall, some 70 square miles of parkland illuminate London. In many squares there are public gardens, or gardens at least available to the neighbouring residents (such as Cadogan Square in Chelsea), and a large number of urban churchyards have been converted to public spaces.

The largest of the royal parks in inner London is Hyde Park, appropriated from the monks of Westminster by Henry VIII in 1536, and opened to the public in James I's reign. Kensington Gardens, originally attached to Nottingham House, which became Kensington Palace, were added to it by William IV in the early 19th century, making the combined area by far the biggest green space in central London.

Regent's Park too (see pages 134–5) was acquired by Henry VIII, after the dissolution of the abbey of Barking, the country's greatest Benedictine nunnery, in 1539. The Tudor and Stuart monarchs used it as a hunting ground, and then rented it out to farmers, who supplied London with hay and dairy products. John Nash, sponsored by the Prince Regent, planned its present 487-acre shape and the surrounding Georgian terraces, and by 1841 it was open to the public. It was badly damaged in the Second World War, but restored by 1980. Primrose Hill to the north was a favourite site for duellists in the 19th century. Green Park and St James's Park, which together make up around 150 acres of open space, are the most central in London and have long royal histories too.

Holland Park was the garden of Holland House, a magnificent Jacobean mansion belonging to the earls of Holland from the 17th century. After it was bombed in the Second World War, the house was left derelict until the London County Council bought it in 1952, restoring as much of it as possible and opening the gardens to the public.

Other parks in the inner parts of London include the little-known Archbishop's Park, formed from the gardens of Lambeth Palace and opened to the public in 1901; and the much larger Battersea Park, where the Duke of Wellington fought a duel in 1829 with Lord Winchilsea (both survived it). The present park was designed and laid out in the 1850s, with the lake and sub-tropical gardens added later. A Buddhist peace pagoda was built on the northern edge in 1985, visible from the north bank of the river.

Park Village
East

Park Village
West

Outer Circle

Cumberland
Terrace

Winfield
House

Chester
Terrace

London Central
Mosque

Open Air Theatre

Inner Circle

Chester
Gate

Hanover Gate

Cambridge
Terrace

Hanover and
Kent Terrace

1

2

The Holme

Marylebone
Green

Sussex Place

Park Square

Clarence Terrace

Clarence Gate

Ulster Terrace

Park Crescent

York Gate

Cornwall Terrace

Portland Place

York Terrace

All Soul's Church

Regent Street

REGENT'S PARK AND REGENT STREET

The future George IV assumed power as Prince Regent (because George III was suffering from senile porphyria) in 1811. In the same year the leases in Marylebone Park reverted to the crown. The architect John Nash (1752–1835) was closely associated with the Prince Regent (his wife is believed to have been the Prince's mistress), and his proposals for developing the park, and linking it with the Prince's residence in Carlton House, won a competition to determine the best design for the new estate.

The plan for Regent Street was approved by Parliament in 1813 and work began with the straight approach from Carlton House up to Piccadilly Circus, involving a huge amount of compulsory purchase and demolition. The curved quadrant was finished in 1820, and the whole route completed by 1823, making it the largest and most spectacular street development ever achieved in London.

The original idea was to turn the park into a garden city for the nobility, with a royal villa on the east side facing Cumberland Terrace and 56 other villas. Fortunately it didn't turn out that way. Only eight villas were built (one of which is the home of the US ambassador), and instead the sides of the park were lined with Nash's magnificent terraces, decorated with pediments and statues. The Zoological Society took over the gardens at the northern end in 1828. London Zoo opened to the public 20 years later, and it remains a highly popular attraction.

In Queen Mary's Gardens (which were originally called the Ring) the popular Open Air Theatre began to stage Shakespeare plays in 1932. Birdwatchers love the park for its sparrow-hawks, kestrel and tawny owls, and the herons and grey wagtails along the canal and around the lake. There are also children's playgrounds, tennis courts, rowing boats on the lake and a huge, grassy area for sports.

One of the oddest reminders of early 19th-century London is Regent's Canal, which threads across the north of the park. It opened in 1820, starting at Grand Junction in Paddington and running – occasionally through long tunnels – all the way to Hackney, where it links with the Hertford Union Canal and down to Limehouse. It was meant to be a commercial triumph, allowing goods to be transported cheaply across north London, but the arrival of the railways a few years later made it obsolete. Today it is an esoteric pleasure for Londoners in boats and narrow barges.

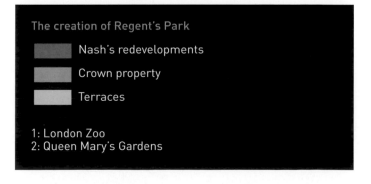

The creation of Regent's Park

Nash's redevelopments

Crown property

Terraces

1: London Zoo
2: Queen Mary's Gardens

PROTESTS AND RIOTS

London has a long history of violence, not least in protests against injustice or oppression. The best-known medieval example is the Peasants' Revolt in 1382, which began outside the city, in Kent and Essex, as a protest against the status of villeins and the unpopular and corruptly instigated poll-tax. The Kentish peasants, led by Wat Tyler, marched on London and arrived at Blackheath on 12 June, where they met Richard II; and the Essex men camped in the fields beyond Aldgate. With the support of Londoners they raided Marshalsea Prison, set fire to the archbishop's house in Lambeth, opened Fleet Prison, and assaulted John of Gaunt's Savoy Palace. The rebellion was suppressed by the end of the month, but left a powerful memory in the minds of the ruling classes. Even more violent were the Gordon Riots in June 1780 (see pages 138-9).

There have been plenty of other popular uprisings against the domination of the ruling classes, but the race riot is a particularly unpleasant modern phenomenon, of which the worst examples were at Notting Hill in 1958, and in Brixton several times in the 1980s. Poverty and unemployment are usually cited as the causes. In the 1960s a number of marches took place in protest against the Vietnam War, often involving assaults on the police. In 1990, when the government introduced plans to change the local council tax ratings system, demonstrations took place throughout the country, and many normally respectable home owners refused to pay the so-called Poll Tax – a reminder of the Peasants' Revolt. In March a demonstration was organised in Trafalgar Square, attended by at least 100,000 protestors, and ending in violence and many arrests.

In more recent times the most notable protests have been the annual countryside marches, in which country people demonstrate against urbanite ignorance of the issues which affect them; and the huge demonstrations in 2003 against the war on Iraq. Although many marchers clearly showed their intense feelings about both these issues, no violence was involved.

626 YEARS OF VIOLENT DEMONSTRATIONS

1377 Londoners riot and attack John of Gaunt's Savoy Palace (15).

1450 Led by Jack Cade, rioters revolt against excessive taxes, encamp at Blackheath (16), occupy Southwark, pillage London and kill the Treasurer and the Sheriff of Kent.

1497 Rebels against taxation, led from Cornwall and Somerset by Lord Audley, are defeated by Henry VII's troops at the Battle of Blackheath.

1517 Evil May Day riots. Artisans and apprentices, led by John Lincoln, attack properties of foreign workers in Stepney. 135 Flemings are killed.(17)

1605 On 5 November a group of extremist Roman Catholics attempt to blow up Parliament and King James I. The foiling of the Gunpowder Plot has been annually commemorated by Londoners ever since. (18)

1642 In October, after the first major battle in the Civil War at Edgehill in Warwickshire, Parliament erects a massive circuit of defences around London – banks and ditches running between a series of forts, from Millbank (2) to Hyde Park Corner (3), up to Shoreditch and down to Wapping, and from Bermondsey to Vauxhall (see opposite).

1710 Anti-Whig riots in support of Dr Henry Sacheverall, on trial in the House of Lords for preaching a sermon at St. Paul's (19) attacking the Whig government and the proposed Hanoverian succession.

1719 Spitalfields (20) weavers riot against Indian calico imports.

1736 Spitalfields weavers riot against Irish immigrants, accusing them of accepting work at low wages.

1767 Riots in support of the radical John Wilkes, elected to Parliament for Middlesex, but excluded by the House of Commons. His statue stands in Fetter Lane (21) (see pages 38–9).

1780 The Gordon Riots, 2–9 June (see pages 138–9) (22).

1809 'Old Prices' riots take place for 61 nights (September to November), protesting about the increased seat prices at the newly built Theatre Royal in Covent Garden (23).

1810 Riots occur in April in protest at the arrest, and imprisonment in The Tower (24), of Sir Francis Burdett for advocating parliamentary reform.

1816 A meeting in December at Spa Field in Clerkenwell (25), to urge the Prince Regent to initiate parliamentary reforms including universal male suffrage and secret ballots, leads to a riot, attacks on The Tower(24), robbery of a gunsmith's shop in Snow Hill (26), and an assault on the Royal Exchange.

1817 The Prince Regent's carriage is mobbed in Westminster (27).

1820 A group of conspirators led by Arthur Thistlewood, planning to assassinate the Cabinet, are arrested for treason in Cato Street (28). They are subsequently hanged, and then beheaded.

1834 In April, police disperse 30,000 trade union protestors, gathered at Copenhagen Fields (29), Clerkenwell to support the Tolpuddle Martyrs. Juries acquit the accused of injuring police, on the grounds of self-defence.

1848 In April, a major Chartist demonstration is organised on Kennington Common (30), campaigning for political equality and social justice. The Duke of Wellington organises defences including enlisting 170,000 special constables.

1855 Protestors fight police in Hyde Park (31) as 50,000 demonstrate against Lord Grosvenor's Sunday Trading Bill.

1859 In June, violent anti-ritualist demonstrations at St-George's-in-the-East (32), Wapping, continuing for several months.

1866 Police break up violent demonstrations at a Reform League meeting in Hyde Park (31).

1886 In the coldest February for 30 years, unemployed Londoners demonstrate in the West End and around Hyde Park.

1887 Police and soldiers ride down impoverished demonstrators in Trafalgar Square (33) during 'Bloody Sunday' (November). Skirmishes continue into December, including a major brawl in Westminster Abbey.

1911 The Siege of Sydney Street (34) in January, in which police and troops, overseen by the Home Secretary, Winston Churchill, are deployed against two alleged Russian anarchists.

1912 Suffragettes smash shop windows in the West End (35).

1913 In April, the suffragette leader Mrs Pankhurst is imprisoned for inciting her supporters to bomb Lloyd George's home in Surrey (36).

1914 The Women's Social and Political Union is banned from meeting in Hyde Park (31), leading to numerous clashes with the police.

1914 A suffragette bombs the coronation chair at Westminster Abbey (37).

1932 The culmination of the National Unemployed Workers Movement's fourth hunger march sees police driven out of Hyde Park (31).

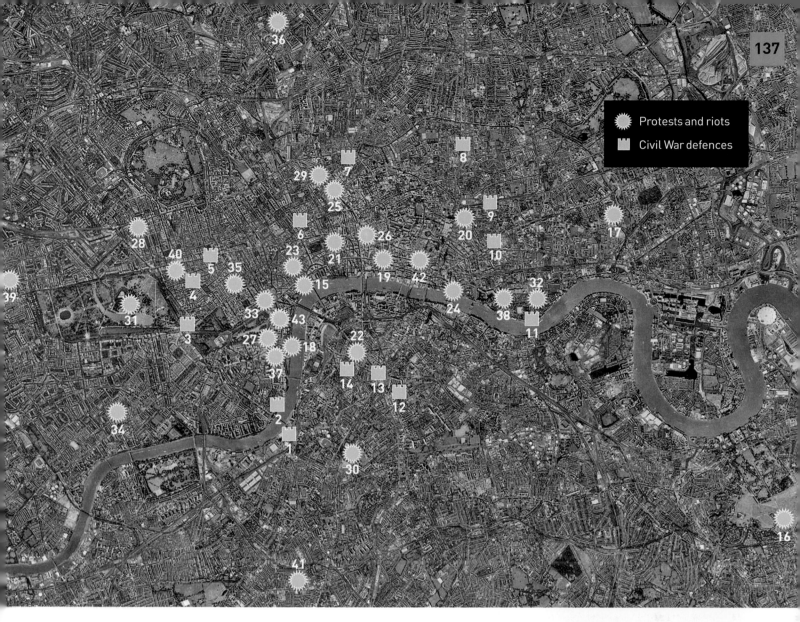

Protests and riots

Civil War defences

1933 In July a rally is held in Hyde Park (31) to protest at the treatment of Jews in Germany.

1936 In the Battle of Cable Street, anti-fascists halt Oswald Mosley's provocative BUF march into Whitechapel (38).

1958 Notting Hill (39) racially motivated riots in August.

1968 In March, up to 100,000 people demonstrate in anti-Vietnam War protests outside the American Embassy in Grosvenor Square (40).

1976 In August, rioting occurs at the end of the Notting Hill Carnival.

1981 Severe rioting and arson in Brixton (41) in April, motivated by racism, housing shortage, and hostility to the police.

1985 Riots in Brixton (41) and the Broadwater Farm Estate in Tottenham on successive weekends, following the death of a black woman in police custody. A police constable is killed.

1987 A woman is stabbed during rioting at the Notting Hill Carnival.

1990 Poll Tax riots in Trafalgar Square (33).

1994 Demonstrations in Hyde Park (31), against a new Criminal Justice Bill.

1999 Heavy rioting during anti-capitalist protests in the City (42).

2000 A Countryside Alliance march, from Hyde Park, across Blackfriars Bridge to Whitehall (43), involved around 400,000 peaceful demonstrators.

2003 Over 200,000 peaceful marchers demonstrate against the Iraq war, converging from different directions at Piccadilly Circus and heading for Hyde Park (31).

London Civil War defences
 1: Vauxhall Fort
 2: Millbank Fort
 3: Hyde Park Corner Forts
 4: Mount Row Battery
 5: Great Russell Street and
    Wardour Street Forts and
    Batteries
 6: Great Ormond Street Fort
 7: New River Head Fort
 8: Kingsland Road Forts
 9: Brick Lane Fort or Battery
10: Whitechapel Road Fort or
    Battery
11: Wapping Fort or Battery
12: Old Kent Road Fort
13: Elephant and Castle Fort
14: Imperial War Museum Fort

Clerkenwell Prison ⑥

Moorfields ⑤

Newgate Prison ⑥

Lincoln's Inn Fields ④

Bank of England ⑥

Bow Street ⑥

Fleet Prison ⑥

Warwick Street ④

The Clink ⑥

③

②

King's Bench ⑥

House of Commons

①

Geraldine Mary Harmsworth Park

● Sequence of events

👥 Asssembly point, 2 June 1780

⬅ Movement of rioters

👑 Locations burned

⬛ Cavalry troop

❚❚ Infantry companies

━━ Government patrol routes

THE GORDON RIOTS

After the Reformation, anti-Catholic feeling ran high throughout Britain. Anglicans believed that the prime allegiance of Catholics was to the Pope, and that therefore they were all potential traitors to the monarchy. 'Papist' was a term of abuse, and a cry of 'no popery' would rouse English fear and anger. A series of laws penalising Catholics was passed in the reign of William III, excluding them from voting or from holding any professional or public office. They were also banned from university education, from buying land, and even from marrying Protestant women.

By the second half of the 18th century a rather more liberal view was growing in some political circles, and the first Catholic Relief Act was passed under Lord North's government in 1778, repealing a number of these penal laws in Ireland. The Act aroused passionate anti-Catholic fears among many Londoners, and in 1780 Lord George Gordon, the leader of the Protestant Association, agreed to lead a protest march.

A crowd of 50,000 anti-Catholic protestors assembled on Friday, 2 June in St George's Fields in Lambeth (now Geraldine Mary Harmsworth Park, from which many other protests have since begun), marched across Westminster Bridge and began to invade the House of Commons. A squadron of dragoons was called up, Gordon lost control of the crowd, and although some were arrested in Parliament Square, the majority broke away and made their way towards the City. That evening, riots broke out in Lincoln's Inn Fields, and the mob plundered and set fire to the Sardinian ambassador's private chapel.

The next day was relatively quiet, but on Sunday morning Catholic chapels in Moorfields and further east in Spitalfields were looted and set alight. By Monday, it was no longer an anti-Catholic riot: attacks on the Irish, and indeed the London authorities, spread all over the city. Londoners supporting the rioters wore a blue cockade to show their allegiance, and displayed blue flags marked 'No Popery'. Shops everywhere were closed. Some of the troops ordered in to control the riots seemed sympathetic, and the attacks snowballed. Newgate Prison was set on fire, allowing prisoners to escape, and then the same happened at other prisons: Clerkenwell, the Fleet, King's Bench and the Clink. Other targets included Langdale's distillery, next to Barnard's Inn in Holborn, the Lord Chief Justice's house in Bloomsbury Square, Sir John Fielding's house in Bow Street; and even Downing Street and the Bank of England were attacked, but defended.

By 9 June it was over. Hundreds of rioters were arrested, and in due course 25 were hanged. Gordon was arrested for high treason and imprisoned in the Tower, but eventually acquitted. He subsequently converted to Judaism. Seven years later he was arrested again for criminal libel against Marie Antoinette, and he died in Newgate Prison.

Chronology of the Riots
1: Friday, 2 June 1780 – 50,000 anti-Catholic protestors assemble in St George's Fields.
2: Marchers cross Westminster Bridge and attack the House of Commons.
3: Rioters move towards the City.
4: Evening of 2 June – Rioting in Lincoln's Inn Fields. Sardinian Ambassador's chapel burned. Chapel in Warwick Street attacked.
5: Sunday, 4 June – Catholic chapels in Moorfields and Spitalfields attacked.
6: Tuesday, 6 June – Attacks on prisons at Newgate and Clerkenwell, the Fleet, King's Bench and the Clink. Holborn distillery of Mr Langdale burned. Sir John Fielding's house in Bow Street attacked. Bank of England attacked.

	1847 Street plan		Street names c.1847
	Buildings that have disappeared		Modern street names
	Buildings that still exist		

LONDON IRISH IN 1850

The devastating famine and disease that afflicted Ireland from 1845, when the potato crop failed for several years, led to massive emigrations. Hundreds of thousands of Irish people left the country, mostly for the USA and Canada, but as many as 250,000 came to Britain, nearly half of whom ended up in London. Most were desperately poor, and in London they tended to make for the most decayed areas, little better than ghettoes.

St Giles-in-the-Fields was the worst of these. There has been something sinister about this area from the earliest times. Henry I's wife, Queen Matilda, founded a leper hospital there in 1101, dedicating it to St Giles as the patron saint of outcasts. Condemned prisoners stopped at the chapel there on their way to execution at Tyburn. And this was where the Great Plague started in 1665, overcrowding its graveyards with the victims. By the 19th century, it was a notorious area of drunkenness, slums and desperate poverty, although the opening of New Oxford Street in 1847 had cut through some of the worst of it. The area circled by Dyott Street, Bainbridge Street and St Giles High Street was the 'Rookeries', a maze of narrow alleys and yards with rotting tenements and cellars. This is where most of the Irish immigrants found themselves, and soon it was known as 'Little Dublin'.

Henry Mayhew, in his masterpiece *London Labour and the London Poor* (1851), identifies what he calls the 'Irish nests', where the Irish communities were confined. There was Brook

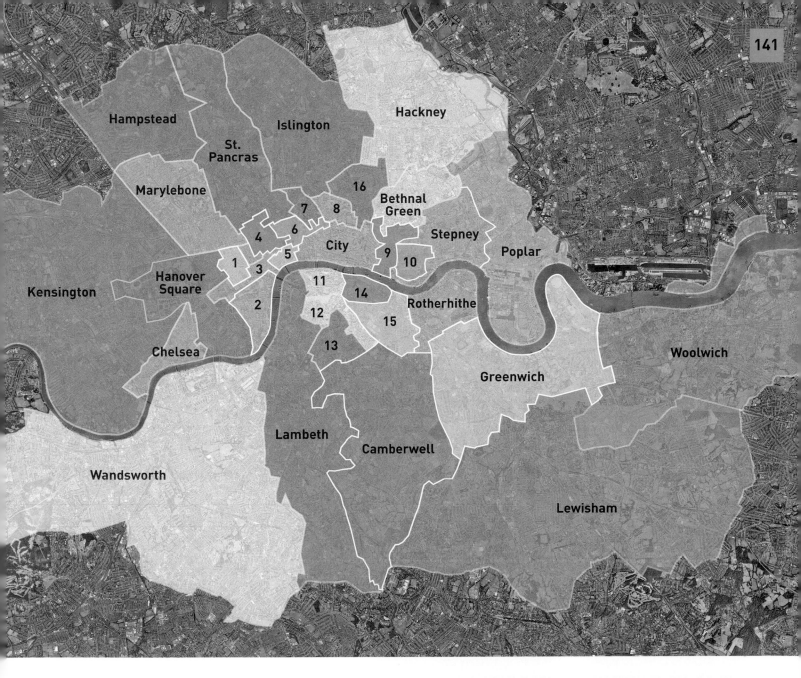

Street in Hackney, near the church of St Barnabas; Cromer Street in St Pancras; Saffron Hill and King Street in Holborn; but apart from St Giles the biggest Irish community was in Whitechapel, particularly down Commercial Road, at Ratcliff Cross, and in the yards and alleys adjoining Rosemary Lane. One of the five Whitechapel murder victims was Irish. Charles Booth's poverty map (see pages 94–5) shows that some of these streets in Whitechapel were still, 30 years later, among the poorest slums in London, or as he put it, 'lowest class, vicious, semi-criminal', or 'very poor, casual, chronic want'. The worst were just to the west of Brick Lane.

Today the Irish community in London is large and energetic, and contributes substantially to the city's economy. On St Patrick's Day, along with other Londoners, the Irish community can be seen celebrating in public houses all over the city. A popular central meeting place is O'Neill's in New Row, Covent Garden.

London Irish population 1850
Proportion of total population

- 0–1.9%
- 2–3.9%
- 4–5.9%
- 6–7.9%
- 8–9.9%
- 10% and over

1: St. James
2: Westminster
3: St. Martin
4: St. Giles
5: Strand
6: Holborn
7: Clerkenwell
8: St. Luke
9: Whitechapel
10: St. George in the East
11: St. Saviour
12: St. George
13: Newington
14: St. Olave, Southwark
15: Bermondsey
16: Shoreditch

IMMIGRANT COMMUNITIES

For many centuries London has housed immigrants from all over the world, attracted by economic opportunity or seeing it as a refuge from persecution. Foreign communities have expanded and prospered here throughout history, contributing to London's energy and growth. As the British Empire rapidly expanded during the 19th century, immigrants from China, India and the Caribbean were the main newcomers. After the Great Famine, one in twenty of all Londoners were Irish. Pogroms in Russia and Poland towards the end of the century led to the arrival of many Jews; and 30,000 Germans were living in London before the First World War. The 20th century has seen the arrival of many more immigrants from the West Indies, Africa and the Indian subcontinent, as well as Greek and Turkish Cypriots, Poles, Indonesians, and Vietnamese. Since the 1960s, the West End has developed its own Chinatown.

But every time a large group of foreigners has appeared in London, they have had to endure hostility and discrimination. The Jews and Irish faced widespread religious intolerance and opprobrium, and at different times racial hatred and harassment has afflicted incomers from all parts of the world. This is still the case, particularly in poorer areas such as Tower Hamlets. And yet London remains one of the most ethnically and culturally diverse cities in the world, with nearly one and a half million non-white citizens.

Sometimes the incoming communities adopted particular areas of the city – the Huguenots in Soho, the Sephardim Jews in Whitechapel – but more usually they became integrated within the indigenous population. Certain areas are still associated with particular communities, even though many live outside of them, often because a native institution is based there. The Polish Social and Cultural Association is based in King Street, Hammersmith, and many Poles live in the neighbourhood. There is a Vietnamese Catholic church in Bow Common Lane, so many Vietnamese live in Poplar and Mile End. The Turkish Advisory and Welfare Centre is in Sydenham Road (SE26), so many Turks live nearby. There are Japanese communities in East Acton and St John's Wood.

Southall is home to a large proportion of Londoners with Indian, Pakistani, Sri Lankan and Bangladeshi origins. Many Jamaicans and other Caribbeans live in Brixton and Stockwell, and although there have been racial crises in recent times they have played a major role in revitalising these London areas and forging a new identity for them.

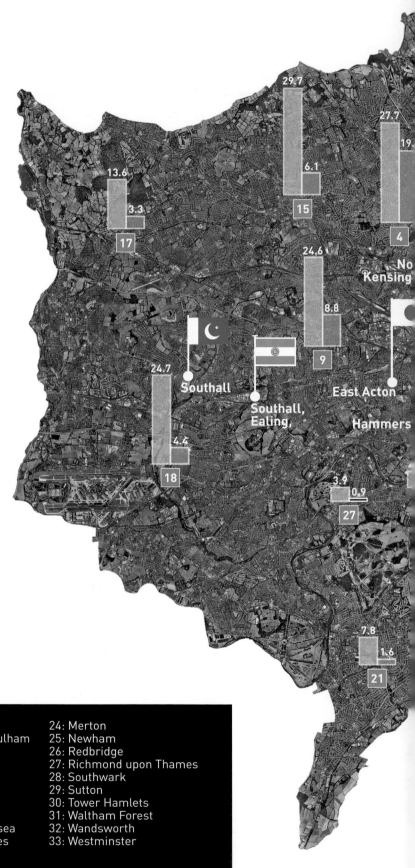

London boroughs
1: Barking and Dagenham
2: Barnet
3: Bexley
4: Brent
5: Bromley
6: Camden
7: City of London
8: Croydon
9: Ealing
10: Enfield
11: Greenwich
12: Hackney
13: Hammersmith and Fulham
14: Haringey
15: Harrow
16: Havering
17: Hillingdon
18: Hounslow
19: Islington
20: Kensington and Chelsea
21: Kingston upon Thames
22: Lambeth
23: Lewisham
24: Merton
25: Newham
26: Redbridge
27: Richmond upon Thames
28: Southwark
29: Sutton
30: Tower Hamlets
31: Waltham Forest
32: Wandsworth
33: Westminster

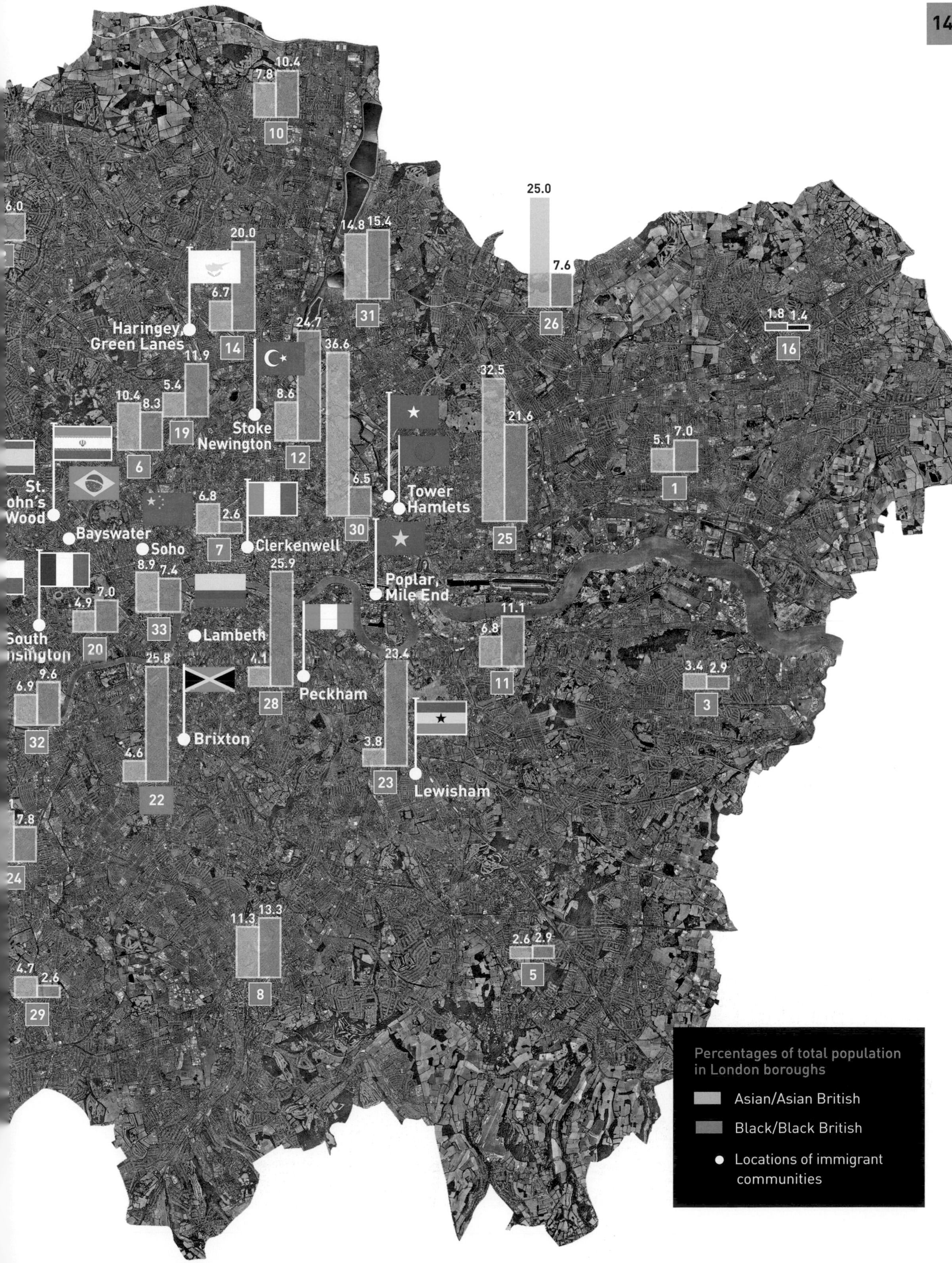

6.0

10.4
7.8

10

25.0

14.8 15.4

7.6

31

26

20.0

6.7

Haringey,
Green Lanes

14

24.7

1.8 1.4

16

11.9

19

5.4

36.6

32.5

8.6

Stoke
Newington

12

21.6

5.1 7.0

1

10.4
8.3

6

6.5

25

30

Tower
Hamlets

St.
John's
Wood

6.8
2.6

7

Clerkenwell

Bayswater

Soho

Poplar,
Mile End

8.9 7.4

25.9

11.1

3.4 2.9

3

4.9 7.0

33

6.8

20

South
Kensington

Lambeth

4.1

11

9.6
6.9

25.8

32

23.4

28

Peckham

Brixton

3.8

23

Lewisham

4.6

22

1
7.8

24

11.3 13.3

8

2.6 2.9

5

4.7 2.6

29

Percentages of total population
in London boroughs

Asian/Asian British

Black/Black British

● Locations of immigrant
communities

THE MEDIA

Fleet Street was the centre of printing and publishing in London for hundreds of years. Wynkin de Worde, who took over William Caxton's business in Westminster after his death in 1491, set up his own printing press in 1500 opposite Shoe Lane; and Richard Pynson (Henry VIII's printer) established his press at the corner of Fleet Street and Chancery Lane in the same year. Dozens more followed, until in 1986 the main newspapers moved eastwards.

By the 18th century, daily and weekly news journals were on offer in the growing mass of coffee houses and taverns in the City, all printed in or around Fleet Street. The printers were the publishers, and produced newspapers as well as books. A publisher called J. Shuckburgh, one of my ancestors, owned a printing works at the Sun, next to the Inner Temple, in 1749. William Woodfall, editor of one of the first newspapers, the *Morning Chronicle*, lived in Salisbury Square, and set up the *Diary* in 1789. The publishers John Murray were based at 32 Fleet Street until they moved to their present premises in Albemarle Street in 1812.

In the 19th and 20th centuries the road was dominated by national newspapers such as the *Daily Telegraph* (founded in 1855) and the *Daily Express* (founded in 1900). Today, only Reuter's, the world's leading electronic publisher, founded in 1851, remains there at number 85. The cause of the move was Rupert Murdoch's determination to suppress the restrictive 'Spanish practices' of London printers and their trade unions, in order to introduce new technology. He dismissed 5,000 employees who refused to sign a no-strike deal when his News International business moved to Docklands.

Just down the road off the Strand, at Savoy Hill, the BBC started broadcasting its first daily programmes in 1922. Within five years it was hopelessly overcrowded, and a striking new building was designed for them on the corner of Portland Place and Langham Street. It was completed by 1932, and expanded in the 1960s. The world's first television transmitter was erected in 1936 at Alexandra Palace, and in 1949 the BBC acquired a three-acre site in Shepherd's Bush, on which its Television Centre was built by 1960. Independent television broadcasting began in 1955, and today two companies – Carlton (based at 25 Knightsbridge) and LWT (in Upper Ground on the South Bank) – are licensed in London, although Londoners have access to hundreds of different commercial channels. Sky television, now based in Grant Way, Isleworth, launched the first British satellite service in 1989, and digital television in 1998.

Magazines have been the growth journalistic product in London in the 20th century. Many hundreds are produced weekly or monthly, on every conceivable topic from Acoustics to Zoology. Among the best sellers, *Vogue* has its headquarters at Vogue House in Hanover Square.

Locations of Fleet Street newspapers

1: Next to the King's Arms by Fleet Bridge
   Daily Courant (1702–35)
   Daily Post (1719–46)
   Daily Journal (1721–37)
2: Red Lion Court
   Gentleman's Magazine (1731–1907)
3: Printing House Square
   The Times (1785–1986)
4: Bouverie Street
   Daily News (1884–1930)
   Star (1928–30)
   Punch (1930–69)
   News of the World (1932–86)
5: 85 Fleet Street
   Reuters
6: 120 Fleet Street
   Daily News (1846–84)
   Daily Express (1930–1988)
7: 127 Fleet Street
   Morning Advertiser (1815–1928)
8: 141 Fleet Street
   Daily Telegraph (1882–1988)
9: 183 Fleet Street
   Political Register
10: 186 Fleet Street
   Dundee Evening Telegraph
   People's Journal
11: Corner of Shoe Lane and Fleet Street
   Liverpool Daily Post
12: Corner of Shoe Lane and Plumtree Court
   Evening Standard
13: Crane Court
   No.9: *Punch* (1841–1930)
   No.10: *Illustrated London News* (1842–?)
14: Salisbury Square
   Lloyd's Weekly Newspaper (1842–1914)
   Daily Chronicle (1869–1930)
   News Chronicle (1930–60)
15: Whitefriars Street
   Evening News (1894–96)
   Daily Mirror (1905–25)
   News of the World (1892–1932)
16: Carmelite House, Carmelite Street/
   Tallis Street
   Daily Mail (1896–1927)
   Daily Mirror (1903–05)
   Evening News (1896–1960)
17: New Carmelite House
   Associated Newspapers (1936–86)
18: Bream's Buildings
   Daily Mirror (1925–60)
19: Tudor Street
   Institute of Journalists (now in Docklands)
20: Northcliffe House, Tudor Street
   Daily Mail (1927–86)
21: Falcon Court, Fleet Street
   John Murray Publishers (1769–1812)
22: Holborn Circus (now the Sainsbury Business
   Centre)
   Daily Mirror (1960–88)
   Daily Herald (1960–4)
   Sun (1964–69)

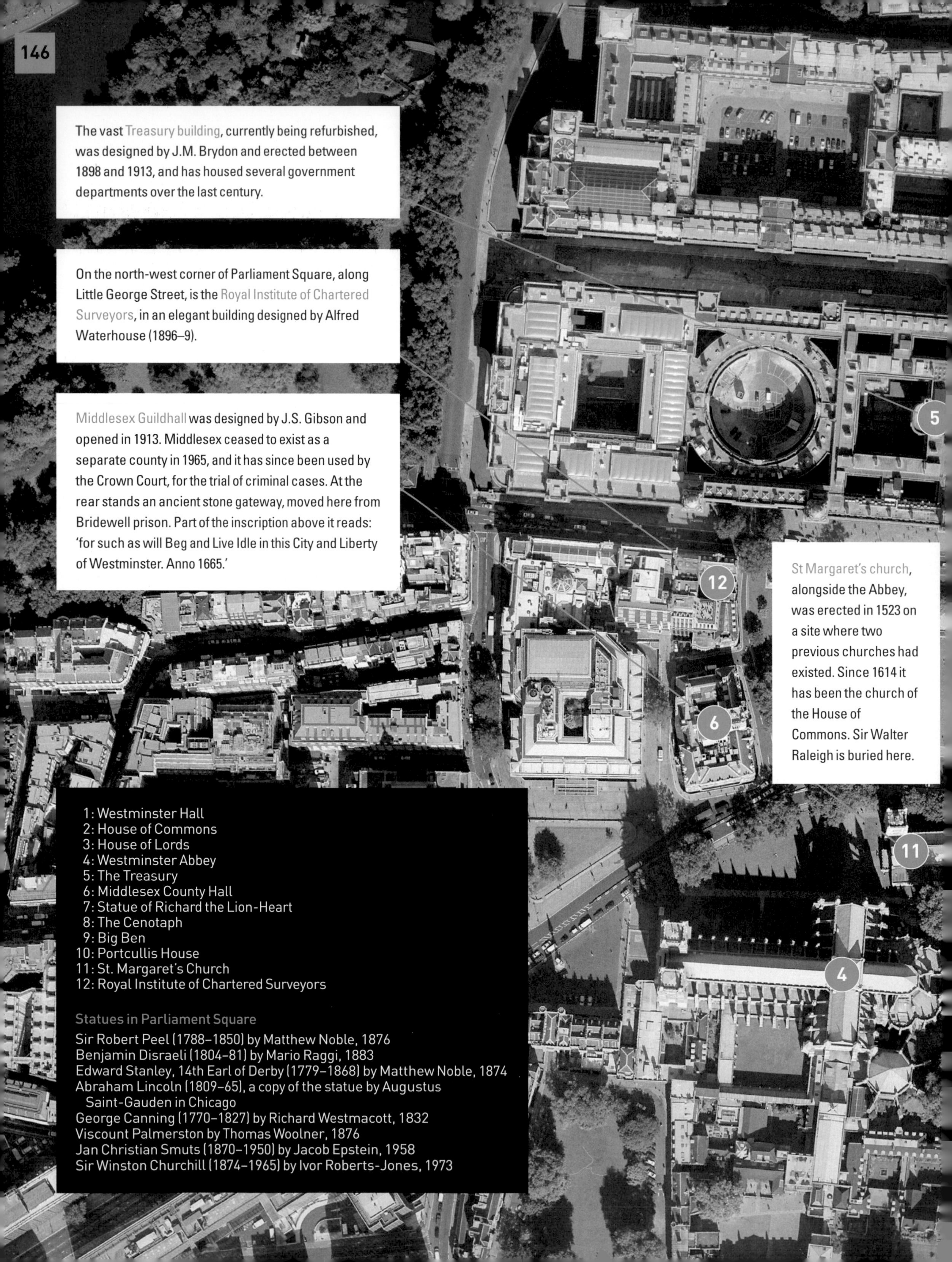

The vast Treasury building, currently being refurbished, was designed by J.M. Brydon and erected between 1898 and 1913, and has housed several government departments over the last century.

On the north-west corner of Parliament Square, along Little George Street, is the Royal Institute of Chartered Surveyors, in an elegant building designed by Alfred Waterhouse (1896–9).

Middlesex Guildhall was designed by J.S. Gibson and opened in 1913. Middlesex ceased to exist as a separate county in 1965, and it has since been used by the Crown Court, for the trial of criminal cases. At the rear stands an ancient stone gateway, moved here from Bridewell prison. Part of the inscription above it reads: 'for such as will Beg and Live Idle in this City and Liberty of Westminster. Anno 1665.'

St Margaret's church, alongside the Abbey, was erected in 1523 on a site where two previous churches had existed. Since 1614 it has been the church of the House of Commons. Sir Walter Raleigh is buried here.

1: Westminster Hall
2: House of Commons
3: House of Lords
4: Westminster Abbey
5: The Treasury
6: Middlesex County Hall
7: Statue of Richard the Lion-Heart
8: The Cenotaph
9: Big Ben
10: Portcullis House
11: St. Margaret's Church
12: Royal Institute of Chartered Surveyors

Statues in Parliament Square

Sir Robert Peel (1788–1850) by Matthew Noble, 1876
Benjamin Disraeli (1804–81) by Mario Raggi, 1883
Edward Stanley, 14th Earl of Derby (1779–1868) by Matthew Noble, 1874
Abraham Lincoln (1809–65), a copy of the statue by Augustus
   Saint-Gauden in Chicago
George Canning (1770–1827) by Richard Westmacott, 1832
Viscount Palmerston by Thomas Woolner, 1876
Jan Christian Smuts (1870–1950) by Jacob Epstein, 1958
Sir Winston Churchill (1874–1965) by Ivor Roberts-Jones, 1973

THE STORY OF PARLIAMENT SQUARE

Although there is evidence of a Roman settlement at Westminster, upstream from Londinium, the origins of the Abbey are obscure. It is mentioned in the regularis concordia of c. 970 which established Benedictine monasticism as the standard for English churches, and it was already associated with royalty when Edward the Confessor decided to move his main royal residence there in order to oversee a spectacular redevelopment of the church, starting in about 1050. After the Norman conquest Westminster Palace remained a favourite of the Plantagenet kings, and under Henry II it became the country's centre of government.

Westminster Hall, designed by William Rufus and built in 1099, and the only surviving part of the palace, has fulfilled various functions in the succeeding centuries: a banqueting hall, a house of lords, the law courts (until 1882) and a shopping mall. Charles I was tried and condemned here, as was Guy Fawkes in 1606. The bodies of William Gladstone, Edward VII, Winston Churchill and Queen Elizabeth, the Queen Mother, lay in state here. The rest of the palace, to which rambling additions were made throughout the Middle Ages, was subject to frequent fires. One in 1698 destroyed most of Whitehall, and in 1835 the whole palace except for the Hall was burned down. For the first time, Parliament could have a building specially designed for the purpose, and architects were invited to submit plans 'in the Gothic or Elizabethan style'. Charles Barry, assisted by A.W. Pugin, won the competition over 96 other submissions, and in 1851 the Houses of Parliament were opened, their whole interior gorgeously and intricately decorated to Pugin's designs. The clock tower, known as Big Ben, was added in 1858. In the Second World War the building was frequently attacked by German bombers, and the north end of the House of Commons was more or less destroyed. It was rebuilt by 1950, following Barry's design but simplifying Pugin's decoration.

None of Edward the Confessor's Abbey remains visible. The present building was conceived in 1245 in the reign of Henry III. Influenced by the king's desire to reproduce the Gothic style of French cathedrals and Sainte Chapelle in Paris, the project took four centuries to complete, though by his death in 1272 much of the eastern end was complete. The nave was added, in the original style, from 1376; and apart from the western towers the entire abbey was completed, with the added chapels, by 1532. The towers above the entrance were designed by Nicholas Hawksmoor, under the surveyance of Sir Christopher Wren, and finally completed in 1745. The abbey is packed with tombs and monuments, from medieval, Tudor and Stuart monarchs to 19th-century statesmen. The first poet to be buried in Poet's Corner in the south transept was Geoffrey Chaucer in 1400. A recent addition to the square is the controversial but impressive Portcullis House (2000), built on top of Westminster underground station. It was designed by Sir Michael Hopkins to provide members of parliament and their staff with more space and facilities

LOCAL GOVERNMENT

Greater London is an area of about 610 square miles, with a resident population of approximately 7 million. London comprises two cities (London and Westminster) and 31 boroughs. The government and management of this enormous and complex metropolis has undergone several changes over the last 150 years.

The first step was the creation of the Metropolitan Board of Works in 1855, with members elected from local parishes. In 1889 it was replaced by the London County Council (LCC), elected directly by London citizens, and housed after 1922 in the monumental County Hall on the South Bank. In the early decades the Liberals held control, from 1907 to 1934 it was Conservative-led, and after that the Labour Party took over until the LCC was replaced in 1965 by the Greater London Council (GLC), part of a major national reorganisation of local government. The GLC too operated on party political lines, with both leading parties in control for roughly equal successive periods. It was abolished in 1986, and its powers diverted to the London boroughs.

For a while thereafter, London was the only capital city in the western world with no co-ordinating authority. New organisations were set up to manage services like London's fire brigade, waste disposal, transport, education and health. In 1999, the Labour government introduced the Greater London Authority Act, providing for a directly-elected London Assembly and a Mayor of London, with a duty to develop London-wide strategies on issues like policing, transport, fire and emergencies, cultural affairs, the environment, health concerns, and the promotion of London to the outside world. The London Assembly works in conjunction with local coucils and other major service providers.

The borough councils are directly elected by their local residents, and most in London are currently Labour-controlled. They are responsible for a range of social services, including care for the elderly and disabled; council housing; nursery provision; primary, secondary and adult education; refuse and recycling; road maintenance; parks and cemeteries; and protecting the local environment. In 2000, the Association of London Government was formed to assist the individual councils in working together on all these issues, and to lobby the national government for resources to benefit London.

Ken Livingston was elected mayor in 2000. He has concentrated primarily on transport problems, creating a new organisation called Transport for London, and introducing congestion charges for those driving into inner London.

London boroughs and their town halls

1: Barking & Dagenham, Civic Centre, Dagenham, Essex
2: Barnet, Town Hall, The Burroughs, Hendon
3: Bexley, Broadway, Bexleyheath, Kent
4: Brent, Imperial Life House, 390–400 High Road, Wembley, Middlesex
5: Bromley, Civic Centre, Stockwell Close, Bromley
6: Camden, Town Hall, Judd Street
7: Corporation of London (City), Guildhall
8: Croydon, Town Hall, Katharine Street, Croydon
9: Ealing, Perceval House, 14–16 Uxbridge Road
10: Enfield, Civic Centre, Silver Street, Enfield

11: Greenwich, Woolwich Town Hall, Wellington Street
12: Hackney, Hackney Town Hall, Mare Street
13: Hammersmith & Fulham, Town Hall, King Street
14: Harringay, Civic Centre, High Road
15: Harrow, Civic Centre, Station Road, Harrow, Middlesex
16: Havering, Town Hall, Main Road, Romford, Essex
17: Hillingdon, Civic Centre, High Street, Uxbridge, Middlesex
18: Hounslow, Civic Centre, Lampton Road, Hounslow
19: Islington, Town Hall, Upper Street
20: Kensington & Chelsea, Town Hall, Hornton Street
21: Kingston, Guildhall, High Street, Kingston-upon-Thames

22: Lambeth, Lambeth Town Hall, Brixton Hill
23: Lewisham, Town Hall, Catford
24: Merton, Civic Centre, London Road, Morden, Surrey
25: Newham, Town Hall, Barking Road, East Ham
26: Redbridge, Town Hall, Ilford
27: Richmond, Civic Centre, 44 York Street, Twickenham
28: Southwark, Town Hall, Peckham Road
29: Sutton, Civic Offices, Nicholas Way, Sutton, Surrey
30: Tower Hamlets, Town Hall, Mulberry Place, 5 Clove Crescent
31: Waltham Forest, Town Hall, Forest Road
32: Wandsworth, Town Hall, Wandsworth High Street
33: Westminster, City Hall, 64 Victoria Street

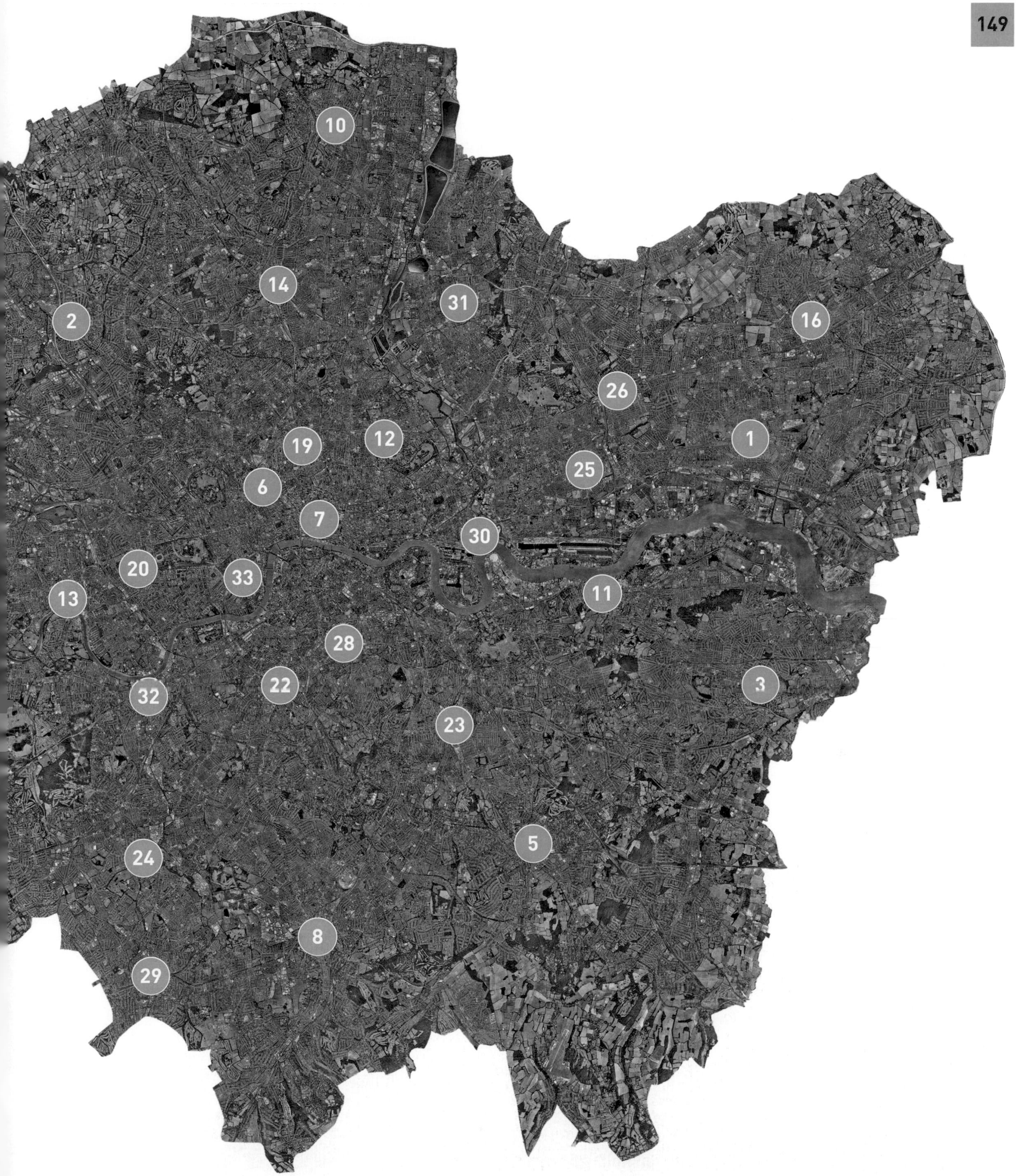
10
14
31
2
16
26
19
12
1
25
6
7
30
20
33
13
11
28
22
32
3
23
5
24
8
29

THE BRITISH LIBRARY

When the British Museum was opened in 1759, it included a Department of Printed Books, some of which had been donated by George II. Over the next two centuries it grew to become one of the largest libraries in the world. Its spectacular domed reading room and surrounding book stacks were built in the Museum's courtyard in 1852–7, and attracted scores of great scholars and writers, including Charles Dickens, George Bernard Shaw and Virginia Woolf, as well as Lenin and Karl Marx. Fifty years later it was already clear that space in the museum would run out, and various steps were taken to alleviate this problem: parts of the collections, such as the newspaper library, were transferred elsewhere. Plans to create a new building next door were overruled in the 1970s, and eyes fell on the nearest large vacant site, a derelict goods yard immediately to the west of St Pancras Station. The site was bought in 1976.

The St Pancras building was designed by Colin St John Wilson, whose original plan was to fill the entire site, from Euston Road to Brill Street. Construction started in 1980, but there were endless delays and rising costs. In 1988, the plan had to be reduced to two-thirds of its original size. It was finally opened in June 1990 by the Queen.

Through a portico on Euston Road, you enter a spacious open piazza. At the front of the library are rooms open to the public, a book shop and an exhibition hall. Beyond are a range of reading rooms, with the King's library, that of George III (donated in the 18th century by his son, George IV) on display on the first floor. Access to the reading rooms is only allowed to those with a pass. To be granted a pass you have to demonstrate that you have reached a point in your research where no other library can supply the information you need. Most of the books are stored underneath the building, in a carefully temperature-controlled environment. In addition to the museum's library, the new British Library comprises three other major national collections, the National Central Library, the National Lending Library for Science and Technology, and the Patent Office Library.

The London Library at 14 St James's Square is a rather smaller, privately-run library founded in 1841 at the instigation of Thomas Carlyle, who had had a frustrating morning waiting for several hours in the British Museum for a book to be delivered. It contains around a million books, and is funded by the subscriptions of its members. Its coverage is mainly in the humanities, with particular emphasis on literature and history.

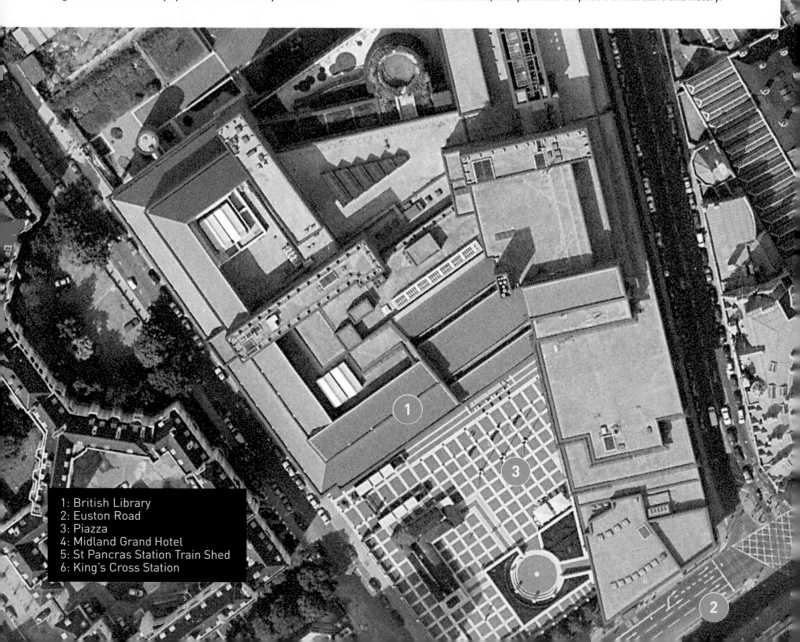

1: British Library
2: Euston Road
3: Piazza
4: Midland Grand Hotel
5: St Pancras Station Train Shed
6: King's Cross Station

ST PANCRAS STATION AND THE MIDLAND GRAND HOTEL

Next door to the British Library is the remarkable St Pancras Station, fronted by its grade 1 listed Midland Grand Hotel. When the Midland Railway company bought the site in 1863, it was one of London's worst slums. They commissioned the long and broad glass and iron train shed from W. H. Barlow, and held a competition for the design of the hotel to form its façade on the Euston Road. The winner was Sir George Gilbert Scott. His high Gothic design of pinnacles, towers and gables, completed in 1872, is the most strikingly beautiful Victorian building in London.

The 250-bedroom hotel, with its long, curving dining room and elegant staircase, was for a while regarded as one of the city's most luxurious. It closed in 1935, was converted to offices for railway staff and was damaged in the Second World War. In the 1960s there was a serious possibility that it might be demolished, but it was saved by a campaign led by Sir John Betjeman and the Victorian Society. Since then, there have been endless debates about its future. In the 1990s British Rail and English Heritage spent large sums restoring the outside, but within it continues to decay.

Now a massive new plan is under way, expected to be complete by 2008. The station will become the principal London terminus for Eurostar trains, with its platforms increased from eight to thirteen. The train shed will be elegantly restored, and the extensions covered with a new roof of glass and steel. A new Underground booking hall, situated beneath the hotel, has been designed by the architects Allies & Morrison. The hotel itself will be converted into luxury apartments on the upper floors, and its grand reception rooms restored as restaurants and bars, with a new four-storey annexe of hotel bedrooms along the west side. All of this has been designed by the award-winning Renton Howard Wood Levin Partnership.

So St Pancras will be reborn. Neighbouring King's Cross station is the next restoration target. Over the coming decade this whole area, once notoriously gloomy and decayed, will be completely transformed.

1: Kensington Central, Phillimore Walk
2: North Kensington, 108 Ladbroke Grove
3: Notting Hill Gate,1 Pembridge Square
4: Chelsea, Old Town Hall, King's Road
5: Brompton, 210 Old Brompton Road
6: Kensal, 20 Golborne Road
7: Hammersmith, Shepherd's Bush Road
8: Shepherd's Bush, 7 Uxbridge Road
9: Askew Road, 87/91 Askew Road
10: Fulham, 598 Fulham Road
11: Baron's Court, North End Crescent
12: Sands End, 59 Broughton Road

13: Charing Cross, 4 Charing Cross Road
14: Church Street, Church Street
15: Maida Vale, Sutherland Avenue
16: Marylebone, 109–117 Marylebone Road
17: Mayfair, 25 South Audley Street
18: Paddington, Porchester Road
19: Pimlico, Rampayne Street
20: Queen's Park, 666 Harrow Road
21: St James's, 62 Victoria Street
22: St John's Wood, 20 Circus Road
23: Victoria, 160 Buckingham Palace Road

PUBLIC LIBRARIES

There have been all sorts of libraries all over Britain for centuries: at work places, in inns, on grand estates for the benefit of the servants, and village libraries provided by benevolent vicars. In London nearly a thousand are recorded as existing by 1850, ranging from major institutions and colleges to circulating libraries, and libraries in hospitals, coffee houses, clubs and churches. There is a long tradition of making reading matter available for the benefit of the general public.

But it was not seen as something that local councils had a duty to provide until in the 1840s William Ewart (1798–1869), an active social reformer and the MP for Bletchingly, began a campaign to introduce the idea. He was supported by various other Liberal and Chartist members of Parliament, including Edward Edwards, a former bricklayer who had educated himself in Mechanics Institute libraries and in 1839 had secured himself a job as an assistant in the British Museum's department of printed books. As with many other proposed liberal reforms of the time, their draft Public Libraries Act, debated in Parliament in 1849, evoked considerable hostility from the Conservative opposition, on the grounds that the local tax-paying middle and upper classes would be funding a service that would be of sole use to the workers. One MP is quoted as saying that 'people have too much knowledge already: it was much easier to manage them 20 years ago; the more education people got the more difficult they are to manage'.

A number of compromises were agreed upon before Lord John Russell's Whig government gave its support to the Act. Ewart had intended for the provision of libraries to be mandatory throughout Britain, but it was confined to boroughs with populations over 10,000; and the councils were obliged before embarking on it to obtain by referendum the consent of two-thirds of local ratepayers. But the Act was passed in 1850, and in the next few years Ewart introduced various amendments which improved it. Most councils thereafter secured financial help from local entrepreneurs and philanthropists in order to construct the buildings and purchase the books. Henry Tate (1819–99), the sugar maker and founder of the Tate Gallery, played a major part in supporting London public libraries.

By 1900 there were nearly 100 public libraries in London, and today they are a major resource, managed by the local authorities and used by 58 per cent of the population.

Kensington & Chelsea
Hammersmith & Fulham
Westminster

Legend

- 🟥 Cabinet-makers
- 🔴 Chair-makers
- 🔺 Furniture-makers
- 🟦 French-polishers
- 🟢 Turners
- 🔺 Carvers
- ⚙ Sawmills

INDUSTRY

Tudor London was a plethora of industrial activities: blacksmiths, small workshops producing glass and pottery, carpenters, armourers, gold and silversmiths, drapers and cloth-workers. There were at least nine commercial breweries, six along the riverside from Blackfriars to London Bridge, another across the river in Southwark, and others in Newgate and Clerkenwell. Commerce and shops tended to be in the centre, and industry outside the wall to the east.

By the 19th century, the pattern was similar but the numbers vastly greater. By the middle of the century only seventeen companies employed more than 250 workers, and 86 per cent of industrial employers had less

Chicken Lane

West Smithfield

St Bartholomew

Cock Lane

Grey Friars

Seacoal Lane

Tanners

Butcher's Meat

Fleet Street

Black Friars

St Paul's Cathedral

Goldsmiths

River Fleet

Carter Lane

Watling Street

Old Fish Street

Cordwainer Street

Watergate

Thames Street

St Paul's Wharf

Fish Wharf

Wood Street

Coldman Street

Poultry

Skinners

Butcher's meat

Brewing, dyeing

Cornhill

Lombard Street

Austin Friars

Glasschurch Street

Holy Trinity

Aldgate Street

Minchen Lane

Mart Lane

Petty Wales

Billingsgate

London Bridge

Tower of London

the Gas Light and Coke company in Bromley (where the London Gas Museum now stands), as well as the Great Eastern Railway's train factory at Stratford. In the first half of the 20th century, certain industries tended to concentrate in particular areas, for example, clothing and textiles in Holborn, Stepney and Hackney, paper and printing in Fleet Street and the City, and chemical works in Westminster, Paddington and Hammersmith. The American Ford Motor Company began manufacturing cars in Dagenham in the 1930s. Industrial zones were set up in many suburban areas all around the city, accessible by the new trunk road networks, in the Lea Valley, Enfield, Isleworth, Park Royal, Hayes, Cricklewood and Wembley.

Through the second half of the century these manufacturing industries declined, many of them moving away from London and some going out of business altogether. The London docks closed in the 1960s. Increasingly the city's economy is dependent on service industries such as the media, tourism, management, accountancy, banking, law and architecture.

A few remain, such as Brass Master, a brass manufacturer, in Uxbridge, and Datasights, a technological glazier, in Enfield. There are still some major breweries: Guinness in Park Royal, Fuller's in Chiswick, and Young & Co in Wandsworth, where beer has been brewed since 1581.

Medieval commercial areas

Principal industrial areas in Medieval times

Principal industrial areas in Tudor times

1 Armourers
2 Brickmakers
3 Basketmakers
4 Brewers
5 Bowyers
6 Carpenters
7 Corn-millers
8 Curriers
9 Cordwainers
10 Dyers
11 Fletchers
12 Founders
13 Glassmakers
14 Goldsmiths
15 Printers
16 Silversmiths
17 Tenter Stretchers
18 Upholsterers
19 Wiredrawers

Zoological Society
(1826)

Royal College of Physicians
(1518)

British Medical Association
(1832)

Royal Society of Tropical Medicine
(1907)

Royal Anthropological Institute
(1871)

Gresham
College (1597)

Royal Society of Medicine
(1805)

Royal College of Surgeons
(1800) – originally Company of
Barber-Surgeons (1540)

Royal Institution
(1799)

Royal Society
(1645)

Royal Society of Chemistry (1980)
Society of Antiquaries (1707)
Geological Society (1825)

Royal Geographical Society
(1830)

Royal College of
Veterinary Surgeons
(1844)

Royal Entomological Society
(1833)

Royal Horticultural Society
(1804)

Royal Pharmaceutical Society
(1841)

SCIENCE

In the Middle Ages scientific and medical progress was slow, and confined to Oxford and Cambridge and to friars such as Roger Bacon (1214–94). But when William Caxton's printing press opened in Westminster in 1476, London began to become an important centre for scientific debate and research. The Royal College of Physicians, by far the oldest medical institution in England, was founded in 1518 by the king's physician, Thomas Linacre, and its early meetings were held in his house in Knightrider Street, near St Paul's Cathedral. Since then it has moved several times, and is currently in an elegant modern building, designed by Denys Lasdun, on the south-east corner of Regent's Park.

In 1597, Gresham College was opened as a centre for the delivery of public lectures on scientific and other subjects, and from 1645 the Royal Society for the improvement of natural knowledge, now called simply the Royal Society, developed from the weekly meetings of the college's professors. It was here that Sir Isaac Newton demonstrated his theory of gravitation in 1683–4. This great institution too has moved several times. It spent 100 years in Burlington House, before arriving at Carlton House Terrace in 1967.

In 1675 John Flamsteed was appointed the first Astronomer Royal by Charles II, and shortly thereafter opened the Royal Observatory at Greenwich. This beautiful building in Greenwich Park, in part designed by Sir Christopher Wren, is now a museum displaying a fine collection of early astronomical instruments.

The Royal Institution has been in Albemarle Street since its foundation in 1799, for 'diffusing the knowledge and facilitating the general introduction of useful mechanical inventions and improvements, and for teaching by courses of philosophical lectures and experiments the application of science to the common purposes of life'. The elegant classical façade was added in 1838. This is where Michael Faraday experimented with electricity, and became Professor of Chemistry.

Among the many 19th-century scientific institutions still operating in London are the Royal Society of Medicine (1805) in Wimpole Street, into which 17 other specialty societies were merged in 1907; the Royal Geographical Society (1830); the Royal Pharmaceutical Society (1841); and the Royal Society of Chemistry (1980) in Burlington House which is an amalgam of the Chemical Society (1841) and the Royal Institute of Chemistry (1877). Burlington House is also home to the Society of Antiquaries (1707) and the Geological Society (1825) – not to mention the Royal Academy of Arts, founded in 1768, which occupies the central section of the building.

Major scientific institutions
(with date of foundation)

Royal Observatory Greenwich
(1675)

FOOD

There have been eating-houses all over London since early times, and even take-aways are recorded in the 12th century. Bread Street was full of cook-shops, where customers could bring their own food to be cooked; and as the population grew there were many others in Cheapside, Bishopsgate Street, Covent Garden, and Haymarket. By the 18th century they became known as beef-houses or chop-houses. Dolly's Chop-house behind St. Paul's Cathedral was a popular restaurant which survived into the 19th century. Coffee-houses proliferated too, and there were thousands all over the city by 1700.

Dining-halls and restaurants opened for business in the second half of the 19th century, mostly associated with the new hotels, and almost at once many became famous for their bad food. On the brighter side, the Café Royal in Regent Street opened in 1865, and the Criterion Restaurant in Piccadilly in 1874. The more popular Lyon's Corner Houses began in 1907, and fish-and-chip shops in poorer areas to the east. Throughout the 20th century London was notorious around the world for its lack of culinary virtues: meat and two veg was the standard London meal.

After the Second World War, things began to change. Starting in Soho, foreign cooking, especially French, Italian, Chinese and Indian, began to spread and become popular. In the 1960s Indian restaurants became particularly popular because they were cheap and stimulating, with amenable and friendly service. Pizzas were another new trend: Peter Boizot opened his first Pizza Express in Wardour Street in 1965, and there are now over 100 in London.

Perhaps influenced by the bestselling post-war cookbooks of Elizabeth David, Londoners began to expect and admire higher standards for eating out. Le Gavroche was opened in 1967 by the French Roux brothers, Albert and Michel; and other high-class restaurants, with different cuisines, followed. In 1995, Marco Pierre White became the first born and bred British chef to be awarded three Michelin stars for his restaurant at the Hyde Park Hotel.

By the beginning of the 21st century, an enormously wide range of cuisines, from Afghan to Vietnamese, were on offer in restaurants in every part of London. Upper Street in Islington is a prototype of the larger scene, with dozens of eating places offering different kinds of food. Not all are successful, but if they go out of business they are quickly replaced. The selection shown here is not a choice based on quality or price, but does demonstrate the extraordinary diversity of food in London today.

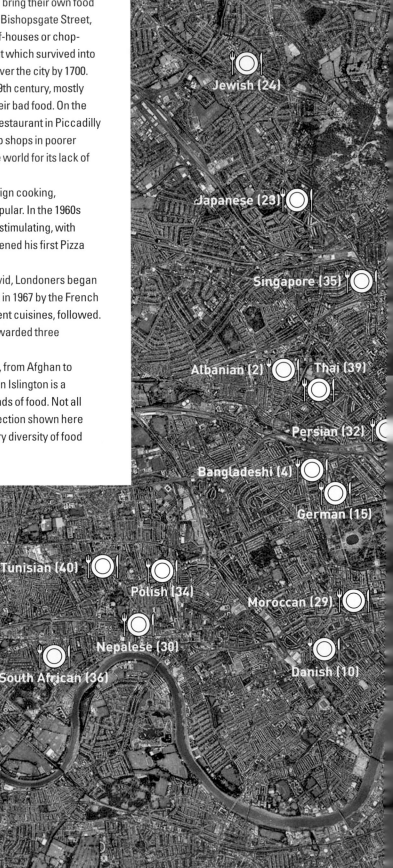

Jewish (24)

Japanese (23)

Singapore (35)

Albanian (2) Thai (39)

Persian (32)

Bangladeshi (4)

German (15)

Grenadian (18)

Tunisian (40)

Polish (34)

Moroccan (29)

Nepalese (30)

South African (36)

Danish (10)

Brazilian (5)

Mauritian (27)

Indian (20)

Ethiopian (13)

Mexican (28)

Georgian (16)

Cuban (9)

French (14)

Afghan (1)

Swiss (38)

Egyptian (12)

Spanish (37)

Greek (17)

Vietnamese (42)

Dutch (11)

Hungarian

Turkish (41)

Pakistani (31)

Malaysian (26)

Irish (21)

British (6)

Lebanese (25)

Peruvian (33)

Italian (22)

Colombian (8)

Chinese (7)

Argentinian (3)

International cuisine in London
1: The Afghan Kitchen, 35 Islington Green
2: Lisi, 5 Malvern Road
3: La Pampa, 60 Battersea Rise
4: Ginger, 115 Westbourne Grove
5: Sabor do Brasil, 36 Highgate Hill
6: Simpson's in the Strand, 100 Strand
7: Hunan, 51 Pimlico Road
8: La Bodeguita, Elephant & Castle Shopping Centre
9: Cuba Libre, 72 Upper Street
10: Lundum's, 119 Old Brompton Road
11: My Old Dutch, 121 High Holborn
12: Ali Baba, 32 Ivor Place
13: Lalibela, 137 Fortess Road
14: Almeida, 30 Almeida Street
15: Jagerhutte, 36 Queensway
16: Tbilisi, 91 Holloway Road
17: The Real Greek, 15 Hoxton Market
18: BB's, 3 Chignell Place, Uxbridge Road
19: Gay Hussar, 2 Greek Street
20: The Parsee, 34 Highgate Hill
21: Mulligan's, 13–14 Cork Street
22: Zafferano, 15 Lowndes Street
23: Wakaba, 122a Finchley Road
24: Blooms, 130 Golders Green Road
25: Al-Hamra, 31–33 Shepherd Market
26: Mawar, 175a Edgware Road
27: Chez Liline, 101 Stroud Green Road
28: Zuni, 134 Fortess Road
29: Pasha, 1 Gloucester Road
30: Light of Nepal, 268 King Street
31: Lahore Kebab House, 2 Umberstone Street
32: Kandoo, 458 Edgware Road
33: Fina Estampa, 152 Tooley Street
34: Patio, 5 Goldhawk Road
35: Singapore Garden, 83 Fairfax Road
36: Dumela, Devonshire Road
37: Moro, 343–36 Exmouth Market
38: Café Delancey, 3 Delancey Street
39: Southeast, 239 Elgin Avenue
40: Adam's Café, 77 Askew Road
41: Sofra, 36 Tavistock Street
42: Bam-Bou, 1 Percy Street

9

Since Britain and Libya resumed diplomatic relations in 1999, the so-called Libyan People's Bureau (17) has been based at 61 Ennismore Gardens, next to the Russian Orthodox Cathedral.
Next to Ennismore Gardens is a larger square, Prince's Gardens (18), dominated by buildings belonging to the nearby Imperial College. The café on the ground floor of Linstead Hall (1968) is constantly packed with students reading and writing essays.

Westminster Synagogue (11) is at Kent House in Rutland Gardens, built in 1870 on the site of a previous mansion rented by Queen Victoria's son Edward, Duke of Kent. The present building was a celebrated salon for concerts and ballet in the 1920s and 30s. The Jewish community acquired it in 1960.
At no. 2 Rutland Gardens Mews (13), a tiny and attractive private square off Rutland Gardens, two exceptional women lived at different times in the 20th century: the ballerina Dame Margot Fonteyn and the cellist Jacqueline du Pré (it was rented by her husband Daniel Barenboim).

Ennismore Gardens (16) and its neighbourhood were acquired and built by the Earl of Listowel, Viscount Ennismore, in 1823. The Ennismore Arms pub, which has recently closed down, was built in 1950 on the site of a previous inn bombed in the second world war.

1: Albert Gate (1846)
2: Hyde Park Barracks
3: Rutland Gate (1838-56)
4: Russian Orthodox Cathedral (1849)
5: Harrods (1901-5)
6: Harvey Nichols
7: French embassy, 58 Knightsbridge
8: Hyde Park Hotel, now called Mandarin Oriental Hyde Park Hotel (1894)
9: Park Tower Hotel
10: Bonhams, Montpelier Street
11: Westminster Synagogue
12: 41 Rutland Gate
13: Rutland Gardens Mews
14: The Brompton Oratory
15: Anglican church of Holy Trinity
16: Ennismore Gardens
17: Libyan People's Bureau
18: Prince's Gardens

The scientific genius Sir Francis Galton (1822–1911), who is today forgotten or ignored because of his politically incorrect formulation of eugenics, lived for 50 years at 41 Rutland Gate (12). The Brompton Oratory (14), designed in Baroque style by Herbert Gribble and consecrated in 1884, is the second largest Catholic church in Britain. It contains marble statues of the apostles by Giuseppe Mazzuoli (1643–1725).

Tucked away behind the Brompton Oratory is the Anglican church of Holy Trinity (15), designed in a plain style known as 'commissioners' gothic' by the architect T.L. Donaldson and consecrated in 1829. Today it is a lively centre for evangelicals and enthusiasts for the Alpha Course, described as 'an opportunity to explore the meaning of life'.

THE STORY OF KNIGHTSBRIDGE

Close to where Albert Gate now stands on the south side of Hyde Park, the river Westbourne flows underground, down to the Thames. A thousand years ago it was crossed by a bridge, with a road leading down to the rural village of Kensington. There is an 11th-century legend that two knights once fought each other to the death on this bridge. Henceforth, the street and its surrounding village have been called Knightsbridge.

In the early decades of the 18th century, London stopped at Hyde Park Corner, and to the west were open fields and farms, and a few grand mansions like Kensington Court (later Palace), and Holland House. The open Kensington Road was blocked halfway down by a seedy and ramshackle inn, the resort of highwaymen, called Halfway House, which only came down in 1846. But by the 1780s Knightsbridge had been joined to Chelsea by the Hans Town development (Hans Town is now a ward in the Borough of Kensington and Chelsea), with Sloane Street as its spine, the Life Guards barracks had gone up on the side of the park (replaced by Basil Spence's Hyde Park Barracks in 1970), and Rutland House and its park and gardens dominated the area down to Brompton Road. Just inside the park through Rutland Gate were the Riding House Stables,

where the army still exercise their horses today.

The area was rapidly built up over the next century. Grand new houses went up around Prince's Gate, where Rutland House had stood, and in 1849 an elegant church was built off Ennismore Gardens which much later became the Russian Orthodox Cathedral. At the same time a small grocery store on Brompton Road called Harrod's began to expand dramatically, and by the end of the 19th century it was already said 'to serve the world'. Today, it occupies four acres, and has made Knightsbridge a world-renowned shopping centre. Almost equally successful was a linen store on the corner of Sloane Street, opened by Benjamin Harvey in 1813, which today is the fashionable department store Harvey Nichols. The French embassy was built at Albert Gate in 1854, next to Holy Trinity Church (since demolished), and forty years later the Hyde Park Hotel went up, facing the park.

Other Knightsbridge attractions today include the elegantly tubular Park Tower Hotel, designed by Richard Seifert in 1972. The auctioneers Bonhams, founded in 1793, have premises in Montpelier Street, where the gardens of Rutland House once lay.

Filming locations

1: *The Lavender Hill Mob* (1951)
directed by Charles Crichton,
starring Alec Guinness, Stanley
Holloway and Audrey Hepburn

2: *The Ladykillers* (1955)
directed by Alexander Mackendrick,
starring Alec Guinness, Peter
Sellers and Frankie Howerd

3: *Alfie* (1966)
directed by Lewis Gilbert, starring
Michael Caine, Jane Asher, Shelley
Winters, Denham Elliott

4: *A Hard Day's Night* (1964)
directed by Richard Lester, starring
John Lennon, Paul McCartney,
George Harrison, Ringo Starr

5: *Howard's End* (1992)
directed by James Ivory, starring
Anthony Hopkins, Vanessa
Redgrave, Helena Bonham Carter,
Emma Thompson

6: *Sliding Doors* (1998)
directed by Peter Howitt, starring
Gwyneth Paltrow and Virginia
McKenna

7: *Eyes Wide Shut* (1999)
directed by Stanley Kubrick, starring
Tom Cruise and Nicole Kidman

8: *Four Weddings and a Funeral* (1994)
directed by Mike Newall, starring
Hugh Grant and Andie MacDowell

9: *Sense and Sensibility* (1995)
directed by Ang Lee, starring Emma
Thompson, Alan Rickman, Katie
Winslet and Hugh Grant

10: *Notting Hill* (1999)
directed by Roger Michell, starring
Julia Roberts and Hugh Grant

11: *Harry Potter and the Philosopher's
Stone* (2001)
directed by Chris Columbus,
starring Daniel Radcliffe

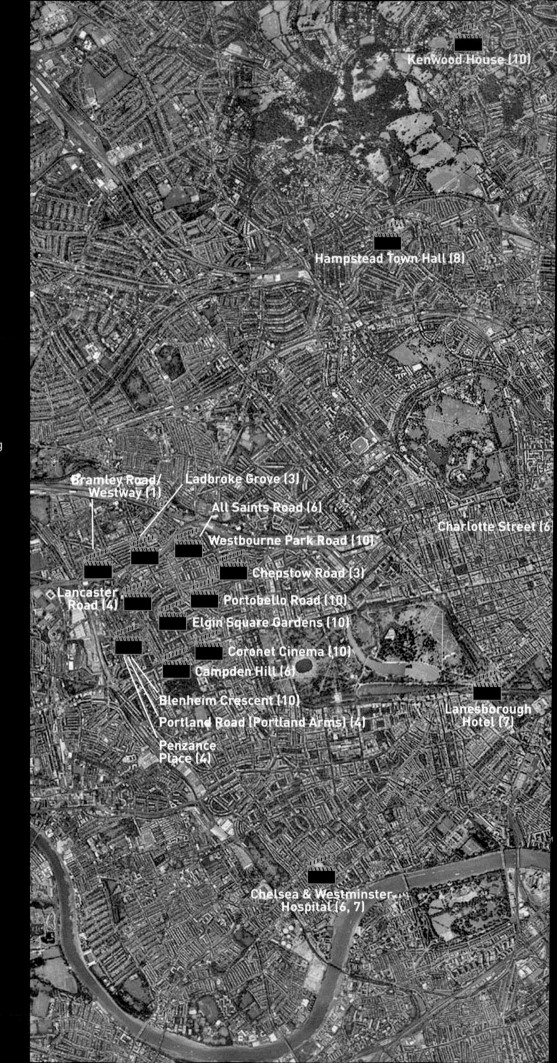

Kenwood House (10)

Hampstead Town Hall (8)

Bramley Road/
Westway (1)

Ladbroke Grove (3)

All Saints Road (6)

Charlotte Street (6

Westbourne Park Road (10)

Chepstow Road (3)

Lancaster
Road (4)

Portobello Road (10)

Elgin Square Gardens (10)

Coronet Cinema (10)

Campden Hill (6)

Lanesborough
Hotel (7)

Blenheim Crescent (10)

Portland Road (Portland Arms) (4)

Penzance
Place (4)

Chelsea & Westminster
Hospital (6, 7)

LONDON FILMS

Among the London areas that have been most often used by film-makers are Southwark, Greenwich, King's Cross, Camden and, more recently, Notting Hill. Two of Alec Guinness's masterpieces offer a memorable view of London half a century ago. *The Lavender Hill Mob* (1951), about a timid bank clerk who carries out a bullion robbery, has scenes filmed in Bramley Road (since over-run by the Westway), and *The Ladykillers* (1955) drew much of its macabre atmosphere from King's Cross. *Alfie* (1966), starring Michael Caine as its cockney hero, was also shot there, as well as in Ladbroke Grove and Chepstow Road. The masterly Beatles film *A Hard Day's Night* (1964) has scenes set in King's Cross and in various Notting Hill streets such as Penzance Place, Clarendon Road, Lancaster Road, and at the Portland Arms in Portland Road. *Howard's End* (1992), James Ivory's best adaptation from an E. M. Forster novel, has scenes in Borough Market and Park Street, Southwark, as well as in the so-called St. Pancras Chambers which were once, in the 1870s, the Midland Grand Hotel.

Admirers of Gwyneth Paltrow's performance as a Notting Hill resident in *Sliding Doors* (1998) will not be surprised to know that some of it was filmed in that neighbourhood, for instance at the Windsor Castle pub on Campden Hill and Ma's Café on All Saints Road. Other scenes are at Bertorelli's in Charlotte Street, the Chelsea and Westminster Hospital in the Fulham Road, Lincoln's Inn Fields and the Albert Embankment.

In Stanley Kubrick's last film, *Eyes Wide Shut* (1999), starring Tom Cruise and Nicole Kidman, there is not much sense of a London background; but in fact both the Chelsea and Kensington Hospital and the Lanesborough Hotel on Hyde Park Corner feature in the film, as well as Hatton Gardens in Holborn. Among other recent popular films with London settings is *Four Weddings and a Funeral* (1994), which uses the Royal Naval College chapel in Greenwich, as well as Hampstead town hall. Greenwich Park and the College, including the Queen's House, also appear in Emma Thompson's delightful filmic version of Jane Austen's *Sense and Sensibility* (1995).

And then of course there's the highly popular *Notting Hill* (1999), starring Julia Roberts and Hugh Grant, the most recent and successful film ever about a specific London location. Portobello Road, where the hero's bookshop is set, appears frequently, and there are scenes filmed in Kenwood House, at the Coronet Cinema in Notting Hill Gate, and in Elgin Square Gardens and Westbourne Park Road. Harry Potter's many fans will of course know that Hogwarts Express departs from platform 9¾ at King's Cross Station.

Guildhall

**St. Paul's
Cathedral**

R i v e r   T h a m e s

Christopher Wren's plan for the
reconstruction of the City

London City Walls

Plan showing grand squares
and broad avenues . It would
have looked rather similar to the
sixteenth arrondissement in Paris.

Custom House

The Tower

UNREALISED PLANS FOR LONDON

Destruction heralds reconstruction. Perhaps the best chance to change the shape of London arose after the Great Fire in 1666, and Sir Christopher Wren took full advantage of it a week later with his plan to rebuild the medieval City with grand squares and broad avenues lined with elegant buildings suited to London's status as a great trading capital (see opposite). In 1796 William Revely came up with a scheme to straighten the Thames by creating a new channel all the way from Silvertown to Wapping.

When the London cemeteries became hopelessly overcrowded at the beginning of the 19th century (see pages 84–5), the architect Francis Goodwin produced a plan for a vast, 150-acre 'Grand National Cemetery', designed in the classical Greek style with a modern Parthenon at its centre. Such schemes usually failed because they were too ambitious or expensive. One that worked was the fire that destroyed Westminster Palace in 1834, allowing the monumental Houses of Parliament to change the whole appearance of the east side of the Thames.

The Second World War bombing provided another opportunity, and in 1943, at the request of London County Council, J. H. Forshaw and Patrick Abercrombie produced their County of London Plan, which would have solved many of today's traffic problems. The main idea was a series of three concentric ring roads, to dissuade drivers from going unnecessarily through the centre. The inner ring road linked all the main northern railway stations, ran down to a new tunnel under the river east of Tower Bridge, through Southwark, over Vauxhall Bridge, up to Brompton, and through a tunnel under Hyde Park. The outer road would have developed and improved the north and south circulars that exist today. The one between them ran through areas like Shepherd's Bush, St. John's Wood, Islington and Stepney, under a new tunnel to Deptford, then through Peckham and Clapham, over Battersea Bridge and up Warwick Road. A tunnel under St James's Park, close to Buckingham Palace, and another under Bloomsbury, were other parts of the scheme. Perhaps George VI objected to the former.

Abercrombie also produced a Greater London Plan. Most of his specifics have not been realised, but his ideas have influenced London's development over the last half century. His proposal for separate, self-governed outer 'satellite' towns, such as Stevenage and Harlow, were implemented.

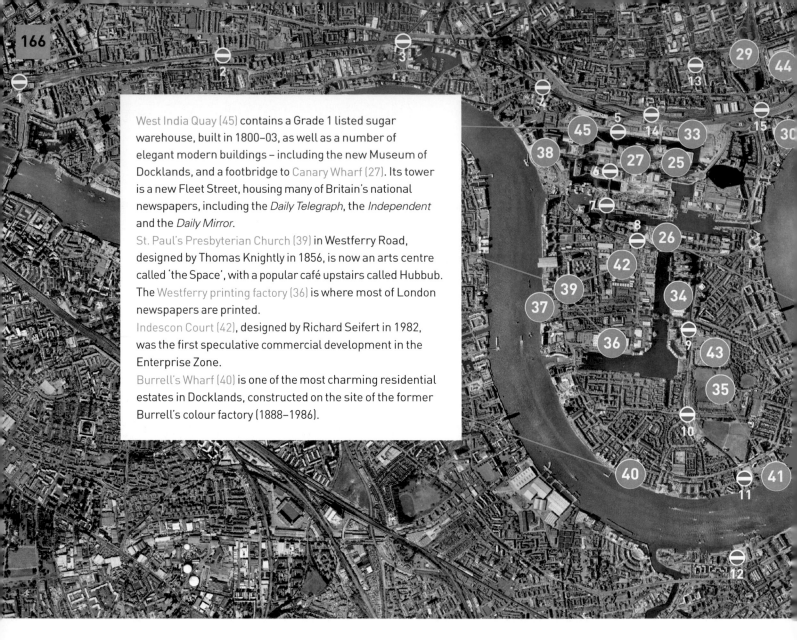

West India Quay (45) contains a Grade 1 listed sugar warehouse, built in 1800–03, as well as a number of elegant modern buildings – including the new Museum of Docklands, and a footbridge to Canary Wharf (27). Its tower is a new Fleet Street, housing many of Britain's national newspapers, including the *Daily Telegraph*, the *Independent* and the *Daily Mirror*.

St. Paul's Presbyterian Church (39) in Westferry Road, designed by Thomas Knightly in 1856, is now an arts centre called 'the Space', with a popular café upstairs called Hubbub. The Westferry printing factory (36) is where most of London newspapers are printed.

Indescon Court (42), designed by Richard Seifert in 1982, was the first speculative commercial development in the Enterprise Zone.

Burrell's Wharf (40) is one of the most charming residential estates in Docklands, constructed on the site of the former Burrell's colour factory (1888–1986).

THE STORY OF DOCKLANDS

When the Port of London docks finally closed in 1981, this huge seven-mile stretch along the river from the Tower down to Woolwich was full of decaying warehouses, empty council housing and desolate open areas. Some local councils were still hopeful that London's role as a commercial port could be revived, but this wasn't happening, and the government decided to set up the London Docklands Development Corporation, which over the next two decades achieved an astonishing revival.

One method of attracting private investment was to offer businesses entering the Isle of Dogs 'enterprise zone' a ten-year exemption from council tax, a 100 per cent corporation and income tax allowance for capital expenditure and much freer than normal planning and building controls. To begin with there were some relatively modest industrial and commercial developments around Millwall Inner Dock. Terry Farrell's famous Limehouse Studios, converted from a former rum and banana warehouse, was built in 1982, but was later demolished to allow the eastern extension of Canary Wharf. Richard Seifert's South Quay Plaza went up on Marsh Wall. But the big breakthrough came with the idea of creating a 29-hectare financial services centre on Canary Wharf, which was eventually taken over by the Canadian development company

Olympia & York. Canary Wharf has the tallest tower in Britain, designed by Cesar Pelli, and visible from all over London. Other towers, almost as tall and called Citygroup and HSBC, have recently risen beside it.

East India Dock also began to attract investors, and in 1989 Nicholas Grimshaw's prize-winning building for the Financial Times went up, followed by the former Reuters recreation facility, part of their data centre building, at Blackwall Yard, designed by Richard Rogers, and others.

A crucial element in the regeneration of Docklands was the issue of transport, which was virtually non-existent at the start – just a few congested roads and the Blackwall Tunnel. The Docklands Light Railway was the first step, linking the Isle of Dogs with Tower Gateway to the west and Stratford to the north. In due course it was extended to Bank, south to Lewisham, and east to Beckton. Equally vital was the opening of London City Airport, on the strip between Royal Albert Dock and King George V Dock, formally opened by the Queen in November 1987 for 'short takeoff and landing' aircraft. Its runway was extended in 1992, and by the turn of the century over one and a half million passengers were using it every year. Finally, the underground Jubilee Line extension opened in 1999, providing an easy connection between Docklands and the West End.

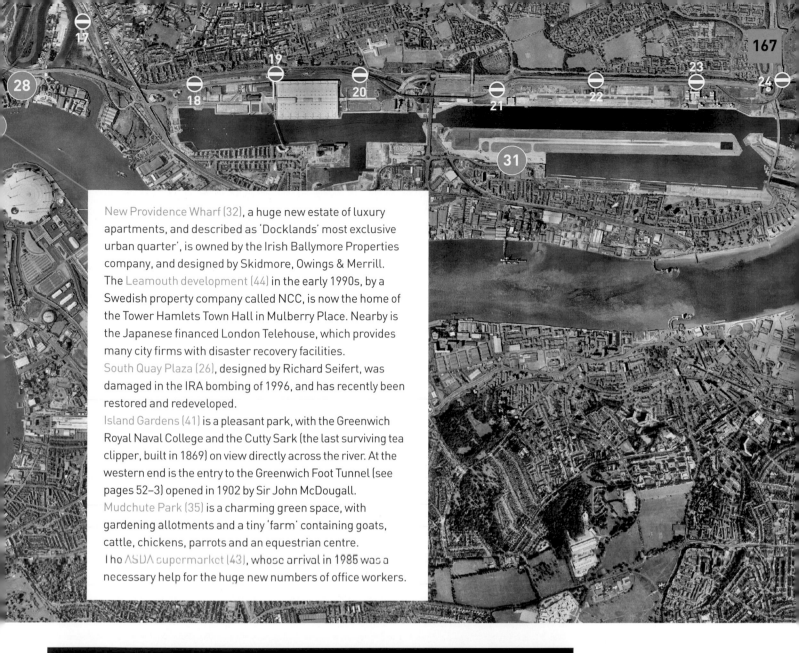

New Providence Wharf (32), a huge new estate of luxury apartments, and described as 'Docklands' most exclusive urban quarter', is owned by the Irish Ballymore Properties company, and designed by Skidmore, Owings & Merrill.

The Leamouth development (44) in the early 1990s, by a Swedish property company called NCC, is now the home of the Tower Hamlets Town Hall in Mulberry Place. Nearby is the Japanese financed London Telehouse, which provides many city firms with disaster recovery facilities.

South Quay Plaza (26), designed by Richard Seifert, was damaged in the IRA bombing of 1996, and has recently been restored and redeveloped.

Island Gardens (41) is a pleasant park, with the Greenwich Royal Naval College and the Cutty Sark (the last surviving tea clipper, built in 1869) on view directly across the river. At the western end is the entry to the Greenwich Foot Tunnel (see pages 52–3) opened in 1902 by Sir John McDougall.

Mudchute Park (35) is a charming green space, with gardening allotments and a tiny 'farm' containing goats, cattle, chickens, parrots and an equestrian centre.

The ASDA supermarket (43), whose arrival in 1985 was a necessary help for the huge new numbers of office workers.

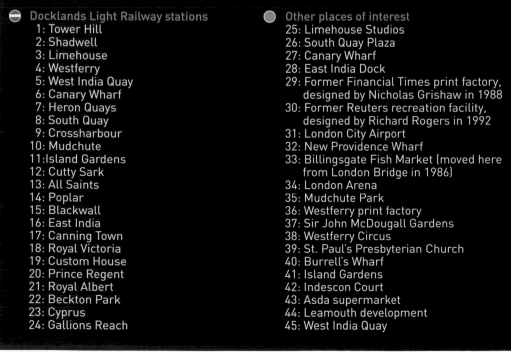

⊖ Docklands Light Railway stations
 1: Tower Hill
 2: Shadwell
 3: Limehouse
 4: Westferry
 5: West India Quay
 6: Canary Wharf
 7: Heron Quays
 8: South Quay
 9: Crossharbour
10: Mudchute
11: Island Gardens
12: Cutty Sark
13: All Saints
14: Poplar
15: Blackwall
16: East India
17: Canning Town
18: Royal Victoria
19: Custom House
20: Prince Regent
21: Royal Albert
22: Beckton Park
23: Cyprus
24: Gallions Reach

● Other places of interest
25: Limehouse Studios
26: South Quay Plaza
27: Canary Wharf
28: East India Dock
29: Former Financial Times print factory, designed by Nicholas Grishaw in 1988
30: Former Reuters recreation facility, designed by Richard Rogers in 1992
31: London City Airport
32: New Providence Wharf
33: Billingsgate Fish Market (moved here from London Bridge in 1986)
34: London Arena
35: Mudchute Park
36: Westferry print factory
37: Sir John McDougall Gardens
38: Westferry Circus
39: St. Paul's Presbyterian Church
40: Burrell's Wharf
41: Island Gardens
42: Indescon Court
43: Asda supermarket
44: Leamouth development
45: West India Quay

CAVERSHAM

GOSPEL OAK,
CASTLE HAVEN

King's Cross
North

KILBURN, PRIORY, WEST
END, FORTUNE GREEN

Camden Town

CAMDEN
CENTRAL

Canalside

Willesden
Junction

Mornington Crescent

Euston

King's Cross

WEST EUSTON

British
Library

KING'S CROSS
BRUNSWICK

Tavistock Square

HOLBORN

Russell Square

Paddington

BLOOMSBURY

Holborn

Farringdon

WHITE
CITY

Bond
Street

Tottenham
Court
Road

Aldwych

Broomyard
Avenue

Uxbridge Road
West

South Bank

Waterloo

Askew
Road

Shepherd's Bush Marketh

Bloemfontein
Road

Shepherd's Bush
Green

St. Geor
Circus

Lambeth North

Imperial War
Museum

Victoria

Elephant
Castle So

Kennington Cross

Oval

IMPERIAL
WHARF

Albert Squre

Stockwell the Swan

Stockwell Green

Academy

Clapham
Junction

Brixton
Popes Road

LONDON'S FUTURE

So where will it go from here? London's mayor, Ken Livingstone, whose job is to define developmental strategies, has so far concentrated on short- or medium-term issues, such as improving public transport, reducing crime, and regenerating the 'brownfield' sites where industries used to be based, and which are often decayed and contaminated.

In the longer term, he has sought to encourage more drastic developments in east and west London. Park Royal has been identified as an area much in need of regeneration, where manufacturing industries could be persuaded to base themselves. There are sites in inner London, around Paddington, King's Cross and Elephant and Castle, where redundant railway lines have left open spaces; and he believes new cross-London railway lines will also be needed. One of his main focuses is on Thames Gateway, about six square miles of land ripe for redevelopment, and close to areas of deprivation. Another example is the Greenwich peninsula, on which the endlessly problematic Millennium Dome was constructed in 1999. This large area had housed a huge gasworks for many decades, and the land was polluted with industrial chemicals, and dominated by the entrance to Blackwall Tunnel. Since the Dome closed at the end of 2000, several offers have been made to acquire it, mostly for use as a sports and entertainment centre.

The introduction in 2003 of congestion charges for vehicle drivers entering inner London sparked passionate debate, and general hostility from the majority of Londoners. Most commentators predicted it would

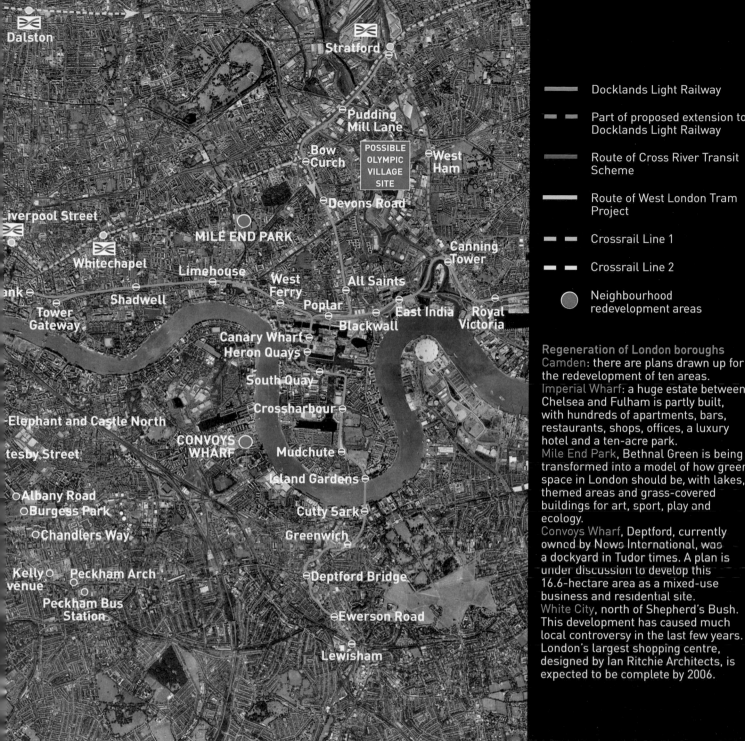

Dalston

Stratford

Pudding
Mill Lane

Bow
Curch

POSSIBLE
OLYMPIC
VILLAGE
SITE

West
Ham

Devons Road

iverpool Street

MILE END PARK

Canning
Tower

Whitechapel

Limehouse

West
Ferry

All Saints

ank

Shadwell

Poplar

East India

Royal
Victoria

Tower
Gateway

Blackwall

Canary Wharf
Heron Quays

South Quay

Crossharbour

-Elephant and Castle North

CONVOYS
WHARF

Mudchute

tesby Street

Island Gardens

Albany Road
Burgess Park

Cutty Sark

Chandlers Way

Greenwich

Kelly
venue

Peckham Arch

Deptford Bridge

Peckham Bus
Station

Ewerson Road

Lewisham

Docklands Light Railway

Part of proposed extension to
Docklands Light Railway

Route of Cross River Transit
Scheme

Route of West London Tram
Project

Crossrail Line 1

Crossrail Line 2

Neighbourhood
redevelopment areas

Regeneration of London boroughs
Camden: there are plans drawn up for
the redevelopment of ten areas.
Imperial Wharf: a huge estate between
Chelsea and Fulham is partly built,
with hundreds of apartments, bars,
restaurants, shops, offices, a luxury
hotel and a ten-acre park.
Mile End Park, Bethnal Green is being
transformed into a model of how green
space in London should be, with lakes,
themed areas and grass-covered
buildings for art, sport, play and
ecology.
Convoys Wharf, Deptford, currently
owned by News International, was
a dockyard in Tudor times. A plan is
under discussion to develop this
16.6-hectare area as a mixed-use
business and residential site.
White City, north of Shepherd's Bush.
This development has caused much
local controversy in the last few years.
London's largest shopping centre,
designed by Ian Ritchie Architects, is
expected to be complete by 2006.

fail for various reasons: that there would be even more congestion on the outer edges, that thousands of drivers would avoid payment or that the monitoring systems would fail. So far, these predictions have not come about, and indeed a recent poll reveals that more than half of Londoners are now in favour of the system. Whether a similar pattern will emerge with the reintroduction of trams remains to be seen.

London's recent rise in population is likely to continue, perhaps by as many as 700,000 by 2016, taking it to over 8 million. There is more controversy about the future of its economy. London's world status as a financial and banking centre is being challenged by Frankfurt, Berlin and Paris, and a lot of modernisation is needed if it is to hold its place, in terms of technology as well as transport, housing and other facilities. But there

is nothing new about this kind of challenge. Throughout its long history London has undergone drastic declines as well as massive growth.

London is currently planning to compete for the right to stage the 2012 Olympics, in order to provide a boost to the city's economy. The proposed main venue is the Lower Lea Valley, running south from Stratford.

Crossrail (see map) is a joint venture between the Strategic Rail Authority and Transport for London, and aiming to improve access for commuters from the home counties. Two main lines are planned, west to east from Reading to Dartford, and north-east from Clapham to King's Cross. And the reintroduction of trams in London, for the first time for half a century, is another of the Greater London Authority's plans to improve public transport (see map and pages 58–9).

CHRONOLOGY

HISTORY, POLITICS AND SOCIETY

AD

43	Romans invade England.
50	Foundation of Londinium.
60	Sack of Londinium by Boudicca.
61	Londinium rebuilt and designated capital of province.
125	Londinium destroyed by fire.
200	Londinium designated as capital of Britannia Superior.
457	Britons defeated by mercenaries. Londinium disappears from historical record.
604	Mellitus appointed Bishop of London.
842	Viking attack on London: 'Great Slaughter'.
c.871	Danes occupy London. Recaptured by King Alfred (878).
911	Edward takes control of London after Alfred's death.
1016	Canute captures London, becomes king.
1042	Edward the Confessor becomes king. London made capital of England.
1066	Harold killed at Hastings; William crowned at Westminster Abbey.
1085	Population c.10–15,000.
1180	Population inside walls c.40,000.
1192	Permission granted for mayor and aldermen with own court.
1207	Archbishop of Canterbury takes up residence at Lambeth.
1215	Magna Carta: Mayor of London one of signatories.
1290	Expulsion of Jews from London ghetto in Old Jewry.
1327	First Common Council of City of London.
1348–9	Black Death epidemic: c.10,000 buried at West Smithfield.
1377	Population c.40,000.
1381	Peasants revolt led by Wat Tyler.
1397	First of Richard Whittington's four terms as Lord Mayor.
1415	Henry V leads victory parade after Agincourt (London Bridge to St. Paul's).
1422	First records of the Honourable Society of Lincoln's Inn.
1440	First reference to the Honourable Society of the Inner Temple.
1535	Sir Thomas Moore executed at the Tower of London.
1550	Population c.80,000.
1580	Proclamation forbidding housebuilding within three miles of any London gate.
1583	Population c.120,000.
1603	Outbreak of plague: c.25,000 deaths.
1605	Guy Fawkes' 'Gunpowder Plot'.
1630	Population c.200,000.
1642	Royalist Army defeated at Turnham Green.
1649–60	Charles I executed in Whitehall; the Commonwealth declared.
1662	Royal Society founded.
1665	Bubonic Plague: c.70,000 deaths.
1666	Great Fire of London.
1700	Population over 500,000.
1702–5	Buckingham House built.
1720	The 'South Sea Bubble'.
1732	Sir Robert Walpole offered 10 Downing St as official residence.
1751	Licensing Act.
1762	Westminster Paving and Lighting Act.
1767	Houses in city numbered for first time.
1780	Gordon Riots: c.850 killed.
1811	Population c.1,000,000.
1812	Prime Minister Spencer Perceval assassinated at House of Commons.
1825	Gallows and turnpike removed from Tyburn.
1829	Metropolitan Police Act.
1832	Cholera epidemic.
1835	Animal fighting made illegal.
1837	Buckingham Palace becomes permanent London residence of the Court.
1837	Typhus epidemic.
1845	Mass meeting of Chartists on Kennington Common.
1848–9	Major cholera epidemic.
1850	Board of Health report on cholera epidemic of 1848-9 and supply of water to metropolis.
1853	Smoke Abatement Act.
1853–4	Cholera epidemic.
1857	Thames Conservancy Act.
1858	'The Great Stink': pollution on the Thames.
1859	Metropolitan Drinking Fountain Association founded.
1860	Metropolis Gas Act.
1860	London Trades Council founded.
1865	Foundation of the Salvation Army in East End.
1866	Last major outbreak of cholera, 5,915 deaths in Poplar.
1866	Sanitation Act.
1868	Toll gates abolished.
1868	Last public execution at Newgate Prison.
1870	School Board of London established.
1878	Epping Forest acquired by City of London Corporation.
1885	Highgate Woods acquired by City of London Corporation.
1888	London County Council created.
1890	Housing Act enabling the LCC to clear slums.
1899	London Government Act: 28 new metropolitan boroughs created.
1902	Metropolitan Water Board created.
1908–33	London County Hall built.
1908	Port of London Authority created.
1911	Population of Greater London c.7,252,000.
1915–18	German zeppelins bomb London.
1919	'The Cenotaph' war memorial unveiled in Whitehall.
1920	'Unknown soldier' buried in Westminster Abbey.
1922	First Queen Charlotte Ball for debutantes.
1926	The General Strike.
1929	Local Government Act: LCC takes over hospitals

1931	Population of Greater London c.8,203,000.
1933	London Transport Act (Board formed).
1935	'Greenbelt' established by LCC.
1936	Jarrow unemployed march to London.
1939	Population of Greater London c.8.700,000.
1940	Air attacks on London docks.
1940	Second great fire of London: 30,000 incendiary bombs.
1941	National Fire Service formed.
1944	First flying bomb hits London.
1946	New Towns Act: eight new towns around London.
1948	First immigrants arrive from Jamaica.
1951	King George VI opens Festival of Britain.
1952	4,000 deaths attributed to 'smog' lasting several days.
1953	Coronation of Elizabeth II at Westminster.
1955	City of London declared 'smokeless zone'.
1957	Survey shows no fish in Thames from Richmond to Tilbury (40 miles).
1962	Commonwealth Institute, Kensington opened.
1965	Formation of Greater London Council to replace LCC.
1968	Large anti-Vietnam war demonstration in London.
1973	Statue of Sir Winston Churchill unveiled.
1974	First salmon caught in Thames for 100 years.
1976	Population of Greater London c.7,000,000.
1981	London Docklands Development Corporation formed.
1981	London Wildlife Trust formed.
1981	Greater London Enterprise Board formed.
1986	Greater London Council abolished.
1987	Fire at King's Cross underground station.
1989	Marchioness pleasure boat disaster on Thames.
1990	Population of Greater London c.6,500,000.
1992	IRA bombs Baltic Exchange.
1995	Aldwych bus bombed by IRA.
1996	Canary Wharf tower bombed by IRA.

COMMERCE, INDUSTRY AND INFRASTRUCTURE

AD

50	Road network begun; Thames bridged; provision of port facilities.
125	New waterfront built.
c.290	London Mint established.
c.640	Gold coins minted in London: the first since Roman times.
899	First mention of Queenhithe.
949	First mention of Billingsgate.
1066	William grants London Charter.
c.1130	Charters establishing liberties.
c.1155	Vintner's Company granted Charter.
1170	Weekly horse fair at Smithfield.
1180	First mention of Goldsmith's Company.
c.1199	First building regulations introduced in the City.
1214	City Charter awarded by King John.
1272	First Craft Guild.
1274	First mention of 'Flete Strete'.
c.1290	The Hop and Grapes in Aldgate High Street: London's oldest Licensed House.
1358	138 shops on London Bridge.
1358	First Goldsmith's Hall.
1380	First Skinner's Hall.
1382	First Custom House.
1389	River wall built at Tower.
1394	Farringdon wards formed outside the wall.
1400	Billingsgate Market granted its charter.
1422	111 crafts recorded in London.
1425	First Draper's Company Hall.
1479	Billingsgate Market rebuilt by Hanseatic merchants.
1501	First printing press set up in Fleet Street.
1513	Foundation of Royal Dockyard at Woolwich and Deptford.
1554	First mention of The George Inn, Southwark.
1566	Royal Exchange instituted by Thomas Gresham.
1584	First mention of Ye Old Cheshire Cheese Inn, Fleet Street.
1593	Horse-driven water pump installed near Queenhithe.
1599	First dry dock built at Rotherhithe.
1613	Opening of 38-mile canal (from Herts to Clerkenwell) London's main water supply.
1614	East India Docks built at Blackwall.
1651	Hay's Wharf opened.
1656	1,153 taverns in the city.
1663	First toll roads.
1667	Fleet Canal and Thames Quay project.
1669	Regular 'Flying Coaches' – London-Oxford-Cambridge.
1680	'Penny Post' introduced.
1694	Foundation of the Bank of England.
1720	Charters granted to the Royal Exchange Assurance and London Assurance companies.
1729	2,484 private coaches, and 1,100 coaches for hire; 22,636 horses in London.
1734	Lloyd's List established as regular weekly publication.
1747	Coal Exchange opened.
1756	600 stage coaches licensed to towns within 19 miles of London; fixed routes from 123 stations in London.
1761	New Road from Paddington to Islington (first London bypass).
1780	London bankers issued their own notes.
1785	First publication of *The Times*.
1794	Grand-Junction Canal opened.
1798	7,000 watchmakers listed in Clerkenwell.
1802	West India Docks opened.
1802	Stock Exchange opened on new site.
1803	Surrey Iron Railway (Wandsworth-Croydon, horse-drawn): first public railway.
1803	Dickens and Jones department store opened.
1803	Commercial Road opened: improved access to docks.
1807	Installation of gas lighting in Pall Mall.
1807–9	Royal Mint opened.

1815	First steamboat service on Thames.
1817	New Custom House.
1819	Burlington shopping arcade, Piccadilly, opened.
1820	Regent's Canal opened.
1827	First publication of *Evening Standard*.
1828	Covent Garden Market.
1829	General Post Office opened.
1829	First omnibus service: Paddington-City.
1834	Hansom Cabs introduced.
1836	First passenger railway in London: London-Greenwich.
1837	Euston Railway Station opened.
1838	Paddington Railway Station opened.
1840	Penny Post introduced.
1841	Fenchurch Street Railway Station opened.
1843	Thames Tunnel opened.
1848	Waterloo Railway Station opened.
1851–2	King's Cross Railway Station opened.
1852	Poplar Docks opened.
1853	Harrod's store opened.
1855	Royal Victoria Docks opened.
1855	Metropolitan Board of Works created.
1863	Metropolitan Railway opened first Underground.
1863–9	Holborn Viaduct.
1864	First London bus with stairs.
1864	Charing Cross Station opened.
1864–70	Victoria Embankment.
1866	Cannon St. Railway Station opened.
1867–72	St. Pancras Station.
1868	Millwall Docks opened.
1868	New Smithfield Market opened.
1868	Abbey Mills Pumping Station opened (Bazalgette).
1869	First Sainsbury's opened in Drury Lane.
1869	Last warship built at Royal Navy Dockyard, Woolwich.
1871	Lloyds Incorporated by Act of Parliament.
1874	Liverpool Street Railway Station opened.
1876	First arrival of refrigerated meat from abroad (America).
1879	First Telephone Exchange, Lombard Street (ten subscribers).
1880	Royal Albert Docks opened.
1886	Tilbury Docks opened.
1886	Shaftesbury Avenue opened.
1888	First issue of the *Financial Times*.
1890	First 'Tube' railway: City and South London.
1897	Queen Victoria's Diamond Jubilee procession.
1899	Savoy Hotel and Theatre built.
1901	First electric trams in London.
1902	Spitalfields Market rebuilt.
1904	First double decker bus running in London.
1905	First telephone box in London.
1906	Bakerloo Line opened.
1906	Piccadilly Line opened.
1907	Northern Line opened.
1907	First Taxicabs in London.
1908	Kingsway Tram Tunnel opened.

1908	Rotherhithe Road Tunnel opened.
1909	Selfridge's department store, Oxford Street opened.
1911–22	Port of London Authority Headquarters erected (Cooper).
1912	Whiteley's department store, Bayswater, opened.
1921	King George V Docks opened.
1924	First Woolworths store in London, Oxford Street.
1924	British Empire Exhibition at Wembley.
1925	Great West Road opened.
1926	London's first traffic roundabout at Parliament Square.
1927	Park Lane Hotel opened.
1930	Dorchester Hotel, Park Lane opened.
1930–4	Battersea Power Station.
1931	Liberty's department store, Regent Street opened.
1931	Shell Mex Offices, Strand.
1932	Cockfosters, Arnos Grove, and Manor House Underground Stations (Holden).
1937	Earls Court Exhibition Hall.
1944	Port of London used as base for invasion of Europe.
1947	Last horse-drawn cab licence given up.
1947	King George VI Reservoir, Staines inaugurated.
1951	London Foreign Exchange Market reopened after 12 years.
1952	Last tram journey in London.
1953	London Airport, Heathrow, opened.
1956	London Gold Market reopened after 15 years.
1960–4	Post Office Tower.
1961–3	Hilton Hotel, Park Lane, opened.
1966	Carnaby Street Market.
1968	Closure of London and St. Katharine Docks.
1968	Euston Station opened.
1968	Victoria Line opened.
1974	Covent Garden Market moved to Nine Elms.
1976	Brent Cross Shopping Centre opened.
1979	Jubilee Line opened.
1981	Royal Docks closed, last of London's docks to close.
1982	Enterprise Zone established in London docks.
1982	Billingsgate Market moved to Isle of Dogs.
1982	Thames Flood Barrier at Woolwich completed.
1986	Big Bang in City.
1986	Terminal Four completed at Heathrow Airport.
1987	Docklands Light Railway opened.
1987	London City Airport opened at Docklands.
1991	Spitalfields Market moved to Leyton.
1991	Channel Tunnel Rail terminal under construction.
1991	Queen Elizabeth II Bridge opened.
1994	Eurostar terminal completed at Waterloo station.
1999	Jubilee Line extension scheduled for completion.

BUILDING AND ARCHITECTURE

BC

600	Middle Iron Age domestic sites at Rainham, Dawley, Bedfont, Heathrow.

AD

80–125	Building of basilica and forum, governor's palace, public baths, fort.
200	City wall built.
240	Mithraic temple built
c.600	Saxon London built mainly outside walls.
604	St. Paul's Cathedral built.
606	St. Mary Overie Nunnery established on the site of present Southwark Cathedral.
898	Conference of King's Council rerestoration of London.
c.1000	Earliest reference to London Bridge.
1067	Building of Tower of London and other castles began.
1089	Bermondsey Abbey founded.
1123	Building of St. Bartholomew's Priory and Hospital begun.
1140	Priory of St. John established at Clerkenwell.
1140	Nunnery of St. Mary's established at Clerkenwell.
1176	Old London Bridge begun
1185	Temple Church consecrated.
1205	St. Helen's Nunnery, Bishopsgate.
1212	Southwark Cathedral.
1220	Wakefield Tower at Tower of London begun.
1250	First Gothic arch (at St. Bartholomew the Great).
1256	St. Paul's Cathedral extended in Gothic style.
1290	Wall extended from Ludgate to Fleet River.
1375	First mention of Staple Inn.
1411	First Guildhall built.
1414	Sheen Palace built by Henry V.
1490	Gatehouse, Lambeth Palace.
1512–19	Henry VII Chapel at Westminster Abbey.
1523	Bridewell Palace.
1547	Somerset Palace begun.
1571	Middle Temple Hall.
1616–35	Queen's House, Greenwich.
1619–25	Banqueting House, Whitehall.
1631	Kew Palace.
1635	Piazza, Covent Garden.
1665	Southampton Square, now Bloomsbury Square.
1670–7	College of Arms.
1670–1700	Rebuilding of City churches: 50 by Wren, one by Hawksmoor.
1671–7	The Monument.
1675–1711	St. Paul's Cathedral rebuilt.
1698	Berkeley Square.
c.1700	Bedford Row.
1701	The Synagogue of Spanish and Portuguese Jews.
1711	Marlborough House.
1712	St. Paul's Chapter House.
1714	St. Alphage, Greenwich.
1717	Cavendish Square.
1720	Hanover Square.
1729	Chiswick House.
1729	Marble Hill House, Twickenham.
1730	St. George, Bloomsbury.
1730	St. Paul's, Deptford.
1735	The Treasury.
1739–53	The Mansion House.
1750–8	Horse Guards.
1750	Westminster Bridge.
1758	Kew Palace.
1758	Horse Guards, Whitehall.
1766	City Wall demolished and removal of gates begun.
1769	Kenwood House.
1772–4	Royal Society of Arts.
1775	Boodle's Club, St. James's.
1776–86	Somerset House.
1778	Brook's Club, St. James's
1786	Osterley Park House.
1788	White's Club, St. James's.
1789	The facade of Guildhall.
1802–3	Albany Chambers, Piccadilly.
1804	Russell Square.
1806	Sir John Soane's House, Lincoln's Inn Fields.
1824	Royal College of Physicians.
1824–31	London Bridge rebuilt.
1825	All Soul's, Langham Place.
1827–33	Carlton House Terrace.
1828	Marble Arch.
1829	Constitution Arch.
1829	Travellers' Club.
1837–52	Houses of Parliament rebuilt after fire.
1841	St. George, Roman Catholic Cathedral, Southwark.
1843	Trafalgar Square.
1848–51	Army and Navy Club.
1851–96	Public Record Office.
1853	Brompton Oratory.
1859	Floral Hall Covent Garden.
1862–4	First Peabody Trust buildings erected.
1866	Leighton House.
1868	Royal Albert Hall.
1871–82	Royal Courts of Justice, Strand.
1875–81	Bedford Park Garden Suburb.
1878	'Cleopatra's Needle' erected on Victoria Embankment.
1891	New Scotland Yard.
1899–1906	The War Office, Whitehall.
1903	Westminster Cathedral.
1905	Kingsway & Aldwych opened.
1905–8	The Quadrant, Regent Street.
1907	Central Criminal Court (The Old Bailey).
1908	Rhodesia House, Strand.
c.1910	Ducane Housing Estate, Hammersmith (LCC).
1910	Admiralty Arch.
1930	YWCA Hostel, Great Russell Street.
1931	Daily Express Offices, Fleet Street.
1932	RIBA, Portland Place.
1935	South Africa House, Trafalgar Square.
1936	Senate House, University of London.
1937	Bow Street Police Court.

1937	LCC Fire Brigade Headquarters.
1940	The Citadel, the Mall.
1955	Trade Union Congress HQ, Great Russell Street (sculpture by Epstein)
1957–79	The Barbican Complex.
1961	United States Embassy, Grosvenor Square.
1962	Shell Centre, South Bank.
1963	Vickers Tower, Millbank.
1968	'Roman Point' Tower Block collapses. Fatalities.
1978	Central London Mosque, Regent's Park.
1982	New British Library building founded.
1986	Lloyd's Building opened.
1987	Princess of Wales Conservatory, Kew Gardens.
1988	New Chapter House, Southwark Cathedral.
1989	Great storm causes much damage in London.
1990	Canary Wharf tower completed.
1991	Broadgate Centre completed at Liverpool Street station.
1995	Conversion of County Hall into flats.
1999	Ferris wheel being built on the South Bank.
2000	Millennium Dome to open, Greenwich

INSTITUTIONS AND POPULAR CULTURE

c.1050	St. James's Leper Hospital.
1148	St. Katharine's Hospital founded by Queen Matilda.
1180	Leisure activities include cock fights, archery, wrestling, skating on Thames when frozen.
1213	St. Thomas's Hospital established at Southwark.
1247	Bethlem Hospital for insane established.
1253	Elephant given to King and kept in Tower of London.
1272	Baynard's Castle handed over to Dominican Friars.
1297	Pig-styes banned from streets.
1371	Foundation of Charterhouse at Clerkenwell.
1509	St. Paul's School founded by John Colet.
1539	St. Bartholomew Hospital refounded after dissolution of monasteries.
c.1550	First use of private coaches.
1552	Christ's Hospital founded.
1558	First proper map of London by Ralph Agas.
1572	Harrow School founded.
1579	Gresham College founded.
1598	John Stow complains of 'terrible number of coaches, world run on wheels'.
1608	Great Frost Fair on Thames; taverns and football.
1611	Charterhouse School founded by Thomas Sutton.
1625	First Hackney carriages permitted to ply for hire.
1634	Sedan chairs for hire.
1637	Hyde Park opened for public use.
1637	50 licensed coaches (by 1652, 200).
1648–9	Frost Fair on Thames; printing press set up on ice.
1676	Foundation of Chelsea Physic Garden.
1682	Foundation of Royal Hospital, Chelsea (Wren).
c.1685	Sadler's Music House Theatre (now Sadler's Wells).
1715	Geffrye Museum (built as almshouses).
1718	Maypole removed from front of Somerset House.

1720	Westminster Hospital opened.
1722	Guy's Hospital founded.
1733	The Serpentine created in Hyde Park.
1739	Foundling Hospital, founded by Thomas Coram.
1741	London Hospital founded.
1759	The Royal Botanic Gardens, Kew founded.
1784	Balloon ascent from Artillery Ground, Finsbury.
1805	Moorfields Eye Hospital founded.
1818	Charing Cross Hospital founded.
1819	Brixton Prison opened.
1819	Bedford College for Women founded.
1828	University College, Gower Street founded.
1831	King's College founded.
1833	London Fire Brigade established.
1834	University College hospital founded.
1835	Madam Tussaud's Waxworks opened.
1836	University of London founded.
1837	King's College Hospital founded.
1839	River Police formed.
1839	Highgate Cemetery opened.
1841	Last frost fair on Thames.
1842	Pentonville Prison opened.
1845	Victoria Park opened.
1845	Surrey County Cricket Club founded.
1849	Wandsworth Prison opened.
1852	Holloway Prison opened.
1853	Battersea Park opened.
1860	Battersea Dogs Home founded.
1863	Middlesex County Cricket Club formed.
1865	Metropolitan Fire Brigade formed.
1869	Southwark Park and Finsbury Park opened.
1873	Alexandra Palace opened.
1874	Wormwood Scrubs Prison opened.
1877	First Wimbledon Tennis tournament.
1880	First ever Cricket Test, England v. Australia, at the Oval.
1882	Central London Polytechnic, Regent Street founded.
1895	First motor bus in London.
1897	Blackwall Tunnel opened.
1904	London Fire Brigade formed.
1908	Twickenham Stadium opened.
1908	Olympic Games held at Shepherds Bush.
1910	London Palladium, Argyll Street opened.
1911	'Pearly King' Association formed.
1914	Cinemas in LCC area total 266.
1921	Last horse-drawn fire engine in London.
1922	BBC begins broadcasting from Savoy Hill.
1923	First FA Cup Final at Wembley Stadium.
1927	First London greyhound track, White City Stadium.
1929	Dominion Theatre opened (became cinema in 1932).
1929	Tower Pier opened.
1930	Finsbury Park Astoria Cinema opened.
1930	First Chelsea Flower Show.
1930	Leicester Square Theatre opened (became cinema 1968).
1931	London public buildings floodlit for first time.

1932	Arsenal Stadium, Highbury, built.
1932	BBC moved to new offices in Portland Place.
1937	Empress Hall Ice Rink opened.
1940	Savoy Cinema, Holloway Road, opened.
1948	First jazz club opened by Ronnie Scott and John Dankworth.
1948	Olympic Games held at Wembley Stadium.
1951	National Film Theatre, South Bank.
1953	First 'coffee bar', 'the Mika', opened on Frith Street.
1955	'Bazaar': the first boutique, Kings Road, Chelsea.
1958	The London Planetarium opened.
1961	First Notting Hill Carnival.
1964	The Beatles recorded at EMI Studios, St. John's Wood.
1968	Rolling Stones gave first open-air concert in Hyde Park
1968	London Weekend Television started.
1970	Radio London started.
1973	LBC began.
1973	Capital Radio began.
1985	'Band Aid' Concert, Wembley Stadium; 72,000 attend.
1991	Open-air concert at Hyde Park.

SCIENCE AND THE ARTS

c.1173	Fitz Stephen, London historian, gave first description of the city.
1180	'Miracle Plays' performed at Clerkenwell.
1245	Westminster Abbey began to acquire art treasures.
1253	Sculptured bosses carved in Westminster Abbey.
1349–52	Stained glass windows made for St. Stephen's Chapel, Westminster Palace.
1377	Effigy of Edward III by John Orchard placed in Westminster Abbey.
1396	Portrait of Richard II painted for Westminster Abbey.
1476	First printing press set up in Westminster by William Caxton.
1510	Birth of Thomas Tallis, composer (died 1585).
1552	Birth of Edmund Spencer, poet and writer (died 1599).
1564	Birth of William Shakespeare, poet and dramatist (died 1616).
1573	Birth of John Dunne, poet and Dean of St. Paul's (died 1631).
1577	First London theatre built at Shoreditch by James Burbage.
1587	Rose Theatre built in Southwark.
1598	John Stow's *Survey of London* published.
1599	Globe Theatre built in Southwark.
1620	Birth of John Evelyn, diarist and writer (died 1706).
1633	Birth of Samuel Pepys, civil servant and diarist (died 1703).
1658	Birth of Henry Purcell, musician (died 1695).
1675–6	Foundation of the Royal Observatory, Greenwich.
1685	Birth of George Frederick Handel, composer (died 1759).
1697	Birth of William Hogarth, artist (died 1764).
1705	Her Majesty's Theatre.
1717	Birth of David Garrick, actor (died 1779).

1720	Theatre Royal, Haymarket.
1728	Birth of Oliver Goldsmith, writer (died 1774).
1732	Covent Garden Theatre (destroyed by fire 1808).
1746	Visit of Antonio Canaletto, Italian artist and painter of London views.
1755	Dr Samuel Johnson published his *Great Dictionary*.
1757	Birth of William Blake, poet and mystic (died 1827).
1759	British Museum opened.
1763	James Boswell, biographer, meets Dr Johnson.
1768	Foundation of Royal Academy.
1776	Birth of John Constable, artist (buried Hampstead 1837).
1778	Birth of William Hazlitt, writer (died 1830).
1784	Birth of James Leigh Hunt, poet (died 1859).
1792	Birth of George Cruickshank, engraver for Charles Dickens (died 1878).
1795	Birth of Thomas Carlyle, writer (died 1881).
1802	'On Westminster Bridge' sonnet by William Wordsworth.
1806	Birth of John Stuart Mill, philosopher (died 1873).
1809	Covent Garden Theatre rebuilt after fire (Smirke).
1816	Keats' house built, Hampstead.
1821	Haymarket Theatre opened.
1823	Royal Academy of Music opened.
1824	National Gallery founded.
1827–8	Zoological Gardens in Regent's Park opened.
1829	Cruickshank's 'March of Bricks' cartoon illustrates London's growth.
1833	Soane Museum founded.
1834	Birth of William Morris, artist, writer, designer (died 1896).
1836	Birth of Walter Besant, London historian (died 1901).
1837	Royal College of Art founded.
1838	National Gallery completed (Wilkins).
1842	British Museum new building begun (opened 1847).
1851	Great Exhibition held in the 'Crystal Palace', Hyde Park.
1858	Alhambra Theatre opened.
1859	National Portrait Gallery opened.
1866	Birth of H. G. Wells, writer (died 1946).
1867	Birth of John Galsworthy, writer (died 1933).
1870	Royal Albert Hall opened.
1875	Bethnal Green Museum opened.
1876	Albert Memorial completed.
1881	Greenwich recognised as meridian.
1881	Natural History Museum opened (Waterhouse).
1883	Royal College of Music founded.
1888	Shaftesbury Theatre opened.
1893	Statue of Eros unveiled at Piccadilly Circus.
1895	First Promenade concert.
1897	Tate Gallery opened.
1900	Wallace Collection opened.
1901	Horniman Museum, Forest Hill opened.
1902	*Life and Labour of People of London* published by Charles Booth.
1904	London Symphony Orchestra founded.
1904	London Coliseum Theatre opened.

1905	Strand Theatre opened.
1905	Aldwych Theatre opened.
1907	Queen's Theatre opened.
1909	Science Museum founded.
1911	Queen Victoria Memorial unveiled by George V in the Mall.
1911	London Museum founded.
1914	Opening of King Edward VII Galleries at British Museum.
1926	J. C. Baird gave first demonstration of television in Frith Street, Soho.
1928	Discovery of penicillin by Alexander Fleming at St. Mary's Hospital, Paddington.
1930	Whitehall Theatre opened.
1931	Windmill Theatre opened.
1932	London Philharmonic Orchestra founded by Sir Thomas Beecham.
1933	Open-air theatre, Regent's Park opened.
1934	National Maritime Museum, Greenwich founded.
1935	Geological Museum, South Kensington founded.
1936	First regular television service from Alexander Palace.
1948	'Eros' reinstated at Piccadilly Circus.
1951	Royal Festival Hall, South Bank opened.
1954	'Temple of Mithras' excavation at Bucklersbury.
1955	BBC TV Centre opened at White City.
1957	Imperial College of Science building, Kensington opened.
1959	Mermaid Theatre, Puddle Dock opened.
1961–2	Royal College of Art, Kensington Gore opened.
1967	Queen Elizabeth Hall, South Bank opened.
1968	Hayward Gallery, South Bank opened.
1969	Greenwich Theatre opened.
1970	The Young Vic Theatre opened.
1973	British Library formed.
1975	New Museum of London opened.
1976	National Theatre, South Bank opened.
1980	London Transport Museum opened at Covent Garden.
1982	Barbican Arts Centre opened.
1988	Museum of the Moving Image opened on South Bank.
1989	Design Museum opened on Butlers Wharf.
1990	Courtauld Gallery moved to Somerset House.
1991	Sainsbury Wing opened at National Gallery.
1993	Quaglino's opened.
1993	Buckingham Palace opened to general public.
1996	Millennium site confirmed at Greenwich.
1997	New Globe Theatre opened on Bankside.
1999	New British Library building completed.

INDEX